Memoirs of a Loose Cannon

Other books by
Simma Holt

Terror in the Name of God

Sex and the Teen-age Revolution

The Devil's Butler

The Other Mrs. Diefenbaker

Memoirs of a Loose Cannon

by

Simma Holt

Seraphim Editions

The publisher gratefully acknowledges the financial assistance of the Canada Council for the Arts and the Ontario Arts Council.

 Canada Council for the Arts   Conseil des Arts du Canada    ONTARIO ARTS COUNCIL CONSEIL DES ARTS DE L'ONTARIO

Library and Archives Canada Cataloguing in Publication

Holt, Simma
    Memoirs of a loose cannon / by Simma Holt.

ISBN 978-0-9808879-4-5

    1. Holt, Simma. 2. Women journalists–Canada–Biography.
3. Journalists–Canada–Biography. I. Title.

PN4913.H64A3 2008   070.92   C2008-906260-4

Editor: George Down
Cover Design and Typography: Julie McNeill, McNeill Design Arts

Published in 2008 by
Seraphim Editions
238 Emerald St. N.
Hamilton, ON
Canada L8L 5K8

Printed and bound in Canada

Contents

Introduction

I am not sure I'm the right person to be writing the introduction to this book.

A nagging thought is that asking me to write the intro is Simma's way of rewarding me for what I thought was facetiously suggesting its title. Or, perhaps, she is getting even.

It's true that I admire her, am fond of her, am awed by her energy and sometimes disjointed enthusiasm. But she's not the easiest person to deal with – especially if you are an editor. She's all over the place, following a line of thought here, breaking off to go there, and then winding up someplace she hadn't intended. That's Simma.

There are others who know Simma better than I – and there are many Simmas, some of them contradictory. There's Simma the humanitarian as well as Simma the warrior. Simma the no-nonsense journalist, Simma the soft-touch idealist. She is compassion blended with realism. The political Simma who deplores some of the characteristics of politics, not to mention politicians.

A case can be made that Simma is arguably the most unusual woman in Canada. There isn't much she hasn't done, and yet she remains disarmingly modest and insecure about her abilities.

When she started as a reporter with *The Vancouver Sun* during the wartime years of the 1940s at $25 a week, she was a feisty Jewish girl from the Alberta town of Vegreville, who'd just graduated from the University of Manitoba (which later honoured her). In later years she liked to mock herself by recalling the teacher who told her, "If you ever shut up, you will suffocate." For what it's worth, ever since she has not come close to suffocating.

Today's female reporters tend to think liberation and equality started with them. It didn't. More accurately, it started with Simma's generation of women reporters who in the 1950s and 1960s were the equal of any men, and more determined than most.

Names barely remembered today, like Marie Moreau, Jean Howarth, Dorothy Howarth, Lotta Dempsey, Jeanine Locke, Phyllis Griffiths, Judith Robinson, Yvonne Crittenden, June Callwood, Florence Bird, to mention a few.

In Vancouver Simma made a name for herself – on the labour beat rather than the women's pages. But that was only the start. She endured the jibes and put-downs of the newsroom of that day, which in later years would be branded as sexism and require sensitivity training. Simma gave as good as she got – and not for nothing was known as "the fastest lip in the West." It's been said of Simma that as a journalist she not only looked for stories, but tried to find solutions.

Among her credentials is being named Canada's Woman of the Year and author of the authoritative book *Terror in the Name of God,* about the Sons of Freedom Doukhobors who captured international headlines in B.C. by their attention-getting tactic of burning their homes and shedding their clothes. As a reporter covering the Sons of Freedom, Simma became one of the early experts on the use of terror to achieve goals – even though the Doukhobors were supposedly pacifists.

Covering the police beat, Simma was more that just an observer. She saved three convicted men from the gallows by digging out evidence that got their sentences commuted after she contacted the Minister of Justice. There's more to each of those stories, but it is quintessential Simma that, despite preventing unwarranted executions, her experiences with murderers persuaded her that there should be the death penalty for heinous murders. Just another apparent contradiction in her life.

Simma's social conscience persuaded her to run for Parliament. As the first Jewish woman to become an MP, Simma both intrigued and frustrated her peers. As a Liberal, she had alarming conservative attributes. Whatever she was, she was no lefty.

In the government of Pierre Trudeau Simma could be critical of the PM. When she thought he was wrong, she said so. She was admiring when she thought he was right. But she always was grateful that Trudeau respected her, would hear her views even if he refused to act on them. She could ask no more. PET, himself, had a history of being something of a loose cannon.

Her ideal appointment was probably as a member of the National Parole Board – the one person on that board who understood the prisoner's mentality better than most. As an idealist, her tough realism made her unusual, if not unique.

Simma was appointed to the Order of Canada, an honour based mostly on her "lifetime commitment to assisting those suffering from injustice, persecution and poverty." One of her books, titled *Sex and the Teen-age Revolution,* proved once again that Simma was well ahead of her time.

After her stint as an MP, the media was fearful of her. Didn't want to hire her, largely, one assumes, because she was increasingly her own person, fearless in espousing her beliefs, often disparaging of trends within the media. If she was tough to deal with, reluctant to compromise principles before, she was that much more determined after being exposed to the cut, thrust and machinations of the House of Commons. For a one-term MP she left big footsteps – even noting that Parliament was virtually irrelevant, and that the pervasive bureaucracy really ran the country. Dismayed at the CBC, she even proposed in 1977 that it should be sold, calling it "sleazy, mediocre, bad, dangerous and divisive." It's a refrain that still echoes today.

I admit to being an adamant supporter of Simma. She has something to say (a lot, really), and hers is a voice that should be heard. When I was in a position to do so, I tried to provide a platform from which her voice could resonate. Her columns of the past stand up surprisingly well today.

One of her (many) causes was that of Jonathan Pollard, sentenced to life imprisonment in the USA when caught spying for Israel – one of the inexplicable ironies, if not oddities, of the secret world of international espionage. To Simma, Pollard was no enemy of the United States, and his intelligence-gathering was on behalf of Israel – which America was, and is, pledged to support. So why would a spy from an allied country be treated more harshly that a spy from the Soviet Union, dedicated to subverting America? The question remains unanswered – as does Simma's conviction that George Bush the Elder had anti-Semitic leanings.

My affection and respect for Simma should not suggest that we always agree. We don't. I sometimes feel she is more a creature of visceral convictions than cerebral ponderings. Often (especially in journalism) a "gut feeling" can be truer and more accurate than a reasoned approach. Simma recently visited Cuba and seemed to fall in love with Cubans (easy to do), and viewed Fidel Castro with something approaching approval if not hero-worship. It drove me nuts. We disagreed, and I've always attributed this to her generous spirit, or perhaps echoing Trudeau's uncritical admiration of Castro.

Unlike her Parliamentary mentor, Trudeau, she never felt similar warmth for Mao Zedong or justified what he wrought in China. Today, she campaigns against the inhumanity underway in China of imprisoning Falun Gong practitioners who follow a creed of meditation and generosity. China has been accused of "harvesting" human organs of political prisoners and death row inmates for sale to rich foreigners in need of transplants.

It was an honour long overdue when Simma was appointed to the News Hall of Fame, recognizing her as one of the great journalists of her country.

As of this writing, I have not read Simma's book, other than suggesting the title. To me, in this age of conformity and political correctness, being something of a "loose cannon" is a term of respect. It means Simma escapes the mold, cannot easily be defined and is not predictable. She comes to her own conclusions, and sticks with them until proven otherwise. Whatever she has to say in this book, there are anecdotes and observations that could fill other books – and probably will if Simma has her way.

As a friend, Simma is loyalty personified. Which doesn't mean she won't fight with you and argue that you need a saliva test. But anyone who knows her knows that if you're ever in a foxhole or in trouble, Simma is the one you want guarding your flank.

Simma, in the unlikely possibility that she ever dies, has already proposed her own epitaph: "SILENT AT LAST."

Peter Worthington
August 2008

Rainbow in a Muddy Sky:
A Dedication

We knew we were on borrowed time in our life together. A massive infarction in April 1975 had left Leon with a heart three times normal size.

I was in flight back to my weekday job in the House of Commons in Ottawa, when it all began in our home in Vancouver. As I entered my office on Parliament Hill my secretary advised me that I had to return home immediately; Leon had had a heart attack and may be dying.

When I arrived at the Vancouver General Hospital that night, I found a medical team working on him behind drawn curtains. His face was topped with an oxygen mask, and tubes were protruding from his body. As much of his face as I could see was ashen. The cardiologist told me privately that Leon had died momentarily, that I should be prepared for the worst; he was mortally ill. However, the doctor told me, when he asked Leon when he thought he would be able to return to work, my husband told him: "Two or three days."

Upon seeing me, Leon gave me a weak smile – but it was his beautiful smile, the one I knew so well. He said, "You shouldn't have come back; your job is too important."

I responded with one of my more graphic – hardly ladylike – phrases to describe my job in politics, compared to what he meant to me.

Later, when he began his recovery, I asked him if he was aware he had died for a moment. He described what he thought happened, his own experience, as "very strange ... but real." He had entered a long tunnel, so "wonderful ... so warm ... a brilliant beautiful light drew me towards what looked like the end of that tunnel." Then he added, as if he saw his own mortality: "I will never again fear death."

He refused to live as an invalid, or to stop active sports – tennis, racquetball, skiing or golf – the essence of his very soul. After a second heart attack he undertook a new sport; he began riding and jumping with the Olympic-trained hunter, Transcend (aka Chuckles). A sweet friendship developed between the two gentle creatures, giving Leon renewed strength and purpose.

He did not let his friends at the stables or tennis club know that his heart was failing. When we were together, however, we talked of the inevitable – the realities of life and death. Privately, it was difficult for me to accept the fact that he might leave me behind. However, we both knew that we must live life to its fullest, to get as much of it as was possible. Thus, our last ten together were the happiest and richest years of our 37-year marriage. He died on the tennis court playing doubles with three doctors November 26, 1985.

There was a day almost a decade before that, when Leon and I had left the slopes of Mount Baker early. The snow was coming down in huge lumpy sheets, breaking apart to form a fat pillow of purest white on the hood of our car. On both sides of us, marvellous shapes were created in soft rounded sculptures of snow on trees and rocks.

As we dropped down towards sea level, the clouds above became visible. They were almost inky blue-black, layered, undulating, having turned the early afternoon into the darkness of night. The falling blobs of snow turned into rain, a virtual cloudburst. The only sounds were the hum of the car's heater, the splashing of rain on the roof and the spitting of water from the tires, the road now looking like a black riverbed.

As the darkness deepened and the windshield wipers could not clear the glass for safe visibility, we slowed to a crawl, with cars bumper to bumper in front and behind us. The deep snow that had enveloped us first and now the darkness revived memories of our most interesting and favourite crook, Johnny Waslynchuk. He with a half dozen of his friends (no doubt all ex-convicts) rescued us one time during a freak storm, when our mountainside home in West Vancouver was buried and near collapse under the weight of 102 inches of wet heavy snow.

Leon quipped: "Where is Johnny now, when we need him?"

And that started it. Though Leon rarely repeated himself, he would not drop this one subject.

"I wish you would write the story of Johnny and all the others … Your autobiography … That will be your best book … Please do it."

We talked about some of the thousands of characters who had passed through my life, stories developed into local headlines, national and international discussion and debate. So often, in retrospect, we could find humour and irony in what had been fear, hopelessness, and the macabre as it was happening, the killers on death row and out on lifetime paroles, and victims of social injustice who became a vital part of our life.

As we sat quietly, each of us deep in our own thoughts and memories of these people, I found a notebook from the glove compartment and started writing a few reminder notes of stories that would be in the book. I knew if I ever wrote this book, I would dedicate it to Leon.

I wrote about a dozen words, read them off to Leon.

"That's good ... thanks," he said.

Suddenly the darkness was broken and a nearly blinding white light streamed into our eyes. The low winter sun had crowded under the edge of the black sky.

Then – so awesome! A rainbow. It rose suddenly and was complete in its perfect symmetry, stretching from one end of the sky to the other, each colour vivid and clearly defined. Its remarkable intensity seemed exaggerated by the deep black backdrop of layered, shifting clouds.

I heard Leon saying, so softly: "That's your life, Simma."

I looked at him in surprise. He went on, saying, in essence, "It is like the people who have come and gone – so many of them out of the darkness, their lives so black or bleak ... sorrow, broken families, but always surprising warmth, kindness, love, beauty, humanity, always the colour and sheen of gold."

We believed there is colour and gold in every soul, including those rejected and most despised by society. Leon and I knew the worst of them, from the streets to death row.

I looked at the rainbow with him and somehow saw it as personal – perhaps a message. And so now, finally, I am writing the book I promised Leon that day long ago. As he said that day, my life can best be described as a rainbow in a muddy sky.

1
It Took an Exploding Volcano

My friend Barton Frank told his friends and mine that the most important fact of the life of Simma Holt is that wherever she goes something drastic or dramatic happens. I dismissed this as a crazy supposition, even accused him of insulting my prized skill as a reporter, primarily my hypersensitive nose for news.

"Try to understand," I explained repeatedly, with variations on the same theme, "if some instinct sets off an itch in the part of my nose that suspects a story in the air, nothing can divert me. And so you see it as something happening. Of course, that is what I am looking for – and finding."

He sniffed and obviously ignored it because he continued to introduce me with his over-used mantra, as though he knew nothing else about me that would impress his audience. I told Barton that if he persisted there would be those who would avoid me, fearing they'd risk the sky – well, at least the roof – falling on them if they happened to be near me.

"No doubt you are the greatest concert cellist I have ever heard, stunning in your scholarship, and your copies of van Gogh paintings are better than the originals." He said nothing, so I took a breath to let him pretend modesty and prepare to protest. He was silent. That was a mistake. Anyone who remains silent can expect me to fill the sound vacuum. And, of course, nature abhors a vacuum. So I continued:

"Sure-as-'ell, you are as far off base as possible … I am just a reporter who goes and seeks out the facts where things happen."

Not prepared to give up, he cited examples to prove his point. One was our stop en route to Reno at my husband Leon's and my favourite Chinese restaurant, Hung Far Lo, in Portland, Oregon. Moments after Leon, Barton and I were seated, two women at the next table got into a fight. Fists, dishes, bits of skin and splashes of blood were flying over our speedily-abandoned table, the combatants getting more vicious, only stopping when police arrived. Two years later, the three of us again headed south and made another stop for lunch at Hung Far Lo. It was on fire. As we drove away, all that remained of that two-storey building was the skeleton of burning embers.

Another piece of proof Barton offered was an incident that occurred soon after his arrival in Vancouver. The three of us were walking along Granville Street when suddenly a police car squealed to a stop beside us. Two officers jumped out of the car and tackled a man who was beside us, about to pass us. They knocked him to the ground, handcuffed him, and as quickly as they arrived they were all gone. The next day we heard the man was high on the list of Canada's most wanted.

Barton's perception may have originated from our first meeting at the Peace Arch, the US–Canada border in 1948.

I had been tipped by Jacques Singer, the new conductor of the Vancouver Symphony Orchestra, a man who had a great instinct for a story. He was determined to build a great national orchestra in Vancouver. One of his first attractions would be the presentation of Barton Frank, a young protégé of the great Gregor Piatagorsky. He told me this young American cellist was so talented, his famous teacher claimed he "surpassed the master."

Maestro Singer had already shown his remarkable news – or public relations – smarts. Since coming to Vancouver he had given me leads which, when followed and written, appeared in the general news, something never before experienced by me or the Symphony. One story was that he intended to pay salaries to what was an orchestra of volunteers. Another time, a most unusual picture overshadowed the accompanying story. It was a remarkable way to announce that the orchestra would feature a new piece, called "Tubby the Tuba." The Maestro set up the picture like a stage manager. He produced a ladder that reached almost to the high ceiling of the rehearsal hall, climbed it, and let the score of "Tubby" – folded accordion style – fall till it hit the floor. The picture ran the full column down the right side of Page One – the face of Jacques Singer at the top of the ladder, the score covering the full length of the ladder down to a pile at the bottom.

So as usual, I was confident that there would be a story in the tip Jacques had given me. He said Barton Frank, already famous in the music world, was coming to Vancouver to play solo in the Symphony. When I learned he was coming through the border that morning, I decided I would try to get his story for the home edition that day by intercepting him there. A photographer and I headed for the Peace Arch 30 miles southeast of the city. When we arrived we found the young musician pacing, steaming with anger. Later I would learn to expect his short fuse to blow whenever he encountered what he perceived as incompetence. This he called "stupidity." I would realize he meant what he said, and had chosen the word with forethought, when I happened to interchange "ignorance" with "stupidity" and he replied, "Ignorance is curable; stupidity is not."

It did not take long to "spring" Barton. The reason he was being barred entry to Canada was his travelling companion, which he always hugged, and was clutching as the customs officers stood close to him. It was his priceless seventeenth-century Cappa cello, insured by Lloyd's of London for a six-figure sum. The customs officer was suspicious; he could not know if Barton might sell it, or stay in Canada with his cello. He could not even be sure it was not stolen, given Barton's behaviour.

Barton signed a few papers and left with us. We arrived in Vancouver in time for me to produce the story, and for the cellist to play and receive praise for his performance that night, then return home to his job with the Dallas Symphony Orchestra in Texas.

Singer wasted neither time nor the goodwill of the Symphony Board members – so proud of their new orchestra leader. He quickly moved to pay the musicians who had played as volunteers to create and build the orchestra. Thus he could offer Barton a salary to equal those Barton had received in his previous jobs with the Washington and Dallas orchestras.

Barton soon came back to Vancouver as first cellist, later returning to the United States. Over the years we became like family. When Leon died he was always there as a best friend. No brother could have been closer.

But back to the Barton conviction that there is some sort of crisis that seems to wait till I arrive.

One June day, in my heavily-packed car, I stopped at Barton's home to say goodbye and tell him I was going to be away the whole summer. As I was backing out of his driveway he said, "Be careful ... I know what can happen wherever you go."

Barely 45 minutes out of Seattle, heading east, climbing towards Snoqualmie Pass, I moved to pass a slow car in front of me. Suddenly that car, only a few feet beside me, burst into flames. I pulled sharply off into – my good luck – a shallow ditch. I took pictures of my car with the fire backdrop. When I got the film developed the next morning, after my overnight stop, I sent the pictures to Barton, noting time and place, and wrote, "This does make me wonder."

The full realization that Barton may be right came May 18, 1980. Leon and I made an instant decision the day before to pack the car and leave immediately after work to escape the bad man-made news dominating our world. Florida was riven by riots and fire. Canada had been hammered seemingly forever by the endless feud of French Canada against English Canada. It might end on the following Tuesday by referendum. (A vain hope!)[1]

Perhaps it is the total helplessness of people like Leon and me (and others in the West) in the unending nationalism and power drive of Central Canada, that has always given cause for anger. Our solution was flight to our favourite retreat, Salishan Lodge, 300 miles south to Portland and 80 miles west on the Pacific shore.

As we drove south, Leon and I talked with anticipation of the strong cleansing effect of Nature on our spirit, our souls. We talked with thoughts of peace and excitement of our escape to Nature. We knew it all so well from our many past visits to Salishan. The ocean was so huge, so clean and strong. We loved to watch the huge swells of incoming tide, whipping up logs seemingly bigger than houses, hurling them like toothpicks on the shore, and later with the ebb of the tide lifting some of them back off into the sea. It was always like a miracle that some small scattered clumps of beach grass

---

1   The first province-wide referendum in Quebec on the question of sovereignty-association was held on Tuesday, May 20, 1980. The Quebec government was asking for a mandate to pursue a new agreement with the rest of Canada; that proposal was rejected by almost 60% of voters. Another referendum was held in 1995.

seemed to survive. Occasionally as we walked on the foam-spattered beach we found the coloured floats with the woven ropes still on them, with torn edges where they broke away from fishing nets perhaps as far off as Hawaii or Japan.

At dusk Saturday, May 17, we parked our Revcon motorhome for the night, two-thirds of the way to our destination. It was our usual rest area stop, Exit 52 on Highway Interstate 5, at the junction of the Toutle and Cowlitz Rivers. We knew the mountain was restless. The last time we were there was March 27 (my fifty-eighth birthday), when the mountain first began to rumble, becoming what scientists term "seismically active." Both of us wore expressions that told all who saw us we were there when Mount St. Helens began to roar.

After a peaceful evening meal, we walked down to the bridge and rivers beside the rest area, then went to our home on wheels. We planned to set out about 8 or 9 the next morning. Leon and I listened in on the truckers' chatter on the CB and fell asleep in the quiet black night far from city lights.

When we went outside in the morning we found members of the nearby Castle Rock community had set up a refreshment stand with free coffee and cookies for the travellers at the rest stop. The conversation was focused on the current news and reports from scientists about the volcano. The latest information was that there were thousands of earthquakes registered from below the peak of the mountain.

Incidental discussion included Mount Baker, 150 miles north, and closer to the Washington–British Columbia border. There had been steam rising from the back of the mountain. It – like Mount St. Helens – was in the Pacific Circle of Fire, and possibly could erupt at any time.

A man drove up in the midst of all this talk. He stepped out of the car and announced simply, "It blew."

He told us that he, his wife and guests were sitting on their porch at Mossyrock having coffee when the sky went black, daylight turned to night in an instant, and they could see the mountain "on fire."

Shortly afterward another driver arrived, his car covered with an inch or more of grey pyroclastic dust. The young man told us he had been camping near the base of Mount Rainer, St. Helens' neighbour, when the volcano exploded. He said the sun disappeared into sudden blackness of starless night. He had piled into his car and driven away, and the only light was from his headlights and the fireballs that crashed around him. Suddenly he grew very pale and looked like he would collapse as he said: "… sure I was going to die … a miracle … a miracle … miracle …" He repeated this as though he could not believe he was still alive.

None of us heard, saw, or felt anything. The sky was unchanged, clear and sunny. We learned when we returned to Vancouver – almost 300 miles north of the volcano – that homes shook, doors were blown open, dishes tumbled from shelves and pictures fell off walls. Yakima and Spokane, 130 and 325 miles east, were paralysed by fallen powder-fine ash settling on the roads in a six-to-ten-inch-deep layer. Car motors clogged and roads became impassable.

Exploding from deep in the belly of the earth, Nature's guts broke loose, rose seven miles into the air, then circled the earth at the rate of 220 to 670 miles an hour for days. The last earthquake that set it off was 5.1 on the Richter scale. The blast was recorded by scientists as 300 times more powerful than the atom bomb dropped on Hiroshima. The temperature as the mountain roared down to its drainage rivers – the Cowlitz and Toutle – was 500 to 700 degrees Fahrenheit. It was the biggest mud and boiling glacier slide in recorded history. The texture was like that of fresh-mixed cement, moving at speeds of 100 to 800 miles an hour, wiping out everything in its path, taking the lives of 57 people, burying 221 homes under 150 feet of its debris. In its flow, it crushed or carried away 27 bridges, 17 miles of railway track, miles of roads, cars, trucks, everything in its way. Super-hot pulverised rock and gas covered 230 square miles of forest. Spectacular Spirit Lake, once the mirror for Mount St. Helens, was turned into a grotesque tangle of splintered logs, mud and pumice rocks.

The mountain's magnificent white-peaked pyramid symmetry was left a distorted ugly black crater, its height reduced from 9,677 feet to 8,364 feet.

At the Washington–Oregon border 40 miles south, the mud and debris poured into the mouth of the Columbia River, reducing its water level from 40 to 14 feet, described as "dangerously low." At Yellowstone Park, the world's largest thermal basin was changed. Its mud pots and geysers – including the famous "Old Faithful" – underwent significant changes in size and timing.

Among those missing in the morning were loggers in or near the Weyerhaeuser Mill on the mountainside, four hikers, and a *National Geographic* crew.

Reporters and photographers flew in on helicopters and left quickly to get their pictures and stories back to Seattle and the wire services for the whole world to hear and see. This reminded me that I was writing for *The Toronto Sun* and was excited that I had an inside, or on-site, story for them, the luck which is the stuff of reporters' fantasies. I got to the phone booth, reached the editor and told him of the first volcanic explosion on this continent in a century. He said he did not think there would be space in that day's edition! The big stories were the referendum in Quebec and the riots that were heating up in Miami. Meanwhile volcanic ash was circling the earth, and the northwest was forever changed in this moment of geological history.

As the reporters came and left, I had little interest in what they were recording, until I called my sister that night to tell her our trip was aborted by a volcano. She said she knew; she was watching the news and heard a reporter say, "The major problem is the tourists here." The camera panned on the waiting lineup of cars and motorhomes on the highway where we had been stopped. The first face she saw, dead centre on the small screen, was mine.

If Barton saw it and said, "I told you so," I could justify it by telling him I was being a reporter interviewing the highway patrolman.

"Is there any word on the missing crew of *National Geographic?*"

"Lady," he said, "when the whole anthill is blowing up we can't worry about a few of its inhabitants."

When I returned several years later and saw the history in film and displays, much of the work was by the "missing" *National Geographic* team. Obviously they survived to bring their remarkable record of the exploding mountain out to the whole world.

It is doubtful I had that reaction which is so cliché – and I never believed – that the hair stood out at the back of my neck. But I did feel uneasy at the thought that both times the volcano stirred I "happened" to be there.

Since then the chain of incidents or coincidences has got a new link, although it is a tiny blip compared to the awakening of the volcano after 123 years. It happened in June 2002, after I pulled into the McDonald's golden arches, parked my car and was turning the key in my door lock. I saw a man lift a handgun into the window of a car beside me. He yelled, "Get out or I will shoot … I'll shoot … this gun …" The man with the gun pulled out a young man, naked from the waist up, threw him face down on the hot parking lot pavement, and handcuffed him.

I brought out my cheap little throwaway camera I'd bought a few days earlier, and kept my distance, trying to hide behind the few trees and signs at the back of the McDonald's. Then I saw a man and woman pull in front of the action in a van marked RCMP, both wearing Royal Canadian Mounted Police jackets. When I started towards the McDonald's, one of the first police officers came up to me. I thought, "This is it. I haven't even got the cover of my old job as news reporter for the big old *Vancouver Sun*." But surprisingly, he did not engage in a tough challenge. Instead he was most polite, and told me:

"We are undercover people. It could be a problem if your pictures were published showing our faces."

I assured him that I only took the pictures because I was there, but he was welcome to the film. He said: "No ... You had every right to take pictures and I would not interfere with that right. I just had the one concern ... our cover exposed." Then to my surprise, he asked, "Do you want to know what is happening here?"

I must have grinned like an idiot. Of course I wanted to know. Would any perpetual reporter, or any citizen, for that matter, not want to know?

He pulled a plastic bag about the size of a medium-sized orange from his pocket, and told me this evidence was cocaine and the arrest was of an active drug pusher.

I did not want to bother him with any discussion as he was finishing what was his job. I dropped my card with a note on his car's front seat, thanked him for his information and told him I would deliver the pictures and negatives to RCMP headquarters for his personal rogue's gallery.

Shortly after, meeting a news photographer, I told him the story.

"I could just weep," he said. "I carry around this expensive equipment and hope one day I will stumble on a story, any story ... and there you are with your cheap throwaway and you are a few feet from where it's happening."

And so to Barton: "As you were saying ..."

2

Born with the Roar

I was born with the roar – what became known as the "Roaring Twenties," the short, fast, flamboyant, crazy reversal of all that had been the accepted way for centuries. It was the total rejection of the mores and style of parents and grandparents – of society itself.

Clancy Strock, born in 1924, a contributing editor to *Reminisce Magazine,* described the Roaring Twenties as an "energetic decade." He saw that period as somewhat like a "giant door. On one side was a world that had changed very little in a century or two … while on the other side came an age of eye-popping change, innovation and progress." As a contemporary in era of birth I could identify with the Strock image: "I put my baby feet astride both worlds."

What was known then as The Great War – seen as the last war in world history – ended with the Armistice on November 11, 1918. The news was received with widespread relief, a moment of joy and then a strange quiet, as though in a universal uncertainty – waiting to see if it was really over, if we were free again.

It actually took until 1922 for the United States, through a joint resolution of Congress in Washington, D.C., to declare that "final war" officially over. Agreements were signed and the main one – the Treaty of Versailles in 1919 – incorporated the League of Nations, the organization that would police and act to stop any nation that might attempt to start another war.

At last, the people of the world felt certain the war was truly over, and were assured that it could never happen again. They believed that they were safe and could return to the routines of normal life. And thus in 1922, three-and-a-half years after the Armistice, the Roar virtually exploded. The world had moved from the quiet uncertainty, a sort of postwar numbness, to wild high spirits.

Young women in their late teens, 20s and upwards cut loose in "devil-may-care" exuberance, as if oblivious of public opinion. They replaced heavy cotton stockings and coarse bloomers with silk or rayon. They rejected their mothers' and grandmothers' chin-to-ankle dresses. Their "gowns" were cut to above the knees, their stockings were rolled down below the knees, revealing for all to see – horror of horrors! – naked body skin. They bobbed their hair and donned headbands to hold back their bouncing cut locks. The most daring chucked off the metal bones and strings of the corsets that pulled in their bellies and waists to the tiny circle that men loved.

Syncopated music called "jazz" was the sound that the young – clutched in tight embrace – would sway to in dance halls or in their homes as it came over the airways on radio. The new music echoed the excitement and freedom of the times.

My mother had a liberated mentality always supported by my Dad, who adored her. She would have been among those who would be happy for "the girls" (as she saw the new generation) who broke out of the fetters of corsets and bloomers. Perhaps she could afford to be broad-minded; her children were too young to be part of the wild revolution in style and mores. And in many subtle ways she revealed that she would have preferred to be dancing with the young and following the Canadian suffragette leaders in Alberta.

One day when my mother heard my mother-in-law complaining because I produced no children, my mother whispered, "Forget it." I never doubted that she loved her children. But when we left home to get education, or when we visited as adults now living in cities away from home, she never urged us to stay. It was apparent that she was self-sufficient and enjoyed the company of my Dad in a reduced household population.

One of her most cherished memories was her meeting with a "real author" – Nellie McClung – who wrote *Sowing Seeds in Danny*. It was the one book outside of her old *Blue Ribbon Recipe Book* that my mother treasured most.

Nellie McClung, she told me, came to the village where our family began – Stony Plain. In retrospect, I realized that my mother had been witness at one of the greatest moments in the women's liberation movement in Canadian history. Nellie McClung was there with the famous "Alberta Five," the women who fought through all the Canadian courts up to the final appeal – the Privy Council in London, England – to have women legally declared "Persons." My mother met Nellie McClung and the other "Ladies." Their stage was a hay wagon. But she could not get involved because she "had too many babies."

It was understandable that those who led the first fights for rights and equality under the law should be Prairie women. Necessity made them equal partners with men. Together the male and female settlers and their children endured probably the harshest climate experienced by any pioneers in a huge empty land. Like so many, my parents as young teenagers came with their parents to North America in the late 19th and the start of the 20th century to escape the anti-Semitic pogroms of Russia and the Ukraine. No doubt, most who came to what they called only "America" were seeking freedom, hope and opportunity in the huge blocks of virgin land offered by the Government of Canada in order to settle the empty west. The women shared their partners' struggles through extremes of cold and heat, living in little more than sheds or barns at first. They worked together ploughing up the raw virgin land to grow their food and fields of grain, while birthing and caring for their babies.

In our household my father did as much at home in the care and feeding of family as my mother. And my mother, when free of her duties, worked beside him in business. As long as he lived and was able, he was a true "house husband" – cooking for my mother and the children when she had other duties or even recreation or social events to attend.

Whether it was in a small quiet corner on the Canadian prairies or the huge cities of America, the story of the Roaring Twenties was one of ever-accelerating revolutionary changes. There were changes in technology, music, art, medicine, social sciences, agriculture, food – every aspect of human society.

The timing of my birth set the pattern of my life and career. I believed that my generation lived in the best and most interesting time in human history. It was a treasure trove for a journalist, a recorder of a corner of history.

3
Vegreville

My voice first sounded in this world – no doubt loud, clear, and in protest – on the evening of March 27, 1922 in a small central Alberta town called Vegreville. I was the sixth of what would be eight children of Nassa Rachel (Greenberg) and Simon Louis Milner (known as "Louis"). For almost seven years I would be the "baby" of the family always knowing I was loved by the older members – Mortie, Hannah, Arthur, Leo and Macey, my parents, and for a short time the only grandparent I can recall, my mother's father.[1]

Vegreville was a microcosm of Canada – a French town in one corner and the rest a wonderful mix of varied cultures and religions. It was the centre for villages and farms around it, for medical and hospital services, education, grain storage elevators, shopping of every sort. Our town had two hospitals, one in "French Town" and the second I knew only as "The RMB," personally significant because it was where I was born. It was at the opposite side to French Town. Even though the distance was probably no more than the equivalent of four or five blocks from our home it seemed to be located in the country. Both hospitals seemed to be "way out of town." After all, few of us got much farther out of Vegreville than into the woods, a fringe of prairie trees, or to our friends in adjacent villages or farms.

Our town sat on the edge of the main "highway" and was about equidistant from Edmonton (65 miles west) and Lloydminster (65 miles east on the Alberta–Saskatchewan border). At that time the road was little more than a rutted trail, used by comparatively few travellers, road workers, local resi-

---

1 Birthdates of my brothers and sisters: Mortie, March 8, 1913; Hannah, February 28, 1914; Arthur (Aaron) February 8, 1915; Leo, January 27, 1917; Macey, August 17, 1919; Miriam, September 26, 1928; Earl, February 12, 1931.

The family of Louis and Nassa Milner when there were only six children, before Miriam and Earl were born.

Back row, left to right: Mortie, Hannah, mother Nassa

Front and centre rows, left to right: Arthur (Aaron), father Simon Louis, Simma, Macey, Nassa's father, and the mischievous Leo. (Leo could not be found when the family gathered for the studio picture. He was photographed separately later and pasted in.)

dents and farmers. Situated beside that road was our family business, the Prince Edward Hotel (the tallest building in town) with café, beer parlour, and a large old-fashioned general store.

Bad weather was good for business. Rain – sometimes cloudbursts – would turn the dusty rutted road into a mud trap as binding as concrete. Or in winter, drifting snow would bury that road and travelling salesmen, workmen, farmers in wagons and the few cars would choose – or be forced – to stop overnight or longer at the hotel, depending when the road was passable.

Today that road has an impressive name and is a major route from the west coast through the Rockies to the heart of Canada. It is called The Yellowhead Highway (part of the Trans-Canada Highway system). It links Canada's four western provinces from Prince Rupert on the west coast to Winnipeg at the confluence of the south-to-north Red River and eastward-flowing Assiniboine.

To the people of our town and the surrounding farms and communities, the Prince Edward was a social centre. The beer parlour in our hotel was one of two favourite watering holes for the locals and travellers. Men and women were not allowed to drink together. There was a separate section for women, and the men were allowed in there, but women dared not even cross over the dividing line. Barred completely were Indians and those listed on what was called the "interdict list," people who became problems when they drank and/or were alcoholics. My sister Hannah's first husband, Milton Cohen, an American from New York who moved home with Hannah shortly after they were married, was deported because he served alcohol to what was known then as a "half-breed."

The second hotel in town was at the other end of the two-block long Main Street. It was the Alberta Hotel, and like the Prince Edward it was on a traffic line, the railway. The station then was located in what would probably be little more than an easy golf drive for a duffer – about 200 feet. The Canadian National Railway train went through Vegreville twice each day – about 1:20 a.m. and 4:30 a.m., one time going east, the other west.

Special events seemed to be constant, always drawing people from the neighbouring areas. There was the annual farm fair. Probably best remembered throughout the towns of Canada and United States was Chautauqua Week, the ultimate culture and entertainment under the Big Tent. In its lifetime (1904–1932) it was said to play in 12,000 towns to more than 35 million people. Tent Chautauqua was described as "varied as Joseph's Coat."[2] Harris P. Harrison and Karl Detzer in *Culture Under Canvas* (Hastings House, New York, 1938) wrote that Chautauqua died in 1932 "under the wheels of the Model A Ford on its way to the movies on new paved roads."

The weekly shows at the Vimy Theatre that I first recall were silent with sub-titles and a pianist in the pit in front of the stage playing music to fit the action on the screen. Forever in memory for me was the way the pianist accelerated and enlarged the sound when the action on the screen became wild and hysterical. My first big movie cry – and a never forgotten show – was called "Smilin' Through." All I remember about it was that the beautiful bride was murdered on her wedding day, falling at the altar, her full wedding gown flowing in great folds around her.

Today, the mention of "Vegreville" in any crowd inevitably brings a single response, as if there is only one fact of Vegreville that is significant. "Oh," they say, with great enthusiasm at having special geo-historical wisdom, "that is the town with the huge Easter Egg."

The Automobile Club's tour books use its Ukrainian name, *Pysanka*. It is described as 9.4 metres (31 feet) high, patterned in bronze, gold and silver, in 3,500 pieces of aluminum. It was erected in 1975 in recognition of the Royal Canadian Mounted Police, who were established as protectors of the peace and security of the settlers to the west. During their visit to the town in 1978 Queen Elizabeth and Prince Philip unveiled a commemorative plaque adjacent to the *Pysanka*.

---

2   The names of the thousands who played under Chautauqua's Big Top became famous in politics, literature, stage and later in the talking pictures and vaudeville, right into the television era that began in the 1950s. Among the names that became famous were Mark Twain, Ventriloquist Edgar Bergen and Charlie McCarthy, Calvin Coolidge, Josh Billings, William Jennings Bryant (said to have delivered his famous "Prince of Peace" speech thousands of times), the most famous singer of the day, Germany's Schumann-Heinck, who is said to have brought down the house whenever she sang "Stille Nacht" (Silent Night). The full Mikado with stars that later became famous on the New York Stage, and the full banned drama of the time, Servant in The House, played under Chautauqua's Big Top.

The Egg is said to be a symbol of the great multicultural mix that began with the courageous settlers from Europe, the British Isles, the United States and Eastern Canada, who stopped and settled beside the transcontinental Canadian National Railway. They challenged the harsh raw plains in the extreme heat in summer and extreme cold in winter (ranging from 110 to 45 degrees below zero Fahrenheit).

My memory of the beauty of the *Pysankas* was the originals, real hens' eggs, covered in remarkably detailed geometric designs by the parents and grandparents of my friends. These immigrant elders from the "Old Country" told us their stories, and among the illustrations of their past were the remarkable art on eggs by ancestors in the Ukraine and Russia. They considered them eternal; originally the colours were produced from surrounding plant life. These colours were carried through on the ribbons and trim of the skirts and necklines of their traditional costumes, latterly worn in their stage dances.

And so, when I hear the praise of that massive landmark I wish its huge hollow belly could be filled with hundreds of millions of the little originals (preserved of course).

Vegreville, as we were told, was named for its founder, a French priest called Father Vegre. (His name, actually, was Father Valentin Végreville.) We never questioned this information. It was one of the facts of our simple life – basic, a matter of trust that what our elders told us was the truth. We were also told that in the Alberta north there were tar sands sufficient to pave the entire face of North America. However, we were assured, it could never happen because there would be no way to transport that stuff from the remoteness of Alberta to market. Like most of my friends, I accepted that in these matters our parents and teachers lived longer and had much more knowledge than we could have. It was years later that I learned how to apply the skills of research before I would commit my information to print or in speech.

Life is always simple when you are young and in a protective family. We never knew or thought about whether we were rich or poor. We had a huge garden and chickens, so we were never short of food. We could always have meals or snacks at our café. We were never short of ice cream, candy or whatever we wanted to eat. We simply had to record on a slip of paper what we had taken. I never was good at keeping records and my father would say, "You are eating up my profits."

All of us worked in the hotel and café. I learned to carry about four or five meals on one arm as early as age 12 or 13. My schoolmates who came in for treats after school got the biggest banana sundaes ever created in any ice cream parlour imaginable.

Music came to our home, first through our parents and their friends, later with the eldest children. We had our own "big band" and "choir." Almost every night we would gather around the piano to sing, the wonderful tenor of my father and brother Arthur (Aaron) leading, with my mother (always an "entertainer") giving her strong voice to the sound.

My parents' voices were often heard as they sang together on their walks through the trails and woods of what was prairie parkland. Before I was born, my sister Hannah recalls, they often walked eight or nine miles singing Yiddish and the current (Victorian and wartime) songs. They would pull their three babies – Mortie, Hannah and Arthur, each a year or less apart – in a wagon or sleigh my father fashioned from orange crates. They would all return at night by train.

We had to only mention a word and it would set off a song by our mother applying that word and soon joined in by my father, if he was home, or by individual family members. For example if we were to say "the moon is rising" outside, she might come out side to see, singing "Moon Over Miami." Her favourite song I hear in memory and now find myself linking those words to the reality of my present age: "Darling I am growing old … silver threads among the gold …"

When she was in the age range I am in today – her 80s – she was singing – always loving a microphone – to the "old people" in the senior citizens' home, or chatting with the talk show hosts. They would say, on air, when they did not hear from her for a few days, "Where is Nassa? We haven't heard from you Nassa!" When she lost her hearing in her 90s these activities slowed. Once in the seniors' home when a group of musicians were entertaining the old folks, I told her the music they were playing. She started to sing. A younger woman resident who had been my high school English and Music teacher, hearing my mother singing off key by herself, whispered to me, "Tell your mother not to sing." I thought, "That would be like telling my mother not to breathe."

My brother Arthur was always ready with a song by request or volunteering in shops and concerts. Like my mother, if he felt like singing, he did not wait for an invitation. He could be heard all hours of the night or day, often with some serious consequences when his strong voice rent the night air, heard by my father two blocks away.

One summer night, in our summer bedroom (our screened in back porch) about 9 o'clock Arthur began singing "Can't you hear me calling Caroline?" My father rushed home in anger announcing, "I hear you – yes I hear you calling Caroline."

Many nights, especially on weekends, my earliest memories are of the family singing and our home becoming the core – as big families were in those days – for the community young people. It would begin with the family gathered around Hannah at the piano, Mortie on the saxophone, Macey on the violin. It did not take long for the friends of my older brothers and sister, who came from all parts of the town, to roll up the carpet, and what was called "The Shindig" began. When we got our first radio, the dance music came from that huge machine or records on the gramophone. Soon they were dancing to the famous big bands.

My brother Macey and I were sent to bed. No one noticed or seemed to care when we watched the party through the staircase rails.

Our parents and their friends would have their own card party in the kitchen or would listen to radio news or dramas, still a novelty and broadcast only at intervals. Lux Radio Theatre and Hallmark plays were the ultimate family entertainment.

Nature's wonders sparkled bright into our lives night and day, before neon dimmed the stars and even the moon, before horns of thousands of frustrated car drivers and blasts from boom boxes eliminated the delicate and sweet sounds around us.

In those days when we looked into the skies we saw only sun, moon, stars, and in the daytime on occasion there would be brackets of small rainbows enclosing the sun. That told us there would be a change in the weather. In the summer, the blue of our huge sky stretched as though into infinity to reach its horizon and I thought then: "No wonder people believed the earth was a flat disk." The white puffy scudding clouds with their ever-changing shapes – a face, a tree, an animal, crowds of people – became my game of imagination as I wrote little stories in my mind about those far-off creatures and things that filled the blue of the heavens.

At night, we searched for the many constellations. I saw the Milky Way as the route of diamonds on which angels danced across the sky into the shimmering jets of blue, red, orange, and gold of the Northern Lights. Always my search was for the Big Dipper. And long after that nightly search, as an adult driving a car and without any sense of direction, how I yearned for those dark clear cloudless skies where I could always find my beloved North Star!

This is my family's hotel in Vegreville.

Built in 1906, it was first named the Queen's Hotel. The National Co-operative Co. Ltd. bought it in 1917 and subsequently changed the name to the National Hotel. After moving to Vegreville in 1921, my father bought the hotel and renamed it the Prince Edward, although the sign on the building was not immediately changed. The hotel retained the name Prince Edward Hotel until it burned down on January 22, 1989.

This photograph of Vegreville is dated Oct 25, 1932. It is taken north of the rail tracks, facing south. The Alberta Hotel is on the right corner just south of the tracks. The Prince Edward Hotel is two blocks south of the Alberta Hotel on the opposite side of the street.

Back to Vegreville 58 years later. There were no big welcome signs when I lived there.

4

Murder Came Early

As the 1930s began so did the drama of hard times. The first reality was the ebb and flow of the homeless young men, the hobos. They rode the rails – hiding on rooftops and in empty or loaded cars of freight trains – headed west to seek solution to the massive crisis in their lives. It was their hope that they could find work, food, a new piece of land on which to live.

But on the Great Plains of North America, the worst drought known in the entire history of their settlement burned crops and left the soil dead dust. It became known in history as the "Dust Bowl" of the "Dirty Thirties." It extended hundreds of thousands of square miles on both sides of the 49th parallel.

While Central and Eastern Canada were battered by economic depression, radio reports from the Prairies told of the land of their farms raised into "a heavy black cloud ... between sky and earth." It swept across at 40, 50, 60 miles an hour. After the storm, they said that their once tilled land was smooth as glass, the crops destroyed.

I was old enough to understand some of the results of that disaster. Where we lived in central Alberta we were not as hard hit as was Saskatchewan. Because we had the hotel, store and a huge garden in a region known as parkland, with trees and therefore more stable ground, we were always able to get food and give help to the wanderers from the tragedy of the Dust Bowl.

I remember that the hobos at our door would never take a bite of the sandwiches offered to them until they earned it with work. Even when my parents, noting their fatigue and obvious need for sustenance, urged them to eat and drink first, they declined.

My father, like many other Vegreville merchants, extended credit in the store and restaurant, even overnight rooms in the hotel. He was trained – as he trained his children – in our faith and duty of *Tzedaka* – to share and care for those in need, without reward. Hannah used to tell the story of her curiosity when she heard our father moving around in the early morning for weeks – starting about 5 or 6 a.m. One morning she got up and watched him through a window. She saw him carrying a box of food, perhaps some clothing, to a new family from the Old Country in a house across the road. He left the box by the door. When she questioned him he told her that they must never know who delivered the food. He told her that it is important to be charitable, that under the rules of Talmud she must always give without the recipient knowing who provided the charity, and in no way seeking acknowledgement or credit.

For me, the decade that followed the Roar of the 20s was my first move into what became my lifetime career as a hunter of stories. Seekers of truth and understanding – as I believed I was or I became – often want to find the source and reason for the various directions and twists life takes. Did it take shape for me even before I was aware of life and death drama? I knew as my career progressed, and certainly in retrospect, that it was this interest in life and death that led to my most sensational and publicly-debated stories – the ones that developed from the condemned men on death row who wrote their thoughts, hopes, histories, and sought my intervention to save them from the gallows.

That was at a time when hanging was real, not simply an academic exercise, and years before I had to vote in the House of Commons for or against abolition of capital punishment in Canada. As a journalist I fought and won commutation of death sentences for three men. The residents named me "Pin-up Girl of Death Row."

One of my biggest stories was that of James Carey, who was sentenced to death with Joe Gordon for the murder of a policeman. I got to know Carey's common-law wife and the police officer who recruited him to get guns for ballistics tests in the search for the shooter in a drug war murder. While Carey was doing this "work" one of the gun owners murdered a Vancouver policeman. Because Carey was present when the shooting occurred he was charged as accessory to murder. Though police officers told me they accepted blame for his being with the killer, they did not testify on his behalf. My articles about Carey won his commutation to life in prison 11 hours before he was to take those 30 steps to the gallows. Carey's lawyer, Norman Mullins, dubbed me "The Court of Last Resort … When all else fails, call Simma Holt."

Later still, as a Member of Parliament, I was vice chairman of the Justice and Legal Affairs committee and sat on the special committee investigating violence in Canadian penitentiaries. I voted in the House of Commons to retain capital punishment on the books. The Government Party Whip, Charles Caccia, an abolitionist, was constantly pressuring me to vote with the Party. He could not understand how I could have been so involved in the lives of murderers, that I fought to save three of them, but spoke on all three readings and in committee for retention. I explained that even when capital punishment was a reality, commutation was used more often than not. But at the same time, if it was on the books, killers who were compulsive, psychopathic and would kill again – at any chance – could face the death penalty. There were men who admitted to me that they would have killed, but were deterred by the thought that they could be hanged.

Murder came into my life early.

I was not yet four years old that dark cold Saturday night in January, 1926, when our *Zaida* (Grandfather) Yecheal (Jacob) Milner was murdered. He had been a successful merchant in the Ukraine until he fled with his wife Fiegie, his two daughters (Hattie and Belle) and his two sons (my father and Morris) to escape the pogroms.

It was Grandfather Milner's practice to close his store before sundown Friday night to begin the Sabbath prayers in the Synagogue, then Saturday morning prayers and – as God willed it – a day of rest until evening prayers, ending the Sabbath at sundown. On Saturdays he might do a bit of schmoozing with his friends, then go to his store to close off the week's sales.

When he opened the door to go in and close his week's business, two teen-aged boys followed him. As he moved to the back of the store he picked up his cash in a wooden cigar box. The robbers seized it and shot him, then ran from the store. As they drove away, they discovered they killed for a "take" of 849 pennies and a few nickels and dimes. The pennies were for candy from school children, who knew my grandfather as the "Candy Man." In anger the killers dribbled the coins out the window from their moving car. The coins in the snow gave police the direction of their flight. It was south. Three weeks later police found the killers hiding in a farm hayloft near Leduc.

At home my mother, grandmother (*Baba*) Fiegie, and friends and relatives – primarily women and children – gathered in the kitchen waiting for the return from synagogue of the family patriarch with his son (my father) and any visitors who might turn up for Sabbath prayers. In big families there was always room in the house for an extra person.

When my Dad came home and his father still had not arrived, Grandmother Milner sent the youngest of her four children – our Aunt Belle – to the store to see why *Zaida* was delayed. When she got there she found her father lying in a pool of blood, dead. The family claimed that Belle turned grey over night. Certainly she had grey hair when she was very young and, as long as I knew her, her hair was nothing but that colour.

Hannah said the family wondered if *Zaida* Milner fought the robbers, as his virtually intransigent conviction was that "wrong is wrong" in human relationships. He was known to argue, even fight, for what he believed was right and just. I've been told that I must have inherited this relentless style from my grandfather and my Dad.

Years later I went in search of the story of my grandfather's murder. I found it published in *The Edmonton Journal*. I expected that a murder in the 1920s would be a major story. It was – told with a large double bold print headline:

POLICE COMB CITY FOR UNKNOWN SLAYER
Aged Merchant Shot Down in his store

It was topped with a tag line: "**Milner Murder**"

A picture of his small store was centre-page art above the fold. Over top was: *"East end store scene of murder mystery."*

Hannah, then 11 years old, was in the courtroom as the trial began. She remembered an ugly incident when the two accused were brought to the prisoners' box. Archie Killips and Nick Haryluk were then 19 and 20. Seated behind Hannah were their mothers. One of them said, with her hatred palpable, she could not understand why the "boys" were on trial at all. *Sotto voce* the mother said, "Why the big fuss? He was only a Jew."

Years later I would experience similar racism as a cub reporter. One day, checking a sudden death in Chinatown, I got the details of a full murder story, the victim a Chinese man. When I told the acting city editor the essence of the story, he did not send out a team of reporters. He simply told me, "Just two or three paragraphs. He's only a Chink."

Seven years after my grandfather's murder, when I was 11, there was another homicide in my world. Even then I knew murder was truly "The Big Story." It was and still is the ultimate drama, with the thread of mystery, suspense, violence and a mystique surrounding the main players. Detective work and the limitations and convoluted requirements of the rule of law add to the drama. Rarely are there witnesses to murder. The victim, obviously, cannot testify to the events. The story must be pieced together like a jigsaw puzzle.

Before round-the-clock radio news coverage or television, murder rated headlines. Newspapers would rush to the street with an extra edition. I loved the cry of the street sellers, "EXTRA ... EXTRA ... READ ALL ABOUT IT."

I treated the second case of murder in my young life as personal, a story I wanted to know. The charge was against a farmer, William McLean, and his 15-year-old son Johnny. They were hiding behind a haystack when a shot went through the kitchen window of their neighbour, Walter J. Parsille, and killed him. McLean was angry over Parsille's barking dog.

The trial was held in June 1933 in Vegreville Court House, one block from my home. Only the tennis courts and an empty lot stood between our home and the courthouse. It was across the road from what had become my favourite hangout – *The Vegreville Observer*. Every noon hour and after school my schoolmates and I would race to the courthouse fence to see and listen. The big drama for us was when the father and son were led in and out the side door only about 15 feet from where we sat watching. Mounties were there – in front, behind and beside them. We never saw so many redcoats in one place before. We were quiet, straining to hear the words from the courtroom that we knew from radio crime dramas: "Where were you on the night of ...?"

William McLean was found guilty on July 5, 1933 and was sentenced to hang on October 6th of that year.

It was about this time – as I remember it – that I got hooked to newspapers. Perhaps in the language of the street I began "joy popping" printer's ink – and to this day I love my addiction.

I was hardly tall enough to watch the deaf, very old man I adored without standing on an apple box as he set the metal type. He set it by hand on the top of his huge heavy block table – the type I would see later in his weekly *Observer*. He was A. L. Horton, owner, writer, editor, publisher. Later when I left home and won any award he would publish it in big print.

He never once shooed me away, but often explained what he was doing. And then I would see the paper and marvel that I had watched it being done and that it was my friend who did it.

While I was still in high school I developed scarlet fever. At that time it was a disease that required quarantine. I was virtually sealed into the ground floor bedroom of my parents. My food was delivered through the window. My brother Leo, the most generous person I have ever known, came from the hotel three and four times a day with something for me – ice cream, chocolate and candy bars, magazines, even a radio. After school, my friends would come and sit on the single board fence to tell me everything that happened during the day, test me on new riddles (which I hated) and bring me books and magazines. One day while my friends were sitting on it the fence smashed under all their weight. It was great for a laugh since there were no injuries other than bruises.

My sister Miriam, who was close to me before I was diagnosed with scarlet fever, was vaccinated with something to prevent her getting the disease. Unfortunately, she already had the disease when the antidote was given, and received a double dose of scarlet fever. It caused nephritis, with irreversible damage to her kidneys before dialysis or kidney transplants were available. My mother knew Miriam was dying long before she told the family. My sister had an excellent voice, in the style of Dinah Shore. Miriam's singing of "Always" was recorded for broadcast by CFRN Edmonton. My mother took her to Los Angeles for her one and only major experience in travel. There, my mother recalled, she was mistaken for the daughter of Loretta Young when they toured the Hollywood Bowl.

Miriam's death at age 17 was the first close family death I experienced, and perhaps it was this that gave me the strength and insight to understand and empathize with the suffering of strangers whose stories I had to cover moments after they had met personal tragedy.

Childhood ends and with it the ties of family loosen, and in some cases even break apart when a girl or boy must leave home to seek a future with bigger challenges than can be found in a small town. Mortie, Hannah and Arthur went to Edmonton. Macey, closest in years and friendship with me, won one of the first large scholarships to Queen's University in Kingston, Ontario. My youngest brother, Earl, took degrees in pharmacy and teaching. It was Leo who remained with my parents. Apart from service in the army and air force in World War II, he kept their hotel-and-restaurant business going, ensuring cash flow for the education of the rest of us.

The last time I was with all of my older brothers and sister was in Saskatoon at the end of August 1939, at a Young Judean convention. War was declared in the midst of it and every young man, including my brothers, expected to be in the army. We knew it was unlikely that all the young people with whom we had such a close attachment then would ever meet again.

One day a tall slim man came into our café and sat at the first seat on the counter for lunch. I served him. I soon learned that he was the dean of Journalism at Columbia University. I told him that I knew about journalism schools, that Columbia was the ultimate in the world. I asked him about opportunities there. He advised me to apply first to Barnard College, then work for a short time on a suburban paper, or a small weekly, and then apply to Columbia. He took my name and said if I did make it to New York to call him when I thought I was ready to apply to Columbia.

I immediately applied for a visa to study in New York, and checked daily (in vain) at the post office. I had also applied to the University of Manitoba, and was accepted. Finally when the time for university registrations drew near I knew I had to move ... and I did. I packed for Winnipeg and the University of Manitoba to seek a general Arts degree.

5

From the Safe Cocoon to Winnipeg

It seems absolutely inconceivable today – more than 65 years later – that I could have been so naïve and cowardly. Never before or since have I been more frightened than I was when I left home alone for the first time in my life, moving away mile by mile from all that was familiar and safe, facing the prospect of finding my way around a big city without the help and protection of my older brothers and sister.

It was early September, 1941. I was on my way to Winnipeg to attend the University of Manitoba. I was going two provinces east of Alberta! I cried all the way from Vegreville to Lloydminster, the prairie town that straddles the Alberta–Saskatchewan border. My tears were both of fear and of sorrow, certain that I would never see my parents again; they seemed so old (in their 50s) and would probably die before I got back home.

This would be the fourth time in my life I would be in a city, the first time alone. With my family I had been in Edmonton twice, and in Saskatoon in 1939. Other than that, my whole world had been Vegreville. I was in my teens before I ever saw a city (Edmonton) or a mountain (somewhere south in or near the Crow's Nest Pass, in the Rockies).

Alone, I knew I would have to find my way in Winnipeg to the university, the downtown campus called "Broadway" (long gone). Because I was entering with senior matriculation (Grade 12) I would register as a second-year student and spend one year downtown before going out to the Fort Gary campus. It was at the opposite end of the city from where I would live – on Cathedral Avenue in the North End. I would have to learn how to use public transit, taking the streetcar through long stretches of empty space and around or through other suburbs.[1]

After making my way to Broadway, I would have to register and – what I had not thought about at all – fit into a society in which my classmates at first over-awed me. I saw them as super-sophisticated; also they had known each other from their earliest school days in their neighbourhoods, synagogues, churches, sports and community centres. I was a total stranger in their midst, both in manner and style. By the time I met others who came from outside the city, they had adapted as I had.

It was impossible even months later to relate to that frightened country girl who was old enough to be self-sufficient, who would begin her journalism experience at university interviewing Marian Anderson, Yehudi Menuhin, and more. The wonder of being a student reporter, or university stringer, was that the same celebrities who were available to the big city dailies were receptive – even seemingly more generous in their time – to university students.

Today I marvel that that past fear was possible. I must believe that facing it and realizing I could manage on my own is what enabled me to become totally independent and fearless in my career and in life itself. Since then I have never thought of being afraid, even when surrounded by Outlaw bikers in San Francisco's Haight Ashbury, Montreal or Seattle. I had no fear walking the streets of New York with a 21-year-old gang leader as my guide through (drug) "shooting galleries" to meet his friends in The Bronx who admitted in interviews they had killed. I was not afraid entering cells or standing alone – all five foot two of me – under the dome of the B.C. Penitentiary surrounded by men who looked like tough giants, who wanted to talk with me, among them the spokesman who would be coming out in a month with "a few pieces of unfinished business to settle." Nor was I afraid in Montevideo, Uruguay getting the story on the con man who posed as the Sons of Freedom "Pope" Stefan Sorokin, nor in a women's prison in Israel with a terrorist who was being prepared to be transferred on a prisoner exchange, reluctant to leave the comfort-

---

1   Returning for the 60th Homecoming in September 2004, I found all the suburbs and empty land was continuous residential, small and large shopping malls.

able prison to return to her gang of thugs under the wing of the Palestine Liberation Organization.

As remote and strange as it seems in retrospect, I am sure my initial fear was very real because of a persistent nightmare, recurring with only minor variations that sometimes surfaces even now. In it, I am in a city alone, lost and wandering through back streets blocked by concrete walls and a field of twisted steel rails and pipes from a wrecked building, not knowing the name or location of my hotel.

That first day in Winnipeg, I travelled downtown from my new home and walked the one or two blocks from the bus stop on Portage Avenue to the university.

I circled the campus, confused and feeling I wanted to run. Just as I was thinking my breath would stop in my anxiety, a redheaded young woman came out of the door and asked, "Are you all right? Do you need help?"

She introduced herself as "Clare Gellatley ... the lady stick (president) of Art Faculty." She said she saw me through a window and sensed something was wrong because I was walking back and forth as though I were lost or looking for something. She led me through the whole process of registration and was constantly in the wings of my life for that first while.

By chance, years later I would be able to reciprocate when Clare turned up at *The Vancouver Sun*. She was a good reporter and a good person. She eventually moved on in her private life and left *The Sun*, after which we lost track of each other.

Within the first week, the University Librarian, showing me the routes for research, took me into the hidden world behind the seemingly endless shelves of books. I could not believe what I saw. There was so much knowledge in these books. My dream of knowing all there is to know in one lifetime crashed at that moment. Reality dawned. I despaired of fulfilling my hope of crowding three careers into one lifetime.

Even so, I did have the careers and more, and kept trying to jam as much knowledge as possible into my life – by intensive research and constant reading. I learned I would never stop learning. I keep doing research and making notes as though I am going to write an exam tomorrow.

As much as I wanted the education of literature, history, current affairs, all contained in those books, there was the most powerful pull – like a giant magnet – within the first days at Broadway. It was *The Manitoban,* the University's student newspaper. It did not take long – as is the way in volunteer work – before I rose to the top of the masthead, first as news editor early in my freshman year and then, in my last two years, as managing editor, the first woman to hold the position. I did it despite the fact that I had vowed I would use my last year to concentrate totally on education, making up for what I missed while working on the student newspaper and as stringer on the *Free Press.* When University President Dr. Sidney Smith phoned me personally to ask me to take that leadership a second year I felt I had no choice.

One day, early in my freshman year, the students were called to assembly in the auditorium to hear University Chancellor John W. Dafoe speak. I knew the name as one of the great leaders in Canadian journalism, editor of the *Winnipeg Free Press* for 40 years. I took a seat near the front of the hall. He looked old, his clothes rumpled, seemingly stained with either food or tobacco. His voice was so low that even sitting in the front row it was difficult to hear his words. The din of bored students, their laughter and whispers, did not help. He seemed not to notice.

However, the next day I went to Dafoe's newspaper, asked to see the city editor, and told him I would like to work part-time for him. His reaction: "I can't stand university students; they know it all." I snapped back, "I'm here because I want to learn." I was hired as university stringer and kept the post throughout my three years at Manitoba, doing occasional assignments for the night editor.

The compulsion to find the story behind every person and situation as I found it was virtually inescapable. On the streetcar I would watch the different people and try to imagine what their stories were. I often thought that was the time I should have started writing fiction. But facts were for me more exciting than fiction.

One of the most memorable days even before being a cub reporter on the major city newspaper was at *The Manitoban* when a new friend and colleague, Enid Nemy, and I set out to get three celebrity interviews in one afternoon.[2]

---

2 Enid Nemy's career in journalism began almost on the same path as mine, starting at Canadian Press, Winnipeg. However, when I went west she went east to write in Montreal, from there going on to become an award-winning columnist on *The New York Times* and contributor to *New Yorker Magazine.*

We had only a nickel between us, the price of one student streetcar ticket. Somehow that coin and two transfers got both of us to three different hotels to interview American contralto Marian Anderson (barred from the city's first-class hotels because she was black), the rising young star, violinist Isaac Stern, and songwriter and composer Sigmund Romberg.[3] Romberg, the last on our story run, greeted us with joy, and for the rest of the afternoon played his music for us, including my mother's favourite song, "When I Grow Too Old To Dream." He explained his pleasure at seeing two young fresh faces at his door after "enduring … a tedious hour with an old woman reporter" from one of the local dailies. (That was before my consciousness had developed to the level that his description of his previous guest might have caused me pain and shame for him.)

I never regretted the fluke that brought me to Winnipeg instead of New York, a fast track to my career in journalism. If I had gone through four or more years at Barnard and then Columbia I might have broken into the big time and perhaps even international reputation. The prizes I won in Canada might have been Pulitzer in USA. But I doubt that I would have had the opportunities, the supports and the kind of editors and mentors who trained me towards the career I had.

Perhaps I did not notice the significant divide between Jews and Gentiles – at least, not until I moved to Winnipeg. Winnipeg had a huge Jewish community and nurtured people who contributed greatly to all phases of Canadian life. Most of the Jewish students had grown up together in North Winnipeg and attended the same schools. Having come from the outside, growing up with children of many races, many of them like myself descended from Eastern European immigrant parents, I did not live isolated from the other races and religions in Vegreville. My first realization of ghettoism came as a disappointment. The Jewish women had one locker room, separate and apart from the others, and seemingly smaller.

Shortly after I arrived and questioned the feeling that there was serious racism, I was told that there was a quota for admission to Medicine of only

---

3   Sigmund Romberg (1887-1951), as staff composer for impresario Jacob Schubert, wrote the scores for 40 musicals. Among his most famous operettas are *Maytime, Blossom Time, The Student Prince, The Desert Song*.

two Jewish students a year, no matter how highly they excelled academically and every other way. There was talk of a student who committed suicide when, despite the fact that his marks and his character would have made for an outstanding doctor, he was rejected while non-Jewish students with lower marks and character qualifications were admitted. It was a story I never checked.

One day four of us who had become close friends from the day we registered were having our sandwich lunches in the women's common room. We were all Jewish, but did not meet the stereotype – Caroline Freedman was a brunette like myself, Goldie Bookhalter platinum blonde, and Torchy (Vera) Kerr a redhead. (Caroline Freedman was a member of the family in which one, Sam, rose to Chief Justice of Manitoba, and brother Max, a journalist, became speech writer for Sir Anthony Eden, wartime foreign secretary and later Prime Minister of the United Kingdom.) A tiny young country girl from Saskatchewan joined us. She introduced herself as "Anna" with an apparently Ukrainian last name. She told us she heard there were "lots of Jews" at the University, and went on to explain, "I hate Jews." Caroline, kind and brilliant in her tact, asked if she had ever met a Jew. Anna said she had not, but heard "such awful stories" about them. Carefully Caroline told her how much we hoped she would join us in friendship. We noted our parents came from the Old Country – Russia and the Ukraine – like her parents, in order to be free, with equal opportunity, without persecution. Anna never left us. Like us, she came to share friends from many religious and ethnic heritages – Icelandic, English, German, and French, to name a few.

The most painful experience in religious hatred came one night when I was covering a Catholic priest's speech at the Newman Club meeting. His lesson was the worst anti-Semitism I had ever experienced up to that time. He used the crucifixion of Jesus to make his point of hatred, unnecessarily graphic in blaming Jews who "killed our Saviour." He did not modify his apparent bitterness by mentioning that Jesus was a Jew whose lessons were from the ancient Talmud. Back in the *Free Press* city room, I wrote it straight, a small story with only his words, none of my own editorial thoughts. About 4 a.m., as I was about to leave the city room, the night editor received a call from the priest. He asked to talk to the reporter who covered his speech. He told me he did not know there was a reporter in the audience and begged me not to write the story. I told him it was a short story, with only his own words. I don't remember whether I checked to see if it was published, whether or not he used influence to kill the story, or if anyone really cared.

Conversely, there were good and memorable personal experiences in racial and religious friendships. One was when Torchy Kerr and I were invited to attend the Student Christian Movement Easter Camp. There, the wonder and potential of love between all faiths was demonstrated by the clergymen and religious professors. Themes for prayers and sermons focused on our common Judeo-Christian bonds. In the beauty of the out-of-doors we shared the greatness of a common God, a God of Love, who did not condone racial or ethnic hatred.

War dominated all our lives. The male students were the obvious target of antagonism for being in university while their peers were fighting and dying at the front. In those days, if an able-bodied man was not in the military he was shunned by the community. Conscientious objectors served in alternative service, and they at times were also shunned.

Jack Ludwig, who later became a published author, was the editor of the *Literary Supplement* of *The Manitoban.* Jack had a crippled leg and was therefore classed as "4F" (not acceptable for military service). He published a poem down a wide right-hand column of his front page. In essence the poem, written by Bert Hamilton, the President of the Students' Union, called for the guns of the war to be turned on William Lyon Mackenzie King. The *Free Press* news pages and editorial writers spewed anger that inflamed the public. Male students were seen as virtual draft dodgers. Even worse, the poem's attack was against the prime minister of the nation.

The University took unprecedented action to punish two who would have been Rhodes Scholarship winners if it had not been wartime. The punishment for the author, Bert Hamilton, and *Manitoban* Managing Editor Ken Williamson was that they would not graduate officially – that is, receive their degrees – until they received honourable discharge from military service. Fortunately, both had already enlisted for active service to start after their graduation.

My home in Winnipeg was with Dr. Jack and Clara (Shnay) Lander. I found it through Molly Shnay from Prince Albert, who had been at the Saskatoon convention. (Molly became one of my brother Macey's girlfriends before he went overseas as a young graduate from Queen's University Medical School.) I stayed with the Landers for all three of my years in Winnipeg.

Though books were numerous in their house Clara never came back from a trip to the public library with fewer than eight or 10 books. The Landers soon recognized my eagerness for life and knowledge. They gave me a gift not long after I began to live in their home. The reason they gave it to me, they said, was the title: *So Little Time.*

And how well I know as I write this that no life is long enough for those who seek absolute truth and beauty. Perhaps if I had learned – and accepted – that at the beginning of my days in the stacks and in journalism I might have lived a quieter slower life. But certainly it would never have been as exciting as when I began my education and the route to the career as a journalist.

In May 1944 I graduated. That day, I received an unexpected special award for the two years I served as managing editor of *The Manitoban.*

This award was the first of two honours I received from my University. Twenty-five years later, in 1969, I received the Jubilee Award for public service in the quarter-century since my graduation. The nomination came from another Manitoba alumnus, Barry Broadfoot, a colleague on *The Vancouver Sun.* In the nomination, quoted in the citation on the award, he compared me to a "bulldog on a bone" when I went after a story.

As soon as I packed up my life in Winnipeg, I set out for my first full-time job in the newspaper business. It was with Canadian Press in Calgary.

6

First and Brief
Career Start

Now it was truly the beginning of my total independence, what I would enjoy and cherish to the last days of my life. The job title – at first – sounded impressive. It was "editorial-operator" in the Calgary bureau of Canadian Press (CP). It was a two-man office. With my arrival it would be a "two-person" office. In it, I would work one month on days on the editorial floor of the *Calgary Herald* and one month on nights for *The Calgary Albertan,* alternating with the "Chief Operator" Maurice Tebo. My salary would be $22 a week.

Going west that first week in June 1944, I barely looked out of the window as the train clacked its way across the Prairies. My full concentration was on the 12- or 18-inch narrow beige paper ribbon called tickertape. It meant memorizing the varied arrangement of punched perpendicular holes, each one of the 26 letters of the alphabet, as well as the holes that would space and punctuate for a full well-written news report. There was no doubt or leeway: I had to know everything possible about preparing the stories for dispatch – how to punch it all onto the tape, then run it through the "send" slot. I was told I could correct errors with a small hand punch that I would find with the machine in Calgary.

If I did not recognize the value put on my planned career start as a news reporter by the job title and salary, I should have known it the minute I saw the space allotted for the Canadian Press bureau there. My workplace was a narrow office little more than a ten-foot hallway, the walking space a lane about three feet between the shelf-like tables on which the machines were mounted. The bathroom in my first bachelor apartment in Vancouver was bigger! I should have realized that this was not exactly a dream career move when I noted the indifference to my suggestion that I would be "energetic" in finding stories from CP Calgary. No doubt Maurice Tebo was not one bit interested. He all but yawned and then went on to tell me what was expected of me that first day.

He probably knew my resumé – *The Manitoban* and stringer mostly late nights and weekends for the *Winnipeg Free Press*. I knew in a superficial sort of way that duplicates ("dupes") of my stories – if and when I produced any of my own – would go on the CP wire across Canada. At the same time the newspaper dupes came into my basket to be rewritten or abbreviated for dispatch to what were then the 97 or 98 member newspapers of the CP.

Despite Maurice's apparent – though unspoken – brush-off of my eager offer of finding and producing news and feature stories, I began the job with natural enthusiasm and optimism. I imagined I would find and write stories that would not only be published in many of the Canadian newspapers, but could appear with and carry the prestige of Reuters, the Associated Press and United Press International. Though for a moment I sensed his negativity, still with the confidence and naïveté of youth I was certain he would not be able to resist a good story if I found it. I thought, and hoped, I was at least moderately ready for the job. I had no idea that I would be totally on my own, right from the first day.

Now Maurice was telling me, "Today you will only check in."

He said that the machine must be kept clear for major incoming news. All I had to do was a regular daily duty – that is, to check in at regular times in a sequence started in the Maritimes on the east through to the west coast bureaux. Each of us used initials for identification. Mine was "SM" for Simma Milner.

Unless the whole of downtown Calgary blew up I must keep the line clear. I must only interrupt the news to report Calgary's turn, after Saskatoon and before Edmonton. I had only to punch and transmit seven strokes on the ticker tape – "Cal Clr."

"*Today*" was June 6, 1944. It was D-Day, the beginning of the end of World War II. The allies had finally moved in the huge flotilla to open the second front.

Maurice Tebo left and I was alone.

I punched out "Cal (Space) Clr." I was ready. Copy boys from the *Herald* kept racing back and forth moving the stories off the newspaper receivers to the news desks. The excitement was high and the papers were producing EXTRAs as the news developed through that day.

I waited my turn, nervous, but sure I was ready for my first transmission. Finally, my turn came.

It was simply: "Cal (space) Clr."

Translation "Calgary Clear."

That was it; so simple. The piece of tape was in its slot and I pressed "On" for the transmission of my first dispatch.

Suddenly everything seemed to go crazy. The naked little machine rattled, shifted, shunted all its parts and I was certain it screamed. The echoes off the walls of the narrow corridor office with the row of printers, teletype machines and typewriters lining the corridor made me feel like I was inside a huge drum.

The machine was in perpetual motion. I felt lost, not knowing how to correct it. I typed another "Cal (space) Clr" and still the damned little machine began its non-stop back-and-forth motion. There was no lid to hide the wild race of its parts. I stopped it, started it, stopped, hung out the window gasping for air, hyperventilating. Then back to the crazed machine. I stopped, started, stopped, wrote the seven little punctures again. At every stop a message would come in, from all parts of the nation it seemed to me, like: "Hustle your bustle Cal there is a war on," or "No time for a potty break," or "Pit stops not allowed today." I finally stopped it, waited, and then heard the receiving unit clatter. It read: "I think she is trying to say 'Cal Clr' Edm Clr, DM." It was Don Miller in Edmonton. I knew I would love him for the rest of my life.

And so began my time in Calgary. Rarely did I send out a story bigger than two or three paragraphs, at best a celebrity passing through the city en route to Vancouver or Toronto, or superficial reports from the Calgary Stampede. None originated from my own research. They were all rewrites from the *Herald* or *The Albertan* reporters' dupes, dropped impersonally, totally without human contact in the CP basket in the window between the city room and my closeted workspace.

It did not take a great genius to know that I was hired under false pretenses and there was no way that my dream of becoming a reporter would be realized at Canadian Press Calgary. CP needed a teletype operator. In wartime they would train even a female for the job. The only "news reporting" from Calgary was the same every day, delivered from somewhere. It was the one subject I had no interest in investigating for source and meaning – farm market reports. I typed them onto the teletype tape and put them through for "send."

My career with CP was short-lived. It began June 6 and closed out at the end of October that year.

The entry of a new friend rescued me. He was Ralph Daly, a Vancouver newspaperman, then in the Royal Canadian Air Force stationed in Calgary. Like me, he appeared to have printer's ink instead of blood flowing through his heart and mind. He could not stay away from the newspaper offices. He especially liked to watch the news arrive from across the country and around the world, rolling in large sheets on the news receivers.

He would come in every night at *The Albertan* and occasionally late afternoon at the *Herald,* presumably when his duty on the base was finished. I soon confided in him that with Canadian Press I was going nowhere, that it was as remote as possible from the newspaper career I wanted. He had already told me about journalism in Vancouver, that there were stories everywhere. He urged me to write to the city editor of *The Vancouver Sun,* Himie Koshevoy, "the greatest … sweetest journalist you will ever meet."

Through all this I continued sending out the farm market reports. I showed Ralph the great advance in my career – the ability to copy the tabulated numbers of these canned reports to ticker tape. Now the transmissions went through without a problem.

"Canadian Press Calgary," I remember telling him, "taught me not to dream."

I knew that as a female I was in this "nothing" job because it was wartime and women in normal times would have no place even in this role. All the women I knew and saw in newspaper jobs were isolated in the "Society" or "Women's" department, doing "women's work" – limited to writing fashion, kitchen or "girl stuff."

When I told Ralph I probably would have to return to my family in Vegreville and from there to normal school in Edmonton to become a teacher,

Ralph literally begged me not to give up on my dream. So one day, I wrote a flippant letter to Himie Koshevoy.

As I recall now, 64 years later, I wrote that Ralph Daly, hanging around my office, urged me to write to the "greatest and sweetest journalist in the world"... that Ralph promised I would "learn from the best in the business – not only Himie, but the great and tough Hal Straight." I think I told Himie in that letter that, according to Ralph, Vancouver was a "terrific" news city, the people and situations of a Pacific coast/port city provided the stories I could find no where else.

I also did the face-saving thing, asking that if he was not interested to please file this in the nearest wastebasket.

As if by coincidence, I received one of CP Chief Gillis Purcell's messages with the closing: "Starting Monday you will work nights permanently. Regards GP."

With all the arrogance of a 22-year-old, and confidence that I had a family that would sustain me if I were jobless, I fired back in less than five minutes: "Starting Monday, I no longer work for CP. Regards, SM."

Now that I was experienced on the machine, the message was not garbled.

GP expressed regrets at my decision, asked me to stay on till he could find a replacement. I agreed and stayed for two weeks.

The day of the "Regards GP" message, Ralph and I stood at the mailbox beside the office, where he tossed a coin. "Heads" I mail the letter, "tails" I return to family and become a schoolteacher. I presume it came up "heads" because I mailed the letter to Himie.

An immediate response came by telegram from *The Sun*'s famous managing editor, Hal Straight. He offered me a job starting November 1, 1944, accommodating my commitment to finish the time I had given on notice. As I recall I was to get an increase in salary from $22 to $25 a week. It was a miracle; I was to work in the newsroom of Canada's third largest newspaper, with the impressive job title "Assistant to the City Editor." I read it so quickly I missed the "to" and headed for Vancouver on *The Sun* train ticket.

The reality was that I was a cub reporter who was in essence the lowest on the three-man totem pole of City Desk. But I was confident that at last I was inside the career that would lead to the fulfillment of my life's dream – a real news reporter, a *journalist*.

7
Through Fog and Fire

Early morning November 1, 1944, I was dressed, packed and waiting when the train slowed and squealed to a stop with a male voice welcoming the passengers to Vancouver.

Groggy from the long night sitting up in my coach seat, I looked out the window of the slowing train and saw a grey wall through an opaque curtain of cloud. Railway cars and engines sat still and random on the rows of tracks, like a depot for ghosts. It would be two weeks before I would realize there was a waterway, the great Vancouver Harbour – with a blue-green backdrop of mountains, capped white in winter. This was Greater Vancouver's North Shore – North and West Vancouver. Those mountains would become the substitute for my beloved North Star of my prairie childhood, the directional marker for one totally devoid of an internal compass.

With the majority of the passengers flooding out of the station onto the foot of Granville Street, I saw for the first time the edge of downtown, the city, and the world where I would live and grow professionally, find friends and the love of a special man.

As I came out the front doors of the station, I asked the first person who smiled at me to tell me the way to *The Vancouver Sun*. He pointed to what I soon knew to be east – four blocks, turn right on Cambie, up two blocks, then left and "you will see it a block away … a tower with a big ball of light on top." I could not miss it, I was told. It's visible from every part of the downtown area. I would learn it was the tallest building in Vancouver, and, at that time, in the British Commonwealth.

Several times I stopped to ask people, just in case I missed a turn. Perhaps it was an excuse to put down my suitcase to rest my arm. That suitcase carried all my life's possessions, the only time I travelled so light in the hundreds of thousands of miles of travel since then. It was long before wheels on baggage.

I was dressed in my best "business" garment – a rump-sprung black gabardine suit. I wore a large flat-topped brown hat. It would have been more appropriately used as a frisbee than a topper for one round-faced, five-foot-two-and-half-inch person trying to make a good first impression. That was the first and last time I wore that hat.

On that morning I met the most important person in my professional career – Himie Koshevoy. He was a short gnome-like man, far from handsome, but with a wonderful lopsided smile that immediately revealed a unique beauty. The wonder of that face – and the spirit behind it – grew. It gave truth to Ralph Daly's description of the city editor. His kindness and sense of humour were legendary among Canadian journalists, and all who ever knew Himie. It was a sort of competition for all who knew him to tell the best "Himie stories," as though wanting identity as friends of his. His humour was that of a punster, but never the corn that is often identified with those who use that genre.

His generosity and gentle humility were evident in his own words as a small but untitled foreword to his only published book, *Himie Koshevoy's Treasure Jest of Best Puns:*

"Some day this book may be considered a turning point in the history of publishing.

There are no rights reserved. Its stories may be reproduced without permission and reviewers who inflict any of its contents on their audience do so with the implicit understanding that is at their own peril. It may be stored in a time capsule and retrieval systems or transmitted by any means, electronic, photocopy, records or film without written permission of the publisher. It may be stapled, spindled or folded. It may be used to start fires or prop up tottering furniture. In other words, feel free to enjoy this book to the fuel or fool."

After explaining his book, he explains himself under the heading "The Author."

"Himie Koshevoy is a man named Himie Koshevoy who has spent a lifetime trying to convince people that Himie Koshevoy is not so many syllables seeking a body. Some think he is a Japanese sumo wrestler, and others an aging Cossack. When the real Himie Koshevoy stands up you can hardly tell ... As a writer he has spent most of his time covering his tracks that began when he was born in Montreal. He had the good sense to leave when he was a year old to spend many many years in his beloved Vancouver."

This was the person I met after the receptionist at the entrance to the huge open Fourth Floor Editorial room. He introduced me to the second person on the City Desk – Bill Short, the provincial editor. I would soon discover that both of them were prepared to tolerate my amateur standing until they could turn me into a useful third on the desk with them.

Himie outlined my duties. He was firm in what I had to do and what was expected of me as "Number Three" on the City Desk.

First: I would check all those who would now be called "first responders." These were the fire department, ambulance, police in Vancouver and the sub-urbs (University Area, Burnaby, New Westminster, North and West Vancouver), and sometimes cities and towns throughout the province if we heard a story of a mercy flight to Vancouver or a major incident such as mur-der or fatal fire or accident. My main checks were to be made three times a day before the major deadlines. At that time, with television almost a dozen years in the future, we had seven editions of the paper six days a week. The main ones were the first edition, the city home edition, and the final street (buff) edition. Added to these would be four local editions, usually with little more than the second front carrying the main stories of their communities – Vancouver Island, North and West Vancouver, Fraser Valley, and B.C. Interior/North.

Second: I would follow the police calls that sounded like there might be a story. I would check the area by use of a City Directory, finding neighbours and businesses on site of the breaking story, and/or related first responders – ambulance, fire, police. If it appeared to be developing into a major – or unique – story, Himie would send out a reporter or reporters with one or sev-eral photographers to the scene or scenes (for example, hospitals or the morgue if there were injuries or death), and the reporter on the police beat would be alerted for arrests and admissions to the morgue. The police reporter usually was already on top of these stories since he was closest to a major source.[1] Meanwhile I would write the initial stories, using whatever information I could get from the scene, the neighbours and my contacts by phone.

Third: When I arrived at the office at 7 a.m. each day the National Defence casualty list would be on my desk. My job was to follow up finding the biographies – the human interest stories – of those killed, wounded, missing in action – even, occasionally, those known to have been taken prisoners of war. When possible I was to get pictures of the casualties.

The final duty was clipping paper. Sounds superficial! However, it was the most valuable training any aspiring reporter could wish.

When the papers came off the presses and were delivered by copy boys to our desk, I would clip the stories, even the classified and occasional display ads, and paste them on our short-page copy paper. Then Himie would take over. If it was a "next day" folio, it usually only had the name of the reporter assigned; if illustration or "art" was needed, he would mark the name and the photo department would receive notice of assignment. Stories in which the sequel was days, months, or years away (as anniversaries) would be filed in folders marked by the 12 months of the year and then an open file of "Next Year." Some days Himie would circle one sentence in a story and list questions, and often that buried bit of colour or news turned into a story, sometimes major. I visualized the day that I too could recognize a story in an inconspicuous sentence, paragraph or classified ad. Even press releases were followed, with the initiative implanted on the reporter in the handwritten notes at the top corner of the document.

But before my right ear got its focus set to the police radio, I was advised of the "top priority" job by the new men in my life. The "ultimate duty" approved by most of the men – and no doubt financed by all – was the one fact of my life that gave me acceptance in a man's world. This, if nothing else, I thought, might keep me employed, at least until the end of the war. I was 22, old enough to get a liquor ration book, and didn't drink then. It was all arranged, I learned, from the managing editor down. One of the reporters

---

1   They were always male. I was, presumably, the first female to fill in on the police beat.

or a copy boy delivered me to the place where I applied for and received the liquor ration book. Then back to the office. It was, I think, the only time I was received with enthusiasm – when I delivered my week's ration of booze for their snake room. That was the only outside-office assignment in my first year in the job.

From the beginning of my career at *The Sun,* I was in close proximity to those who controlled and decided on the stories that would be carried in each edition. Jack Cairns, the news editor, was within reach of my outstretched arm that occasionally could hand him a note promising a story of interest I was pursuing. Around the rim of his horseshoe-shaped desk were copy editors, head and headline writers, the people who did the last editorial work and head writing of the stories that came from the City Desk or off the teletype receivers from across the country and around the world. Even as the least of those at the heart of news management, I would soon be adding to the mix of news of the day.

Himie told me that it was better to ask for help than to blunder in dealing with a problem – an unfamiliar word, place or detail about a city and people I did not know. "Never hesitate – or fear – asking us for help if you are not sure of how to follow a story … Simple as this: the best way to get information is to ask."

A job constant for Bill Short and me was taking dictation from reporters on beat and gathering stories in the community. It was before headphones, electric typewriters, and at least four decades before computers and e-mail in editorial offices. In those days we propped the phone on one shoulder, wedged against one ear, as we listened and pounded out the reporters' stories on manual typewriters.

Five months after I began my job, one of the most sensational events in Vancouver history took place. It was the explosion of the freighter *Greenhill Park,* docked at Pier B, at the edge of the financial core of the city, the virtual heart of downtown. The powerful blast and the continuing explosions of chemicals in the ship's hold shattered plate glass windows a mile or more away.

That day, March 6, 1945, the sphere of my job could not have been more clearly defined. I was tied to my assigned seat beside the police radio. I barely moved from my chair until after 5 p.m. – not even to do what came naturally. A non-stop flood of stories poured in such as I never again experienced in my days on City Desk. Bill and I took calls from reporters scattered throughout the city, and recorded and followed up on information and tips phoned in from citizens. That day every minute seemed to be edging towards a deadline.

Bill always spoke candidly when he thought I could improve on my phone interviewing techniques, in the style and phrasing of questions to get the most accurate and probably most newsworthy answers. His professional talent was well respected. His biography was known and accepted. He was a leader in early Alcoholics Anonymous in the West. I was told there were times he would disappear for days. When he returned it was as if nothing was amiss. He would settle in at his desk; his absence from that chair was never cause for comment or reprimand. That was the obvious indication of how valued he was as a member of *The Sun* "family."[2]

Overhearing my phone interviews, Bill criticized me for taking time "chatting" with contacts, in my routine checks or follow-ups of leads. He thought I was "too involved … wasted time in small talk."

I explained that these people, the contacts who tipped me on stories developing or in climax, had become my friends. It was not long before I was receiving calls from them at home. It was as though they got their own satisfaction in seeing my stories develop in the newspaper, whether I did them or others built on them.

It was not unusual within the first year of my career to receive phone calls from firemen, ambulance workers, and friends on the police force. One of my closest friends was a policewoman named Audrey Kirk. Often I worked nights with Audrey and knew the officers when I would go to a story. I always felt safe and sure that nobody else would get the details in even the minor stories.

When Bill criticized me for "chatter" on the phone, Himie said, "No matter how she did it, she got the story."

Years later Pierre Berton, Canada's most prolific twentieth-century author-historian and an established reporter, would say it in a different way. He urged me to write my autobiography and said the foreword "would read something like this: 'She never did the job the way a reporter should. She got too involved … but scooped us all.'"

---

2 Owner Don Cromie referred to it as "*The Sun* family."

It was not long before my scrapbooks had some pasted clippings – done by Laverna Fong, the editorial secretary, who made up her mind she would help me on the job.

My first scrapbook – 11 by 14 inches with a red cover – is a true reminder of how my career grew. Initially it reflected my pride and my rejoicing at the first stories that reached print. Each one was carefully pasted into the book and dated. The earliest were tiny stories under small heads, no more than an inch or two long, little more than fillers. Even on the first page the stories become larger and soon they are topped by larger heads – two columns and placed conspicuously in the paper.

A most precious piece of memorabilia among those loose papers is a small sheet of copy paper with a single-column story about four inches long, the head reading "Husband Saves Wife as Home Catches Fire." Beside it Himie wrote, "Simma's Third Scoop – Award of Oak Leaf & Cluster of Pearls."

In those days bylines were only for the stars. I cannot remember when I had my first byline. I never cared about the bylines; I simply wanted to tell the story for as many people as possible. I loved to sit on the streetcar and listen to people talk about my stories. My anonymity was a blessing then. Later in life, I realized that having name recognition was an advantage in getting people to tell their stories.

In time my work – with or without the byline – drew requests from magazines and other newspapers for enlargement of the story or a different angle. They included the old *Liberty* magazine, *Chatelaine, Reader's Digest, Fair Lady* in South Africa, and *Cosmopolitan*.

I yearned for the time when I would get assignments outside of the City Room. It happened one day after the paper was put to bed and I was finishing the clippings and filing assignments. The voice on the police radio called officers to a fire in Chinatown. I asked Himie if I could cover it – "*There!*" He responded, "Go your best lick."

I ran the two blocks to the address given on the radio. The fire was at the back of a restaurant, the emergency equipment operating from the lane. It seems Himie saw a blast of smoke from the window behind the City Desk – overlooking the streets to and in Chinatown. He sent senior reporters and a photographer to the scene. *The Province* and several radio reporters closed in.

It was drizzling rain. I was wearing the only business suit I had – the rump-sprung black. One of my shoes had a hole in the sole. I could feel the wet dirty water of the lane squishing around my toes. The other shoe was soggy and felt even worse than the leaky one. The reporters, whose names were known in the business, milled around, and finally the old pros decided this was not worth the time or trouble. They were leaving and asked if I wanted to get a ride back to the office.

I told them I'd hang around for a while. I asked the photographer to wait with me and take me back "in a few minutes."

After the others left, I told him why I wanted to stay. I had been watching numerous cats wandering through the wet goop of the alley, all of them converging and entering the back door of a building. Perhaps if I had been more familiar with the life of the people and beasts in Chinatown, I would have ignored it as "normal." But I followed the cats and found them circling around a Chinese man in a chair, who was being treated for burns by other Chinese. I learned that when the fire broke out in the back of this building, the man set out to rescue his cats, and continued even after he was burned. He explained through an interpreter that by saving all his cats he was guaranteed an afterlife in heaven. As I recall, the number was about 60.

A two-column picture ran mid-Page One.

For years afterward Jack Richards, *The Province* senior reporter in Chinatown that day, gave me backhanded praise, telling the story of how this "Girl Cub" scooped all the pros in Vancouver journalism.

I found my way to break out of my career as a "shut-in" by seeking information and knowledge of the new world in which I was now permanently planted, and by working on my own time after hours.

It began during several weeks of fog so heavy that visibility was little more than a foot or two. The fog was so dense that I would have to feel my way along fences and walls to walk the half block from the South Granville streetcar stop to my home at the coast. I could barely see my own feet.

I was curious. I wondered how emergency vehicles and crews could find their way through the opaque ground cloud to reach and deal with crises before tragedy became irreversible. I contacted the fire chief and asked the question, "How do you reach people in time to save lives and property in this black fog?" He agreed to allow me to ride with them and "see for your-self."

When I arrived at the downtown Fire Hall, Number One, I signed the required waiver, absolving the department and the City of Vancouver of responsibility if I were injured or killed. The firemen were prepared for my entry into their super-male domain that night. But they were not prepared when I bounced in through the door without warning ... I bounced out just as fast, hearing a few firemen run for cover.

My first "ride" was really a run. When the alarm sounded in the fire hall my duty was clear; the chief had given me a huge flashlight and I would carry it to mark the edge of the road as I ran beside the lead engine in the parade. The run was not major for me. Obviously, once I learned the answer to my question about "speed" to emergencies in the fog, I decided that one night of research was sufficient. The chief, however, thought I was useful and my research lasted for a few nights until the fog lifted.

That link with Vancouver Fire Department lasted and grew throughout my 30 years at *The Sun*. Added to my five or six phone checks a day was personal "service" (which had many variations, including carrying water in a three-alarm lumber mill fire on a long weekend when the department was short staffed). I made life-long friends and found numerous subjects for features, magazine stories, and writing about the life-saving work of what was called the "Inhalator Squad," later the VFD Rescue Squad, today manned by paramedics.

I learned that firemen, no matter what their attire or lack of it, can be on the engine in seconds. At night their whole outfit, from boots to top cover, seemed to be set in a single piece by their cots in the upstairs dorm. When the alarm sounded they would be down the pole and on the moving fire engines in less than a minute. Their boast was that the emergency services of Vancouver would be at any site within three minutes of the call.

I was eventually named the first Honorary Fire Chief of the City of Vancouver, and given a pass to cross fire lines. It was not only recognition of the advancement my writing had made in the work of Vancouver Fire Department, but also acceptance that I knew how to manage my own and public safety in emergencies.

Honorary Chief of Vancouver Fire Department. The inscribed helmet was presented to me by Chief Hugh Bird in a special civic ceremony, at which time I was also given a pass that allowed me to cross fire lines.

Once when I started into an apartment building on a fire call where a well-known city lawyer was said to be trapped, I was stopped by the police. The Fire Chief himself came out of the building and led me through the line. He told the officer, "She is one of our chiefs."

Firemen have been involved in numerous good causes. They worked with the public relations director of Children's Hospital, Jean Pearce, and me in *The Vancouver Sun*'s annual March of Dimes. This campaign raised the major portion of the hospital's annual budget. I worked on it six or eight weeks every year for seven consecutive years, writing the stories that helped bring in the target amount needed to top off the operating budget.

The firemen marched behind their popular band through the downtown streets to launch our annual campaign, then set up washtubs outside one major department store while the band played on. Workmen would drop large bills in the tubs. One time a logger walked by, casually dropped a $100 donation, and disappeared in the crowd. That generous anonymous donor always stood out in my memory as the whole Talmudic principle of *Tzedaka*.[3] What I usually saw as a journalist was that when people's names were published as donors the donations would increase.

Children's Hospital March of Dimes gave me a degree of pride in the warm and colourful stories that it produced. Best of all, I knew that every cent raised by *The Sun* features and by various newspaper departments' projects in support of the campaign went to the hospital.

Jean Pearce was a dream partner, never failing in stories that would be the best of human interest. The children came from all parts of the province and occasionally from beyond our borders. Celebrities – clowns, singers, and dramatic actors – were always ready to visit, entertain and play with sick and dying children. One of the most widely publicized stories was that of the song "There's A Bluebird on Your Window Sill," composed by Nurse Elizabeth Clarke as she comforted her small charges. Jean had the song printed on sheet music and it was recorded by some of the most famous singers in America, among them Bing Crosby and Dinah Shore.

---

3   As mentioned in Chapter 4, this is the ethical principle of charity; we give without anyone knowing – neither who gave nor who was the recipient.

My detractors liked to call me a "sob sister" when I wrote a particularly poignant story of a crippled or sick child. There were brave children who rarely cried, too young to know they were different or that they were in any way unlucky in their disability and pain. Death was not cause for fear or worry to the younger children, though the teenagers understood and they were remarkably courageous, some even philosophic in their approach to suffering, life and death.

The other campaign in which I worked full-time for *The Sun* was what was known then as Community Chest, later the United Appeal. Every cent raised went to the agencies served by the campaign. Publisher Don Cromie alternated annually as chairman of the campaign with *The Province* publisher. In *The Sun's* turn to lead the campaign, I did the stories for fundraising and recording of progress. One year, half of Page One had a huge picture of me with an editorial by Don Cromie explaining why "Simma Holt supported the Community Chest." It was published without my consent and I believed it diminished my journalistic independence. But at least word got out about the wide range of human service groups that were beneficiaries of the annual campaign.

History records that the war in Europe began to collapse when Soviet troops circled Berlin and Hitler committed suicide April 30, 1945. In May was the signing of surrender by all the German troops. The war in the Pacific continued under the famous General Douglas MacArthur for four months longer, ending with the first and most horrific use of the atom bomb on Hiroshima and Nagasaki on August 6 and 9, 1945. The formal surrender by Japan was signed September 2. The Second World War was over.

However, on August 12, three weeks before the complete and official ending of the war, *The Sun* rushed to the street with a huge extra. The top half of the front Page had simply "PEACE" in huge white letters on a solid black ground.

It was a false alarm. It happened as a result of a person – of course we were informed it was "a girl" operator – practising "war over" or "peace" on a punched tape, which accidentally went through the slot with other news throughout the continent. By the time the correction reached the news desk at *The Sun,* the EXTRA had carried the big news to the street. Runners were sent out to pull back all the delivery trucks and the copies on the street that had not been sold. It was said that 1,200 were gone to buyers. I saved two.[4]

As the soldiers, airmen and sailors came home from war, they expected to have jobs waiting. Soon I was literally hounded by other reporters to get out. In retrospect I saw myself as the Rosie the Riveter of Canadian journalism. "Rosie" was the name given to women who did essential war work – building ships, airplanes, tanks, all the needs of men in war.

I did not fight for my job. I did not have to. Unknown to me at the time, *The Sun* executive – Himie, Hal Straight, owners Sam and Don Cromie, even the Circulation Manager Herb Gates – said I could have the job as long as I wanted it.

Flashing forward I can almost hear what must have been the postwar dialogue that assured my survival in my career. It was about 15 years later; the newspaper was in financial difficulty and was forced to engage in major economic cuts. Whenever a newspaper seeks solution to financial problems, the editorial staff is expendable. The advertising staff is not; they bring in the money.

Hal Straight again fought to assure my job and that of an exceptional and popular columnist, Jack Wasserman. In the episode of economy cuts then Hal told Himie, "I fought for the jobs of the Jewish kids; now you go to bat for the Gentiles."

In the loose papers of my scrapbook is the stub of my first bi-weekly paycheque as a professional reporter at *The Sun*. Salary $54.33; deductions: $7.10 income tax, 90 cents for Workmen's Compensation, medical, unemployment insurance; net pay $46.33.

Another stub is of a $21 cheque dated December 20, 1944, my first career bonus.

---

4   They are in my papers at the University of Manitoba Archives and Special Collections.

City Desk mid-1940's. City Editor Himie Koshevoy and me. He is missing from this picture, but Bill Short, the provincial editor and assistant to Himie, would normally be in the seat across from me.

News Desk where the copy editors and head writers sat in a horseshoe desk within my arm's length.

Himie Koshevoy and I share some memories.

8

Tragedy in the Water

It was probably the worst moment of my life. No matter how many deaths and funerals I have attended in my personal life or on my job as a reporter, none is more painful nor persistent in memory than what happened that Saturday night, July 13, 1947 at the beautiful but treacherous Spanish Banks off Vancouver's Point Grey Peninsula. Though there was nothing I could do to change it, I go through the nagging quest for revision of that moment: "If I had known … if I had been stronger … if I had not so readily accepted the idea of a swim that night …"

And strangely, as hard as it has been to forgive myself, members of the family showed no animosity towards me because of that terrible loss.

Balfour Barish was a student at the University of British Columbia's engineering department, having completed and survived two full tours of duty as an airman over Germany in World War II. His sisters Doris and Lorna hosted a beach party at Spanish Banks to honour his service and give him a send-off into a promising future with friends he knew and some like myself he met for the first time that night.

As darkness settled over the wide long strip of sand, the North Shore mountains turned from the daylight green to deep purple then into black of night. City lights across the bay were the contrast to the quiet peace of the beach in which we were all so young and happy, celebrating the special life being honoured that night. Bonfires of other beach parties told of others celebrating life itself on this wondrous summer night.

Balfour and I were chatting easily together about our different pasts and our plans for the future. I told him that my job had been writing the casualty lists of the war and veterans returning home. And he told me of his flights and life in the war in Europe.

The air was gentle, soft. The sea water was also still and quiet, warm to the toe-dipping test. I do not know whose idea it was to go for a swim. When Balfour and I asked the others if any of them would join us, none were interested. Their reasons: they did not have their bathing suits or were enjoying the party on the dry beach. Balfour said he had his bathing suit in the car and would change. I had worn my bathing suit under my pantsuit.

The peace of Spanish Banks was deceiving, a virtual temptress to those who loved night swims in Vancouver. In the past I had walked on the soft smooth sands, the tiny soft ripples underfoot part of the whole seductive nature of the beach. When the tide was out, the depth of the water in all the times I had been there was little more than that of a child's wading pool. Inevitably, however, the tide turns and then suddenly the dips are carved deep with the rush of water, the accelerated flow creating deadly whirlpools, their suction and pull somewhat like water tornadoes. I had heard about the treachery of this beautiful beach, but never experienced it.

That night, Balfour and I walked parallel to the beach edge, continuing the conversation we had started on shore, enjoying the wash of the water, unaware of its rise. I began doing the only swim stroke that I had developed beyond the dog paddle in the narrow Vermilion River that ran through Vegreville. We noted the bonfires of the parties on both sides of the one where his relatives and friends were gathered. I was facing the shore; Balfour was at my back. We continued to chatter about our interests, about his welcome home and his joy in his new – and "such a different" – world of peace and challenge at the University of British Columbia, so near to the site of the beach parties.

With my back to him, I was unaware that he could not swim and was walking beside me. Suddenly I heard him scream, looked around and saw him disappear under water, his arm stretching upward. I grabbed his hand, and tried to pull him back towards the shore. He was strong and pulled me under with him. I swallowed water and knew I was drowning. I let go, got some air and looked for him to come up. I did not know how to dive. I did the only thing I knew possible for me to survive; I lay on my back and floated, screaming for help. I thought – so naïvely, not understanding the huge sweep of the tide – that if I stayed in that spot, then when help came they would find Balfour there. But of course, the tide swirled me around.

It was the young people at a party far up the beach from ours who heard my cries. They pulled me to shore. I kept yelling, "Get Balfour ... he's right here ... he went down here ..."

Police, firemen, the people on the beach searched through that short night of darkness. In the morning light, the tide having receded, searchers found Balfour in three feet of water.

When I got to the little house my sister Hannah and I were renting on the farthest reach of the city, the east end of Vancouver, about 9:30 that morning, my father was sitting on the rail of the small porch. He told me he was in Banff the day before and felt something "bad" was happening to me. He got on a train, somehow arriving there even before I returned home. I did not know, nor did I ever think to ask, how he got there or how he reacted so quickly to intuition of danger to me. My sister, en route to San Francisco, was on the phone from Seattle shortly after my dad and I got into the house. Her first words: "Simma are you all right?" I knew Hannah always seemed to have a psychic insight or special sensitivity to others. She had left the train to make the phone call.

Hannah used to entertain my friends and me with teacup readings and I wondered if it was the arrangement of the tea leaves or a clairvoyance unique to her. She could always advise me with such wisdom and certainty.[1]

I stayed off work for a day, not only exhausted having walked up and down the beach aimlessly, but also feeling shame and self-consciousness at the thought of facing the people on the job. When I did arrive at the office the next morning, Himie assigned me to Spanish Banks. There was another drowning.

---

1   She had become a graphologist early in life, beginning in our hotel when she compared signatures on the register to the personalities of the guests she got to know. Then while in the United States she used her skills to help army base psychiatrists and psychologists who brought men into the USO where she, like other young women, was a hostess and used her skill to entertain. Hannah Milner Smith is the author of two of the definitive books on graphology: *Between The Lines: The Casebook of a Graphologist*, McClelland & Stewart Ltd, Toronto, Montreal, 1970, and *The Hidden Meaning, A Guide to Handwriting Analysis*, Gray's Publishing Ltd., Sidney, British Columbia, 1979.

We both knew that I had to face the reality. It was a life lesson: no matter how traumatized, I had to accept what I could not change, and move on.

9
Enter Leon

A few weeks after the Balfour tragedy, at a party I attended with a totally different group of young people, I met Leon. He owned a 32-foot sailboat, a yawl called *Zanira*, with two friends, Mitchell Snider and Harold Lando. The boat had a romantic history. A man had built it for a trip around the world on his honeymoon. It was designed to sleep six; on a day trip it held eight, even ten comfortably. The boys used it for two- or three-day stags to their favourite wilderness resort on Vancouver Island, Yellow Point.

At that first meeting, Leon invited me to join him and some other young couples on the boat for an outing to Bowen Island the next day. I hesitated but quickly realized that at age 25 – and living in a community surrounded by ocean and beaches – I had to accept the lifestyle of the time, the place and the people who would be my friends.

That Sunday became the first of many day trips to Bowen Island, described in tourist brochures as "the idyllic getaway ... in sheltered waters, beaches, and 5,261 hectares (13,000 acres) of forests to explore..."[1] Because of the *Zanira*'s deep draw (eight feet), they could not bring it into the dock. The regulars aboard knew the routine; once anchored about 50 or more yards from the shore, the young people would dive off the boat and swim to the dock. Those who did not swim would go ashore in the dinghy.

Leon offered to row me ashore. I said I wanted to stay on the boat and read. As he hesitated about leaving me, I urged him to join the others. I watched him as his beautiful slim body cut into the water, disappeared momentarily

---

1   *Vancouver Coast and Mountains,* Travel Guide, Beautiful British Columbia, Tourism B.C. 2007, p. 17. Today Bowen Island is like a suburb of Vancouver, with residents' commuter ferry ride 20 minutes from Horseshoe Bay in West Vancouver to Snug Cove.

and then surfaced. He looked back and gave me a small smile and then moved slowly in a strong side stroke. Then I thought, *This is silly.* I dived in, and began my elemental side stroke towards the dock where the others were waiting for Leon. He was still in the water and kept looking back, slowing though keeping his distance from me. I was aware of his watchfulness.

I saw that this was a very caring person, and I knew I wanted him in my life. I thought no farther than that he would be a lifelong friend. I could not know then that he would become my foremost and most beloved friend.

We began dating, not seriously, but obviously mutually enjoying each other's company. I had known more exciting men, but hardly any more thoughtful, patient, kind and with a depth of knowledge that would suddenly and unexpectedly surface in dialogue.

When I arrived in Vancouver, I was a new Jewish girl in town, and all the Jewish mothers, I learned later, pushed their sons to be the first to "get" me as their daughter-in- law. It would be like having the "son the doctor" to have a "daughter-in-law the writer." Many funny situations developed as a result of the first rush of attention thus created. Anxious to impress, I was the model good girl, never using the language I learned at *The Sun.* I never let those mothers' sons hear even a word of the graphic language I could provide. Not even the minor "damn."

(I remember the first time I used "damn" in front of my mother, she said, "I do not understand; I did not go to university." These boys' mothers may not have had my mother's tolerance and humour.)

And so when my friendship began with Leon, neither of us was tied to one dating partner. Nor was I interested in doing anything that might minimize my career as a new reporter. Nonetheless we had been dating periodically, often with his partners and their girlfriends on the *Zanira,* and usually to Bowen Island, for a barbecue on one of the beaches. On one of the outings an old (or perhaps current) girlfriend turned up on the island. My suspicions were aroused when Leon disappeared and his closest friend, Mitchell Snider, was totally dedicated to taking care of me along with his own date. I teased Mitchell, "Greater love hath no man than that he sacrifice exclusive time with his own date to keep Leon's date occupied." Mitchell's date was my new roommate Gertrude (later, by official name change, "Tova") Robb. We had been to the University of Manitoba together, she a star in the drama group.

We had never been close at university, since she had her own circle of friends from childhood in Winnipeg. However, when she came to Vancouver and was receptionist at CBC, I discovered she needed a place to stay. She moved into the house Hannah and I shared. She was my dearest and lifelong friend. No one ever was closer or brought more humour or joy.

When Leon returned to the boat, I did not want him to think I had missed the fact of his life that day, so I asked, "Did you have fun? Mitchell didn't."

Another time, a tall slim woman came to the island in a small sailboat. I suspected it was the same one of that day Mitchell took over. She said the motor of her little day sailer had died and wondered if she and her boat could be towed back to dock in Vancouver. The moon rose and, as though staged, Leon's favourite music – Debussy's *Clair de Lune* – sounded through the *Zanira* on the radio. Leon had taken the tiller in the small cockpit, his rescued friend sat beside him with only the tiller between them. I had chosen the seat directly opposite them. I don't know what made me do it, but I did not like her proprietary attitude towards my date and rarely did my eyes leave Leon or his eyes.

Usually the girls brought picnic lunches for the parties on the *Zanira*, but sometimes there would be a barbecue. Bennie Chechik was the chef or barbecue director at these events. Actually he was a remarkable entrepreneur, the capitalist of the group. Ben and his brothers and sisters owned the West End Vancouver Bay Theatre along with several other enterprises, including the first drive-in theatre on the coast. Ben was the one most harassed by his mother, pushing him to court me. With his great sense of humour he finally escaped his mother's badgering by raving about my talent as a cook. He told his mother, "You cannot imagine how talented she is; she makes the prettiest and most tasty livers wrapped in bacon." So ended a mother's dream of a good kosher daughter-in-law!

The first time I was invited for a steak party was one beautiful warm August night. After we anchored outside the little bay, the first six went ashore. While they were getting the fire started for the barbecue, setting up the grates and arranging the log seating, Leon and I loaded the dinghy with the food. We rowed to the shore. When we got to the beach, I climbed out of the dinghy, up a rock onto a log that was the bridge to the beach party. As I stepped onto that log I saw a snake seemingly across it and hanging over the side. I screamed, raced back to the rock and leaped into the dinghy. It rocked as though it might tip over. I threw down the stuff I was carrying and jumped into the water, fully clothed. This was about 6:30 in the evening.

Leon got himself and the food to shore. He knocked the snake off the plank and with great contempt said, "It's dead."

"I don't care," I shouted, "a snake is a snake is a snake and I hate them."

Over dinner and in the boat on the way home Leon did not speak a single word to me. We drove from the boat dock into Vancouver in his old two-seater 1929 Essex, and still he was mute and obviously angry. I also was getting madder by the minute. I remember the exact spot on Burrard Street Bridge when Leon learned who I was, that I was not that "nice girl" who never said a rotten word, the girl his mother wanted him to romance and marry. We were about ten minutes from my West End apartment, Stanley Park Manor, and it happened. I mustered every rotten word I could think of, and words I had never used in my life but had heard endlessly in the man's world where I worked. I let him have it:

"You bastard, you son-of- … you rotten a---hole '…" and on and on. "I am soaking wet, cold, saved your damned stinking life and the food for all of you … was heroic … jumped into the water to save your rotten hide … and you sit here pouting, angry and treating me as though you had suffered. Here I am soaked to the skin, chilled and perhaps will die long before my time … you behaved like a g--damned idiot, dummy." I still had not said the F--- word but used everything else I could muster. "I sacrificed my health, my youth to save your rotten hide and you behave like a martyred a---hole that you are … a rotten pain in the …"

I think I was still yelling at him when I opened the old sticky door of his Essex and started to get out. He followed me to the side door of the apartment block and, of course, opened it for me. Just as I was about to slam the door with a new phrase or two he might not yet have heard, he said quietly and with his little grin I came to love, "When you get out of your wet clothes will you join me for coffee and a hamburger?"

His mother, he admitted was pushing him to hook me. He told me that he had thought I was "too pure … too perfect" and therefore would be a bore.

Not long after that he proposed to me. I told him that if I ever had to choose between him and my career I would choose the career.

Leon and I were married May 29, 1949, exactly one year and a day after Mitchell and Tova were married. Tova was my matron of honour, then in her eighth month of pregnancy with Judith, the first of her four children. I always called Judith "my flower girl" because the flowers rested on Tova's bulging belly.

After our marriage, I rarely used the great flow of language that blasted him the night of the snake. However, there was one phrase that came easily when I expressed my annoyance at some situation: "Oh pee up a rope."

One day Leon, who rarely swore or used crude language, asked me to "please stop saying that." I knew he was serious and I only used it one time again. That was to tell him about an incident in a parole hearing when I was a member of the National Parole Board.

A young offender, barely out of his teens, was in the toughest maximum prison in the country, Kent Institution (in Kent, B.C.). From studying his record I knew he was just a pain in the neck, not very likely to be even a minor threat to society. I wanted him out of prison, especially out of the maximum security institution. Just before the hearing, we were told that he had been in solitary confinement because of his abusive language to prison guards. That made it impossible for the staff to recommend him for parole, nor could we grant him any form of conditional release. When he appeared, heavily guarded, he simply looked like a harmless, clean-cut little boy, confirming my belief that he would be a "fish" (target for the older prisoners) and ought to be out of prison totally.

I led off by telling him of the predicament we were in because of his offending in the prison the very day he was coming up for his parole hearing. When I asked him why he rated punishment at this crucial time of his life, he wasted no time lipping off at me. I told him I knew from his record that he was basically a "good kid" and usually got along well with the staff. He again got his angry words out at me, and I responded by saying that that stuff simply "makes you a boring kid … and I know you have more to you than that big mouth." I did not have to remind him of the danger of a young inmate in a prison with heavy-duty criminals, many of them lifers.

He became more agitated and angry. I assured him that if he had behaved even minimally he would be a good candidate for some form of conditional

Leon and me on our wedding day.

We had a small breakfast wedding with only our parents and about 15 close friends. The classy convertible was provided by a friend for the picture. For our honeymoon trip we travelled in Leon's 1929 Essex.

release, that we could review the file in a few weeks if he stayed out of trouble. "Being a pain in the butt is no reason to be kept at Kent or any prison."

Finally he admitted what he said to one of his keepers that got him locked into solitary. "I told him to pee up a rope and suck the wet end."

I almost choked and struggled to keep a straight face, saying only that was "pretty bad stuff to say to an officer."

When I got home, I told Leon that my old phrase could have been worse. After I gave him the next line I had heard from the kid, he commented dryly, "I'm glad you did not learn from him, before we met."

I was away from home a great deal as a journalist and then as an MP commuting across Canada for five years, 2,200 miles, through three time zones, at least 16 hours in transit every weekend. Before I left, I would say to Leon, "Have a good time, but change the sheets before I get home."

One day when I got home from Ottawa, in a strange formal way he invited me out to dinner. Usually he said, "Let's go out to eat." We ate out a great deal, partly because of the travel, but also because I was not exactly the greatest cook in the world and he liked "real food." I remember trying to make coffee when we were first married. The first time he said delicately, "It's kind of weak." So the next day I doubled the coffee and he remarked, "It is kind of strong." The third day he said, "Well, at least it is hot."

This night that he invited me out to dinner I knew something was wrong or different. We were barely seated when he said, "I have something to tell you."

He was nervous and upset. He told me that one of his female tennis partners invited him home, and when they arrived there he saw a man looking through the window, through curtains left (in retrospect) conveniently slightly open.

I didn't ask what the man saw, or perhaps photographed. I didn't want to know.

Leon told me she intended to name him co-respondent in her divorce action. It was a "set-up" he said. I laughed because, even though I knew women liked him, and he was well-endowed, I never thought of him as a sex athlete. I put his mind at rest and told him not to worry, that we would talk to our lawyer-friend, George Murray, if she did act on her threat. He was upset that anyone had to know, but I assured him it would elevate his status among the men.

A few days later, he answered the phone. As I walked by I heard him exclaim in obvious shock, "Two thousand dollars?"

I moved close to him and whispered, "Is it her?"

He nodded. I came close to the phone and said in a voice loud enough to be heard through the walls of our house and a block away, "You tell that broad that I am going to sue her for alienation of affection, and it won't be $2,000 but $20,000."

He never heard from her again.

Leon, born September 10, 1914, in Portland, Oregon, was the only son of Molly and Ben Holt. His mother was born in New York. His father, born in Czechoslovakia, emigrated to the United States early in the 20th century.

A group of wealthy New York entrepreneurs persuaded Ben Holt to transfer his great talent into a fashionable high-end fur store on the main street (Granville at Robson) in the growing young city on Canada's west coast. Leon was four when the family moved from Portland to Vancouver.

Holt Fur Company soon had customers among those in high society in Vancouver and from as far away as Washington, D.C. and Hong Kong. Leon worked in the family business as accountant, manager and salesperson. The family prospered and lived well until several events and changes, mostly beyond their control, ended the prosperity. First, Ben Holt, along with millions of other independent small businessmen throughout North America, invested in the stock market when it peaked, shortly before it crashed. Then, while on a buying trip to New York, he lost his high-priced inventory in a major robbery. The insurance company would not pay for his loss, claiming it was an "inside job." The adjusters neither cared nor would hear anything other than what they chose to hear in order to save money for their company. It did not matter how many people of recognized reputation, social and business stature testified to the absolute integrity and honesty of Ben Holt, known as "a man of the old school" whose word was his bond and who would "never take even a penny he did not earn."

Several years later, a seamstress who had worked with Ben Holt in the creation of his fur garments moved to a large new exclusive fur store in downtown Vancouver when Holt Fur Company could no longer afford a full-time worker. Not long after she began there, she went into the basement storage area and recognized the distinctive Ben Holt cut and design, some with her own stitching in them. But it was too late to do anything. Even if he could have acted, Ben Holt was not a fighter; he would rather forget his loss than open an ugly wound and go to police or the courts, with the attendant investigations, the inevitable stress and publicity that would weigh down on his small family.

The end to the Holt Fur Company was inevitable when the department stores began mass producing fur coats and the new furriers could make product quickly, without the detail and perfection that Ben Holt would never abandon for fast money.

At age 65, Leon's parents, sold their home in south Vancouver and rented an apartment in the West End. That was the beginning of the end of the life they loved in their bungalow home, he with his garden, shrubs, flowers and little birds. When all their bills were paid they had about $25,000 left. It was held in the Royal Bank of Canada, at Robson and Granville, the site of the Holts' original store in Canada. Leon and I made sure their bank balance never dropped below the amount they saw as security to the end of their lives. It could remain our little white lie, since Leon handled all their affairs and all they ever saw was that small blue bank account book.

Leon always hated business. He was an outdoor person and started towards his goal of becoming a geologist by entering the University of British Columbia in the early depression years. There were no summer jobs then for university students, so he had to return full time to the family business. Before he could advance his education the war broke out and he was conscripted into the army. He never forgot the day that he appeared before the head of the draft board in Vancouver, Judge Alex Manson (a man I knew later as "the hanging judge"). Leon told Manson that he was an American citizen by birth. Manson responded with the words, "What's the difference if you die as an American or a Canadian?"

Leon became an instructor in the earliest radar and planned, upon discharge, to join with his friend Mitchell Snider in an electronics business. Mitchell had enlisted in the Royal Canadian Air Force and was seconded to the Royal Air Force, serving in the earliest air war in Europe. Both Leon and Mitchell were natural "techies." But when the war ended both returned to their family businesses – Mitchell to San Francisco Tailors and Pawn Brokers, a Vancouver establishment and landmark for over 100 years.

Leon continued to hate the life in business, and yearned for jobs out of doors. In order to help me and his family financially he bought a speed-graphic camera with attachments and set out to learn how to use it. His aim was to help me with illustration for my features and take pictures we would spot that would be saleable. His first photograph was a springtime classic, a child dipping its foot in the water of English Bay. He was soon asked to take assignments with other reporters and became established as a freelance, almost a regular staffer in *The Sun* photo department. In time he was producing photo features and I would do his captions.

Though there were male reporters (not one of them great successes or memorable in the business) who enjoyed harassing me, I always had a good relationship with the photographers. We had won awards together. They would go out of their way to help me on my job and I would find ways to make their pictures better by our working together to get interesting or unusual angles.

One of my favourite moments in Leon's relationship with the photo department was the day they challenged him, "How come you stayed with her so long?"

His answer: "I stick around to see what will happen next."

But Leon's career in the photo department of *The Sun* ended suddenly.

It happened when a City Hall employee was charged with theft of tires and Leon was assigned to get the picture of the man coming out of city lockup on bail. I went with Leon to serve as lookout for him. I had many friends in the police department and could rely on their help when I had a job to do. This night, when the city employee was about to be released, the jail staff advised me as the time arrived and told me he would be leaving from the front door, presumably where his family or a friend was waiting. I rushed out to tell Leon to get ready. When the city worker opened the door and began to walk to the street, Leon's camera was behind his back. Neither he nor the camera moved. The man walked past us. Leon did not budge other than to let him pass without obstruction. I howled and complained. Leon responded quietly, "I'm not going to help ruin a man's life over a silly charge like that."

I howled some more, and my husband listened as usual, without a word of protest over my noise and my criticism.

"You shouldn't have taken the assignment if you were unwilling to follow through." My tirade was an act; I was proud of his integrity. I told him that later.

That night he told me he'd had his fill of the job. At age 40, Leon went back to university.

He was told there were only two careers he could effectively enter at that age – teaching or law. He chose teaching. His first school was in the new, large and impressive Gladstone Secondary School on the east side of Vancouver. There were times that my job as a journalist and his as a teacher there were an embarrassment to both of us.

It was early in the life of this new school that police had uncovered a girls' shoplifting ring, traced back to Gladstone, and I had to find the story.

Another time, the principal, Ralph Thomas, who had become a good friend to both Leon and me, faced a large group of boys who were told that they could not enter the school until they pulled their pants up over their navels. They refused. I was assigned to the story. The staff photographer and I raced to the school and out of the corner of my eye I saw Leon inside the front door with other teachers, behind the principal. I wanted to be invisible. Minutes after we arrived and witnessed the scene, Ralph Thomas had a camera in his hand. He announced, "In five minutes I am going to take a picture of all of you who are left out here. Whoever is in this picture will be sent home, maybe even expelled." The boys waited about two minutes, then pulled up their pants and walked into school. The crisis was over. The story did not even become a filler.

When I ran for the Liberals in the riding of Vancouver–Kingsway, Leon had been at Gladstone about 20 years. We went knocking on doors together, and many times the interest was in Leon. My campaign was irrelevant. I knew that if those households voted for me they would be giving me their vote as much for my husband as for my record.

One day Leon and I were in a long lineup waiting to get into a vintage hotel that had been restored and converted into what had become the favoured after work meeting place for the new generation of young swingers, yuppies, even some left-over hippies. We had come here with my long-time friend from Toronto, Doris Anderson, editor of *Chatelaine* magazine, as a way to show her the town and at the same time see what had become an interesting spot to enjoy happy hour. As we chatted in the line, an ex-policeman friend, apparently the bouncer, recently released from prison in the famous Holey Money case, was keeping order in the line, soothing the impatient ones.[2] He saw me and immediately rushed over. We had corresponded while he was in prison. However, I was unaware of his release and his new career. This was the first time I had seen him since he was led away to prison from the courtroom. He told me he was out on parole, that this job was approved by the National Parole Board. He did not waste time in dialogue, but instead took the three of us out of the line and led us inside. The place was jammed with young people, hardly space to walk through the tables. He finally brought us to a table that seemed only to have about one butt-space left. He introduced me with a great flourish, full of the details of my resumé. They were totally bored – their eyes seemed actually glazed – as he listed my credentials. Then suddenly one of them saw Leon, presumably hovering behind Doris and me.

He cut the ex-cop off. "Hey that's Mr. Holt ..."

Then all the others chimed in with "tough math teacher ... but smiled ... he should never have smiled; we knew he was not as mean as he tried to pretend." Others chimed in and it became a fan club for Leon, each of them – it seemed to me – trying to get him to sit beside him or her. They told him that they got jobs in the business world because of his patience with them. They were dressed in suits, obviously straight in the city's work force. They jammed tighter together. One of the young men moved to the crowded bench against the wall and gave Leon his seat at the head of the "party." Placement of Doris and me was more difficult, given butt sizes at least twice that of Leon. My bouncer friend brought chairs for us. But even before that happened the rave for Leon was on. The young people remembered so many details and stories about his involvement in their school days. One recalled, "You were sure tough, but we learned ... and your smile told us you did not hate us." Listening to this, and knowing Leon's smile so well, I recalled one of his closest and first teacher friends at Gladstone, the Art teacher Don Joplin, warning him, "Never smile or you will lose control."

---

2   A group of policemen involved in the high jacking of $1.2 million from the CP Express destined for the Canadian Mint in Ottawa. When the robbers opened their huge take they found the money all punched with two holes, for destruction at the end of the line. This policeman did the patchwork of the holes.

My husband was the celebrity that day and many times since. I would watch for that small sweet grin when one or several of the thousands of students he taught in his 25 years at Gladstone Secondary School recognized him and what he meant to their lives. Today, almost a quarter of a century after his death, his students, who are now parents and grandparents, still recall the positive role he had in their lives.

He shared and endured some of the most troublesome and interesting people in what we both knew as ever-changing and interesting adventures. There were killers, hippies, street people, drug addicts, bank robbers, celebrities, corporate leaders, rich and poor, many in crises, at turning points. Leon somehow was involved with all of it.

The people we shared included Alvin Karpis, of the notorious Karpis-Barker gang. He had heard of me in McNeil Island Corrections Center (in the state of Washington) and when he came through Vancouver, he had a commitment to a radio station. He found a way to contact us and had dinner at our home. He asked us to see him to his plane, and kept in touch with us until his death in Spain. While in Vancouver the stalking by the radio station reporters made him feel, he said, like he was still surrounded by prison guards or FBI agents.

There was also Jimmy Glover, my favourite drug addict, who suddenly went straight and became a "consultant ... wanted to be a counsellor, but could not spell the word." He ended up in Calgary advising the police on crime prevention – he who had turned up at his worst and lowest addiction moment at my office, asking if I knew a certain person of Jewish name. When he started out the door, I pulled him back, asked for an explanation. Finally he told me, "I really need the money, Simma. It is offered for a little roughing up of this guy, who is problem, and I will do it – if he is not a friend of yours." Needless to say, it did not happen. Not only did I tell him he could never come around again, but also I made him promise me to back off from the job or else I would let the police know.

Joey McKenna was one of almost a dozen men condemned to death for murder who wrote to me from death row.[3] He was convicted for the murder

---

3   Several guards on the death watch in Oakalla Prison Farm in Burnaby, B.C. (later renamed Lower Mainland Regional Correctional Centre, and now closed) would sneak out their writings – most of which were in scribblers addressed to me – and drop them off at my door. I never saw the person who delivered them. I would open my apartment door and find the scribblers rolled up leaning against the wedge or stuck in the doorknob.

of an off-duty ambulance driver who called McKenna's date at a night club "a whore." He left the east-end club, returned shortly after with a gun and shot the man who had offended his date. "Even if she was a whore – and I am not saying she was – he had no right to insult her, to hurt her," he explained to me. His sentence was commuted to life in prison. I visited him frequently and when the time came for him to go out on a day parole, Leon agreed to give him a place in our apartment. He was a good person, very bright and with an intellectual honesty I respected. I believed he had the character that could have made him an executive in life if he had had a different kind of family. His mother was a teenager when she married a much older man, and the pair were constantly in bloody fights. Nonetheless, when anyone tried to help or guide Joey or his sister Maureen, the mother would pull them back home. Maureen became a drug addict. As temporary matron I had escorted her to Kingston Penitentiary. Like Joey, she was very bright and caring, but could never survive much longer when released again to the Vancouver streets and to heroin.

On the weekend Joey came to us, he wanted to go for an evening walk shortly after he arrived, to see how much the world had changed since he was last free on the streets. I also knew that there was a degree of fear in the return from the tight control and protection of prison. When he did not return after several hours, I panicked. Leon waited at home while I went out to find him. While I was out, he returned. When Leon told him of my worry, he beamed; it was a mark that someone cared.

That had happened to me before. I had written a series on what I called the "house of horrors" – an old and potential fire trap for juvenile delinquent girls. During the work on the series I went to an institution for girls in Washington State which was a model for rehabilitation or rescue of troubled teen-aged girls. While I was there, one of the young inmates fled. She was found and held in California. The Matron flew down to pick her up and return her to Washington. The youngster was laughing and beaming when she was brought back. I asked her why she was so happy and she replied, "She really cared about me." The girl talked of how "super" it was that the head of this "school" would actually spend money to find and bring her back. Nobody had ever cared about her before.

Another time I was searching for a story and pictures in response to *The Toronto Star*'s request for an account of the 17-year-old hippie named Rick

Jesmer who had laid criminal charges against the Prime Minister (Pierre Trudeau). When I found Jesmer, I ended up with about 10 hippies in our apartment. All of them wanted a shower first before they would tell me anything. It was not long before we became friends, the wandering children hanging out at the office or my apartment. But that first day, Rick Jesmer threw up in my bathroom and the whole gang went to work cleaning it up. When Leon came home late that afternoon the place was crawling with kids, and the evidence of a sick boy was still in the air.

I cannot remember whether it was that day or several days later that I kept a young girl, about 16 years old, at our place for several days. I was waiting for the YWCA to provide a place for her until they could get her home. It was as a result of this that The Y opened a shelter for female hippies.

After they settled this young girl at The Y, I got a phone call suggesting Leon and I should get tested. The girl had hepatitis B. Leon said, "Okay, Simma – out hippies, out killers or out wife."

It never did end. In his quiet, patient way I always felt that Leon was as much involved as I was – though perhaps with less sympathy, believing able-bodied people can find a way to live and work in society. But no matter who came into my life Leon shared it and in many cases found the people – no matter whether they were exemplary leaders in society or outcasts – to be an enrichment of our lives.

I really liked Leon. It was something greater than love. I guess the time I smile most is recalling the day I had a lesson from the tennis pro, while Leon sat in the gallery and watched. When we were gathering the tennis balls, Leon said to the pro, "Pretty good for a little old lady, eh?" It was shortly before his death. I was about 60. I laughed and adored him all the more.

I suspect even if I was terrible on the court, Leon would have supported me. He was always on my side, even when I suspected I was in the wrong.

10
Token Girl Reporter

Usually, newcomers at *The Sun* were introduced to Vancouver readers with fanfare on Page One. Their arrival stirred quiet but intense repercussions inside the newsroom. Managing Editor Hal Straight was a boss who openly found and recruited some of Canada's top journalists, even trolling abroad for "stars" whose training and record far exceeded the Canadian standard. Hal, the owners-publishers Don and Sam Cromie, and Circulation Manager Herb Gates made no secret of their love of *The Sun* stars. Each addition was a matter of pride – and also led to increased income in advertising sales as the newspaper's circulation grew. Most of all, these were real newspapermen who loved to produce the news.

So when Hal brought in new reporters – who usually went near or to the top of the newsroom ladder – there would be murmurs of discontent among the resident (often younger) reporters. The newcomers would diminish the others' hope and expectation that with each departure by death, retirement or "personal reasons" of senior reporters, they would rise up on the editorial ladder, a few rungs closer to the top and to coveted assignment and beats. When the men shared their frustration with me, I responded appropriately with sympathy for their decreased hope of promotion.

The new arrivals were interesting but made no difference to my career. It was a man's world and the competition for promotion was open to men. Not once did I seek or expect a raise in all the years I was there. I was presented with a raise with two others in what Hal Straight called "merit pay."[1] But for

---

1   The other two were Evelyn Caldwell and Barry Broadfoot. Evelyn Caldwell was Penny Wise, the shopping columnist who also did many offbeat stories, including one of the first interviews with Elvis Presley. She got into Russia with a Canadian Women's Press Club group and wrote about the life of a family she observed by lying on a concrete windowsill of a hotel watching and writing them throughout the night.

the men who expected promotion, the gossip and rumbles of discontent were understandable. I could not expect – nor did I seek – the plum assignments. The big stories were assigned to men. My goal was to grow and maintain my contact friends, find and follow up on tips, and search and find stories wandering through the streets and the places where stories are born and grow. I was happy riding fire engines or ambulances, or being picked up by a police car racing to a bank holdup or murder. From the beginning I knew there was a story in every human being for those of us who had the patience and energy to find it. I had both. Churchill's words were always with me: "There is gold in every soul."

I never was sent to far-off places to watch the earth shake, mountains blow their tops and flow in rivers of fire over towns below, nor watch men kill each other in battle or amid slaughters directed by genocidal tyrants. The longest trip I had in the first dozen years there was on the old interurban streetcar, about 30 or 40 miles into the Fraser Valley in one of the rare major west coast snowstorms. It was to witness and report on the train and the people, those who cut through snow-covered tracks and those in the towns served, and how they survived the brief but unusual isolation.

I loved finding my own stories and writing them, stories nobody noticed and which brought so much pleasure to the city editor. He had no trouble expressing his appreciation and pleasure at what I brought to him.

Despite the fact that there were two older women reporters on their beats, I was the only "girl reporter" in the office. Even the copy runners were male. It was apparent I was the "token girl" when – as I learned – other females applied on several occasions and were told: "We have one girl." After I got married one female reporter told me that she was advised, "When Simma gets pregnant we might hire another female reporter."

My friend Barry Broadfoot always called me "Girl Reporter" even after I left the business and entered other careers.

Only one of Hal's imports made a difference in my life. That difference was massive, actually leaving an indelible and damaging imprint until my old age. Now I can finally say, "I don't give a damn." But I can never forget.

It was the arrival of Earl T. Smith and the power he had over my career and psyche. It was not his ambition that seemed to drive him as much as his overt resentment of women in the newsroom. I was the only girl reporter, there were then no copy girls, and that made me an easy target.

There were two older women on beats when it all began for me there. But they were so highly regarded and sophisticated professionally, and were so rarely seen in the newsroom, that they missed the bullying as far as I could tell.

A magnificent role model for any young journalist, male or female, was Doris Milligan, the City Hall reporter. She was tall, arrow straight, white-haired, with class and confidence. She had the style of one raised in the social and economic elite. Mae Garnett, who was shorter and stocky, with salt-and-pepper hair, held the courthouse beat for 30 years. She was never the subject of a lawsuit despite working in the most vulnerable job for assault by predator lawyers. It was said that she "only had a Grade Eight education." However I saw and heard the most learned judges and lawyers consult her for her opinion. Several prominent lawyers invited her to article in their firms and take her bar exams, the way to entering the profession at that time.

It was weeks before I knew anything more of these women than their voices as they dictated their stories to me by telephone from the beat press rooms. If they came into the office it would have been after hours, to deliver their copy. Both were impatient with me at first for slowing their thought processes as they dictated from notes. I questioned them for the spelling of names and places that would have been known by those who lived in Vancouver.

However, it did not take long for Doris' wonderful kindness to emerge. Throughout the years we were together, working and then as friends after she retired, she gave me strength and valuable counsel.

Mae never did develop patience with me or most other people. Nonetheless she soon became a strong ally. In mutual respect for each other we worked together on her beat when I was sent there to share the heavy load of the many courts and trials. We often handled 10 or 20 cases in a week, including the start and disposition of civil cases processed in the Court Registry.

I have a vague memory that when Earl Smith arrived at *The Sun* his stardom came from an award he won for a series he had written on Canada's worst catastrophe, the December 6, 1917 collision of two ships (the Mont Blanc, carrying a cargo of explosives, and the *Imo*) in Halifax Harbour. The explosion flattened the north end of the city; almost 2,000 people were killed, thousands injured and left homeless.

Earl came to *The Sun* after me, some time in the early 1950s. First he was provincial editor, then city editor. In both jobs I was often assigned to help on his desk, even after I became a street reporter. He always seemed to have the power, because of senior position or my own lack of confidence, to bully the "girl reporter."

I knew – and he knew – I had the energy, tenacity, and instinct for a story, that I could get any story I tackled. No matter how often he attacked the most subjective aspect of journalism – my writing ability – he never criticized my ability to find and produce a story. He couldn't; the evidence was clear to all those who were his superiors – the publisher, managing editor, news editors, and circulation manager. They were vocal, strong and generous in their praise. They should have been the voices that blurred Earl's assaults. But sadly, when one is young, it is the bullies who hold sway. Self-confidence at that time did not come naturally for many of the women I knew in the workforce.

It is Earl's words and voice that I can still hear in memory saying for all to hear: *"If we could cross Simma Holt with Mac Reynolds, we would have the world's greatest reporter-writer."*[2]

In his admiration for the stories I brought to the City Desk he never failed to add: "If only you could write." He did not hear – it seemed to me – the words of the news editor and others on the news rim: "Oh knock it off, Smith."

I knew I could produce a story on deadline, written in simple and basic style that would allow editors to have the basic facts. I once heard News Editor Jack Cairns say: "Her copy is easy to handle."

But there are no absolutes or formula for great writers, so it took little for a bully to undermine my hope that I would be a great writer. Even after I had numerous requests for news and feature stories from magazines and newspapers from all parts of Canada, and some from the United States, I remained insecure about my ability as a writer. Never did I offer a story to the desk or

---

2   Mac Reynolds was a colourful writer who took days to find the perfect words for his beautiful prose while the rest of us had to write or dictate our stories from the field, off the top of our heads, for deadlines five minutes or an hour away.

elsewhere – even to those who wanted my work – without fear that the writing was not acceptable.

Earl could never take away my confidence in my ability to beat him or any other reporter in finding stories and getting pictures to illustrate them. He did recognize that part of my reporter skills. I remember one time several people tried to get pictures relating to the murder of a city policeman. Earl said, "Go get the family album." When I came back with dozens of pictures he said, "I don't understand it. How do you do it?"

"I care, and they know it."

He responded with something like: "I don't care and I guess people know that too."

My 17-year-old sister Miriam died when I was young. Before that, a schoolmate drowned when the ice broke while he was skating on Vegreville's Vermilion River and another schoolmate died from a ruptured appendix. Having gone through a death in my family, and in the families of close friends, I knew and understood the tremendous pain people suffer in these tragedies. It was so poignant in our own home, where so many shared with us the sorrow as Miriam lay in our living room before being moved to the cemetery 60 miles west, in Edmonton.

Whenever I had to go to a home to find the human part of the story in a sudden death – sometimes, which was most difficult, before the police or relatives could notify those in the home – the grief and sorrow I felt with them was real. I could say honestly (though never out loud), "I know your pain."

Earl could not understand my explanation.

On several occasions when I was assigned to work with him on the provincial desk, later the City Desk, Earl would pull pictures out of his top centre desk drawer and throw them across at me. They were naked women. He literally leered at me as he challenged me with, "How do you like dem lungs?"

In those days I was shy and had never been confronted with anything like this. But there was nothing I could – or would – do about it. If I complained, I feared I might be forced out of this career I loved. Actually, I could have caused him worse embarrassment by reporting his collection. It was illegal then to have what would have been considered "pornography."

I recall the last major attempt to drive me out of *The Sun*. It happened one day when I arrived at my desk. There was a sheet of copy paper in the centre of the blotter with a small advertisement pasted to it, a Hudson's Bay Company (department store) ad seeking a copy writer. Beside it was the pencilled message, "Simma: this may interest you."

I walked directly to Hal Straight's office, without knocking (his door was usually open anyway). I stomped in, dropped the sheet of paper on his desk in front of him and asked, "Do you want me to quit?"

He looked up, flushed a rare red and said, almost as if in anger at me, "No I don't want you to leave. You have a job here as long as you want it."

That was the last time Earl Smith was blatant in his harassment.

Another *Sun* import was Bruce Larsen. His move was simply across the hall from *The Province* after the two newspapers merged within Pacific Press. With the end of competition, the effort for the "scoop" died, except in those who still took pride in their work and never lost their ambition to produce the best.

Bruce began as the sports editor. After I left he was promoted to city editor and finally managing editor. As a reporter, Bruce Larsen was a generous professional. We first met in the Kootenays on the Sons of Freedom Doukhobor stories.

The Doukhobors were a Russian sect that brought reporters from around the world to record and photograph their antics (arsons and bombing attacks). Bruce was an expert, with close contacts within the leadership and the most active participants in their style of civil disobedience, what they considered revolt against "government." Bruce had won the trust not only of the Freedomites but also of the Royal Canadian Mounted Police, at the highest levels.

When I arrived in Nelson, B.C., the base for the reporting and trials of the Freedomites, Bruce Larsen did not hesitate for even a moment to offer me help. He provided backgrounds and information – even introduced me to the leaders of the sect and officers of the court and RCMP. He told me what to expect in the *modus operandi* of the terrorists. I knew him as a true professional. When my book on the Sons of Freedom (*Terror in the Name of God*) was published, he was quick to congratulate me and praise the work.

When he came onto *The Sun* he remained a supportive friend. But like so many men of that time, he did not realize how offensive his sexual stereotyping could be. He would call out loud and clear, so that no one on the floor could miss his joke: "What Simma needs is a big football player to service her ... I will check out Emery Barnes."[3]

It was like the racism that is intended to be a way to connect with a Jewish person: "Some of my best friends are Jews."

Emery's first wife, LaVerne Barnes, became one of my close friends. She was not surprised to hear that it was Emery whom Bruce considered a potential volunteer for this "duty." However, when we discussed it in our senior years, long past sensitivity to male dalliances and immature sexist clichés, we could laugh at Bruce's choice. Her ex-husband became an NDP Member of the B.C. Legislature and Speaker in the House.

Bruce married a beautiful young stewardess who became a manager on the City Desk of *The Sun*. She was a multi-talented woman who no doubt could undertake any management job and rise to the top. Jennifer Lloyd Larsen turned up at my campaign office when I ran for and won my seat in the House of Commons in 1974.

There were always those stereotypical clichés, pronounced by men with such pride as if they had a unique line.

"Women are too emotional."

"Women's place is in bed."

"Women's place is in the kitchen."

"When they can do nothing else they cry."

Himie Koshevoy and others told me that these phrases and sexist assaults were designed to "get a rise" out of me. In retrospect I believe the piling-on came because I would respond with some smart-ass remark in order to avoid the appearance that they hurt.

I cannot remember how many times I heard them say, "The female rushes to the washroom to cry when things do not go her way." Never once did any

---

3   Emery Barnes (1929-1998) played for the B.C. Lions football team in the early 1960s. He was a Member of the B.C. Legislature from 1972 to 1996. He became the Legislature's Speaker in 1994, the first black person ever to hold that position.

of them get the satisfaction. I think in those years I lost crying skills; I did not get them again until the death of my husband, and that was big time, 11 years after I left *The Sun*.

My survival was because I loved the job so much that I vowed not even the worst bully would force me out. Along with this I got strength from the majority of the men – and Doris Milligan – at the worst of times. When I advanced to senior reporter status I sat as though encircled by three strong friends. The four of us were almost isolated in our row of desks at the back of the large City Room. I was sandwiched between John Arnett and Arnie Myers, with Barry Broadfoot in front of me. We shared jokes and story ideas, found rationalization for some hurt feelings, and chuckled over office gossip.

Arnie Myers was the medical reporter, totally self-confident and able to say, "They pay me well for what I know, not for what I write." He remained strongly supportive, then pressured me to write my memoir, and in fact edited much of what I wrote after he retired, adding his personal memories. One day Arnie gave me some advice, his remedy for dealing with the abuse: "When it starts just tell them where to go and walk across to the Lotus Gardens Lounge and get drunk."

John Arnett was a quiet, cool personality, who began his life and career in New Zealand covering everything from an oyster-eating contest and country fairs to rowing regattas and municipal councils. The last of his 60 years in journalism was as publisher of a small-town Vancouver Island newspaper, *The Sooke News Mirror*. His brother Peter, who followed him in journalism, became a world-famed war correspondent in some of the most dangerous countries in the world.

Tom Ardies was another in this circle of close male friends. As much as I admired his dry sense of humour, my envy was even greater for the courage few others had; he had the self-assurance to leave the paper in search of change, confident that he would always be welcomed back. He returned often. And whenever he returned he would want to know who the new faces belonged to, and their credentials for being there. A classic moment was his first sighting of Mike Grenby.

Mike worked in the finance department and posed as – or perhaps really was – a cheapskate. His boast was that he could travel around the world for less than most of us would pay to fly to Toronto. He planned his travels carefully, he said, finding friends or friends of friends and then visiting the places where he could crash free and have bed, breakfast and all the rest of his meals in the household. He claimed he netted pigeons for family food.

Grenby was totally bald and wore a beard. On seeing Grenby, loud and clear Tom asked, "Who's that guy with the face upside down?"

Barry Broadfoot was my closest friend throughout our years together at *The Sun* and to the last days of his life. He always gave the impression of absolute confidence, almost to the point of arrogance. Even if he lacked strength, Barry would never let anyone see hurt or embarrassment.

In many ways his life ran on a similar track with mine. Like me, Barry had something of the prairie roots that remained constant in our basic characters. He was born in Winnipeg in 1926, attended the University of Manitoba, entering about the time I graduated. He also worked on the student newspaper, *The Manitoban*. He served in World War II in the infantry for two years, while I lived the war in a safer way on the home front.

Finally, when our careers were ended, both Barry's and my papers became part of the University of Manitoba's Archives and Special Collections for study and research by students who followed us in that great university.

In a sense Barry and I worked in common cause. Both of us wondered at the terrible experience of Japanese Canadians during the war. My work on the waterfront beat led me to the sequel to Barry's book about the terrible time when those people were forcibly relocated off the coastal area – their homes, their fishing boats, everything they owned seized by the Government and sold at fire-sale prices to other Canadian fishermen. I interviewed many of them and wrote of the past and the return of these Canadians, some of whom left Canada to resettle in Japan (where they were also distrusted as aliens).

Barry had a low-key style of telling the most dramatic or fantastic stories. With a few drinks, he admitted, the stories improved. I knew it was the telling rather than the facts that improved. They were hard to believe, if you did not understand the mischievous character of the raconteur.

On the morning of November 22, 1963 Barry walked out of the teletype room and said, "Jack Kennedy has been shot." He said it in a quiet cool way as if he was telling everyone, "It is raining outside." That was his style. The city editor said, "Oh Broadfoot, get lost." Barry walked back to the machine, pulled off the sheet of paper headed "Flash," walked slowly but deliberately to the City Desk and dumped it in front of the editor.

Barry was the first person I allowed to read my Terror manuscript. I was terrified that he might find it wanting. I was afraid to let anyone see this work. But he was such a special kind of friend, whom I trusted and knew would be honest.

. He called me from a phone booth in what he called "The Rock" (Bowen Island, his place of retreat). He had gone there to read my manuscript, said he was halfway through it and had to call to let me know both his "joy and surprise … it is so good … fantastic …" and other words to that effect. Because of Barry's call, I immediately booked a flight to Toronto and left a few days later, in February 1964. I carried my copy of the manuscript for delivery by hand to my publisher, Jack McClelland. Jack had been nagging me to complete the book.

When I handed the manuscript to Jack, I asked that he assign someone to read it and tell me what was needed to fix it. I assured him I am no prima donna about my work, that any cuts, changes and improvements would be greatly appreciated. Before he could comment (and I talk long and fast when I want to make a point) I told him I was prepared to do whatever was necessary, even rewriting the book. He finally managed to cut me off, saying, "You will never get it back because I will never get a book from you."

He knew – as I knew – I would never be satisfied, and would keep on revising and rewriting. Within a few weeks I received eight pages of questions from a super editor I cherish to this day – Joyce Marshall. The book went into production in August. On September 11, 1964 Big Fanny (Florence) Storgoff died in Vancouver General Hospital. She was the leader of most of the Freedomite's sensational incidents, including the so-called "march" (by bus) to Vancouver. When I told Jack, he asked me to write a paragraph or two and he would have it inserted in the book.

Even in this, Barry added to my life and career. He seemed to be everywhere that a story was born or grew. He learned from a friend on staff in Vancouver General Hospital that in the last days of Big Fanny's life she was in character to the end. She led a protest against the morning orange juice on the ward. It was so successful that every glass on the ward was returned to the kitchen, untouched.

Terror in the Name of God was published in Toronto by McClelland & Stewart in November 1964, and by Crown in New York the next year. There was a 14-page "Introduction to the American edition" which included a study of comparative sects throughout North America and updated the changes in the Sons of Freedom terrorist leaders since the publication of the Canadian edition. New pictures were added to the illustration pages, including two pages of my headline stories. Included also was a single-page handwritten letter from one of the terrorist leaders, George Kinakin, recalling my interview with him June 12, 1965. He wrote that he was "thankful for the book that it was published," added detail from his own involvement, and gave assurance that his life as an arsonist and terrorist was over.

One day, after *Terror in the Name of God* was published, Tom Ardies, Barry and I were at lunch in one of our favourite Chinatown eateries when one of them said, "If Simma can write a book so can we." And they both did – with great success.

Barry produced his important Canadian historical books one after another, several of them in less time than it took for me to complete my research, writing, and publication of just one book. His technique was to interview hundreds who lived in and survived major periods and crises in Canadian history. He taped them and then transcribed their own words into what became – all of them – bestsellers: *Ten Lost Years, 1929-1939; The War Years, 1939-1945; The Pioneer Years 1895-1914; Years of Sorrow Years of Shame: The Story of Japanese Canadians in World War II.*

Tom produced bestseller fiction – *Their Man in the White House, Kosygin is Coming, This Suitcase Is Going To Explode, Pandemic.* His personal inscription to me in *Pandemic* reads, "Thanks for teaching me all I know about sex and violence … Love and kisses." That, in spite of the fact that he or Barry dubbed me the "sexless wonder of Canadian journalism." The autograph in *This Suitcase Is Going To Explode* is more to my liking: "Canada's top woman reporter, in awe and affection."

Barry, at about age 50, told me, "I am younger than you, but you will out-live me. I live in an old man's body." He attributed this to what he called "my wild lifestyle of booze and f---ing girls."

The letters he wrote me while I was a Member of Parliament had the name and address scrawled in huge sloppy writing – "Simma Holt Girl Potato." Shirley Strean, as gatekeeper, thought they were hate mail and dumped them unopened in the waste basket. After she met Barry, his letters were the first she would open if they turned up in the daily pile. They were always short. One in particular that brought a laugh was: "I haven't heard from you in a long time. I guess you are dead. I'm glad. I never liked you anyhow."

Barry died at age 77 in November 2003.

Shortly before his death, a group of his closest friends met in a dockside restaurant beside the Nanaimo ferry terminal for our last lunch together. We all told "Barry stories". Our reward was the gentle smile in his tired face, his eyes no longer able to see us clearly, if at all. His hearing and mind still had some of their old strength – enough to elicit a laugh at the gossip or the history we all shared with him. I reminded him of the time we met for coffee near the university entrance, close to his home. It was no time for delicacy; I used Barry's exact words: "We have been such good friends, how come we never f---ed?"

Ian Macdonald was one of the old friends there. Ian had become a star in the Ottawa press gallery and their barbershop quartet. He came home for this reunion. One Ian story I recalled with joy had to do with Managing Editor Erwin Swangard, who was the favourite subject of gossip. Erwin had returned from a trip to Japan and was rushed to hospital. When I came into the office that day I asked Ian what happened, if it was serious. He replied, "It's not serious … but better than nothing."

11

The Other Sex Comes Marching In

Suddenly the City Room changed. The first breakthrough came for women at the annual editorial department Christmas party some time in the late 1950s.

We were presented with gifts. Doris and Mae, near retirement, were given end tables topped with sewing boxes. I was given a portable Royal typewriter. But the most precious gift of that day was the management's announcement that, because of the quality of service by the three female reporters, *Sun* policy would be to seek and hire women as general news reporters.

It was gradual, as if to avoid shock of a precipitous end of the status quo; female reporters began arriving in our City Room one, two, perhaps three at a time over the weeks or months, presumably to avoid causing emotional disturbance to the natives. Some stayed. Others left, either unwilling to take the stuff that was endemic to the place or moving out and upward, some returning to their previous jobs. I loved the work and was determined not to be driven out. In fact at one point, when one of the latter-day managing editors got a bully moment, I assured him that I intended to stay and, if nothing else, to outlive him professionally.

I had remarkable freedom to move and work wherever I chose. During the British Empire and Commonwealth Games in 1954 I said I would be working at home, since it was close to the action and particularly the athletes' village, and I would phone in or deliver the copy to the office. Bill Galt, one of the transient but mature bosses, replied, "I don't care where you write. You can do it in the sh--house, as long as you keep writing."

By then I was surrounded in the office by friends – Barry Broadfoot in front of me, sandwiched between Arnie Myers and John Arnett, with three new strong women encircling Barry.

The female newcomers were Marian Bruce, Pat Moan and Lisa Hobbs, welcome reinforcements for the four residents in our semi-isolated corner away from the "madding crowd" and the few but vocal neanderthals who still believed the only places for women were in the bedroom and the kitchen. Lisa Hobbs had credentials and self-confidence that far surpassed Hal Straight's most highly touted stars. At that time I was rarely in the office. So I heard of the new reporters before I met them.

Lisa Hobbs came north with a huge reputation on a major metropolitan newspaper, the *San Francisco Examiner*.[1] Her resumé was the most impressive of any of the new recruits, perhaps in the whole history of *The Sun*. Born into a family of respected Australian journalists, her record included winning some of the most prestigious journalism awards, including the San Francisco Press Club Award, the AP/UPI Award and the coveted McQuaid Award for a series she did on abuses in California nursing homes. Not only was she recognized for her crusading campaigns that created new law in the United States, but she had an international reporter's record that stretched from London (accredited reporter to Buckingham Palace during coronation year) to India, Cambodia, and Vietnam.

Lisa was in her early 40s when she came to *The Sun* in January 1970. By then she had made international headlines when she did the impossible for any journalist – male or female – at that time. She sneaked into Red China and published the first newspaper stories – and then a book – on that tightly closed society. Although a staff reporter in San Francisco, she had claimed on a visa application to be a housewife residing in Sidney, and thus obtained one of 20 visas given to the Australia–China Friendship Association. She did it, as her publisher described it, "as a mission of faith … because she had to find the truth."

---

1   Lisa Hobbs is now writing as Lisa Hobbs Birnie, and is married to artist John Koerner. The Koerner name is famous in British Columbia for exceptional philanthropy, most notably their endowments to the University of British Columbia.

Lisa's first book – *I Saw Red China* – won massive publicity and positive reviews, hitting the *New York Times* bestseller list. It was read around the world, printed in four languages.

Despite all this, she recalled, "I remember one of the chief honchos on the City Desk (at *The Vancouver Sun*) telling me in front of the entire desk: 'You can't write a decent sentence and you don't even know how to spell.'"

I Saw Red China was followed by *Love And Liberation: Up Front with the Feminists* (McGraw-Hill, 1972), Lisa's book about the feminist revolution of the mid-20th century, my favourite on that topic and most relevant to my life experience. It was not only because my friend was the author. It was that her book was built on a simple but basic principle for successful relationships. Lisa's thesis was that there cannot be love without liberation, nor liberation without love. I knew the accuracy of her thesis personally and its importance to those who seek strong friendships in their relationships. I knew this from the comfortable and happy friendship in love Leon and I had for 37 and a half years, despite my freewheeling life style.

From the moment I met Lisa Hobbs she became a friend, a soulmate, and most of all a teacher and partner in the new ways of women's liberation. Later we would work together internationally in the lead towards equality and respect for women throughout our entire craft, from editorial writers to those in advertising, sales and circulation departments.

When I asked Lisa her recollection of our first meeting she wrote:

"… one male from the City Desk stuck a big (beautiful) nude on the wall behind the precise spot where you, Arnie, Barry, Marian Bruce and I were sitting. The poster advertised a new night club and the words suggestive, something like, 'Why don't you get me to come?' as she (the subject on the poster) pointed to the nether region. Coming out of a S.F. newsroom where crap like that was not part of the interior decor, I was stunned. The National Organization of Women (NOW) was already strong in the United States so I guess my consciousness had been raised. (I voiced) my objection to you, pointing out how disrespectful and degrading it was.

"Your eyes started to flame. Enlightenment broke on you. You leaped up with a cry and clawed the whole poster off the wall.

"Next day another one was up in its place, with an anonymous typed note saying, in an authoritative tone, that it was not to be removed.

"You entered the City Room, saw it, charged at it, and removed it. 'The City Room War' was on.

"The women in the Women's section agreed with those of us on city side … (There were) one or two exceptions (who) stayed off the field of battle."

It did not take long to recognize the reason Lisa was the target of the most vicious – and bitter – gossip by men, usually those with small hope of major advancement in the business. She walked as if she still had the pile of books on top of her head, the way we were trained and practised for erect and perfect posture. Everything about her style and manner yelled "class." Her appearance was one of total confidence and her speech was refined. Most disturbing to the local gerbils was the obvious: none of them could match the professionalism and the big international reputation she had acquired before she arrived in our office.

Never was I surer of Lisa's fame than when she made the leading American tabloid, *The National Enquirer*, with its gossipy item: "Lisa Hobbs is alive and living in Canada."

One of the best moments within the new demographic of *The Sun* newsroom was the result of a "study" undertaken by the youngest and most radical of the newcomers. She was the petite Pat Moan. Pat was about the age I had been when I began my career there. However, Pat had self-confidence that would have ended my career if I had dared to show even an iota of her independence. She had courage and cheek I could never match, even with seniority. She set out to rate the male sexism in the newsroom. She polled all the women of the editorial department, including those in the Women's, Social, Fashion, and Home-Making sections. I was then spending most of my time outside of the office, filling in on beats or following my own leads on stories. Not only was I unaware of Pat's study, but my vote was not sought or available. One day I came into the office and, as usual, I checked the bulletin board. The result of Pat's study was posted there. Earl T. Smith won the top spot.

Another unforgettable moment of my liberation was the way the new women celebrated International Women's Day. It seemed to me that was the first public reference to International Women's Day in our newsroom, or in the office of any other publication. The women prepared well in advance and secretly. We sought male "art." We could not find a single picture of a totally nude male, so had to settle for several well-stacked semi-naked males, their status symbols discreetly covered with jock straps or things that resembled a fig leaf. These were posted throughout the newsroom and in each of the urinals within male firing range. Added to the illustrations were the sayings:

"Men don't need the money as much as women do."

"Men can't cope with pressure the way women can."

"Men are too emotional."

"We appointed a man once and he didn't work out."

"Men rush to the washroom to cry."

Our male friends, especially those in our backroom circle, were amused, even seemed impressed. Not surprising! The angriest were the very people who had long relied on their "cute" attempts at humour at the expense of women. It was sheer joy as we waited and watched the return of each of those from their trek to do what came naturally. Needless to say the worst of the sexists were the angriest. They emerged flushed and frustrated in impotent anger, using colourful phrases. They almost hissed as they passed the other sex on their way back to their desks.

Pat Moan would not tolerate the slightest hint of sexism. She was not long on the job when her impact was felt by Jim Kelly, a gentle, kindly man who was in his mid-50s. One morning as I arrived in the City Room, Jim approached me, obviously upset by an encounter with Pat.

"I thought I was complimenting her," he said. "I told her she looked so pretty in a dress. She almost chewed me up. She was so angry, told me not to be so damned patronizing … and more language I cannot speak."

This was classic of this historic time of change for women in the mid-20th century. Many older men were confused by "Women's Lib." The change may have been too fast and too big for their understanding.

The confusion became evident to the extreme November 20–22, 1970 in Chicago. Approximately 100 women were called together from all parts of the United States, Puerto Rico and Canada by the executive of the American Newspaper Guild (ANG). The original theme of the conference was "Equality Now." The ANG was believed to be the first trade union to undertake what was a unique and courageous initiative. The goal was to study and find ways to end discrimination against women in the workplace. Because the Guild was a craft union, the convention dealt with women in all areas of the trade – from advertising sales to editorial departments.

There were only five delegates from Canada – Sheila McCook, Eleanor Dunn and Jan Hunt from Ottawa, and Lisa and I from Vancouver. Both Lisa and I were elected unanimously to the five-woman drafting committee. The other three were American, and almost half our age. Lisa was then 42; I was 48.

There was no question that the all-male ANG executive called the historic convention with the best of intentions. Nonetheless, the men were baffled by the anger of the young women. It was so intense that several times there was revolutionary talk of walkouts. One time it was sparked by a note Lisa sent to me that circulated through the convention hall. Her message reflected the staging of the first business meeting. On the dais in front of us was President Chuck Perlik, with the western regional organizer and western (Canada and USA) troubleshooter Chuck Dale beside him, and other headquarters and regional executives at a long table at the front of the big hall. At every round table of female delegates was one male – the executive secretaries of the American union locals. In this setting Lisa sent me a note: "Doesn't this remind you of the plantation owners telling the sharecroppers what their problems are?"

I passed the note to the young women beside me at our table. It circled the table, and the male local executive secretary in turn read it, puzzled and unsmiling. Then one of the young women passed it to the adjacent round table. Within what seemed like only minutes, a message came back to us. One of the young women whispered to Lisa and me that the "note summed up the situation so well that a total walkout was planned." That was the last thing we wanted. Our table sent another message around the room, assuring the delegates it was important that we carry this conference to conclusion, because by forcing through strong recommendations we could make changes for women not only in the newspaper industry, but also in other jobs. The publicity from the recommendations for ways to bring equal opportunity and freedom from discrimination in journalism would, we were sure, have an impact everywhere.

The keynote speaker at the banquet was Caroline Bird, author of *Born Female – The High Cost of Keeping Women Down,* a bestseller in 1968. In her speech she told the delegates of the disappointment and hurt she felt when she was forced out of the writing career she had chosen. She had been desperate and upset, she said, and told of how her father rescued her financially, allowing her to write this book that turned her into a hot, high-profile feminist author and public speaker. The ANG convention planners had brought the top author of the time to speak to us.

That night Lisa and I decided to write a satire on the "heroic" survival of the keynote speaker. Our title was something like *The Crisis of Barolyn Curd.* The miraculous rescue came from Daddy's money, allowing her to continue her career and rise to greater celebrity than was possible as a journalist. Lisa was on our manual portable typewriter, with her freshly washed hair in curlers turbaned with an item of lace and silk lingerie. We were laughing at our "creative" humour and silliness, actually free-wheeling perhaps intemperate prose, knowing we would never publish our story. We were still at it at 2 a.m. when the phone rang.

It was ANG Guild President Chuck Perlik. This usually restrained man, obviously trying to maintain his cool, told us that a "very serious problem" was looming and asked us to join him and the other executive officers in his suite to help them deal with it. It could not wait till the morning. When we arrived in the President's suite, all the men in the room looked strained and tense. President Perlik told us that the executive was "totally baffled" by the anger they were facing from the female delegates. Here they were, intent on taking the lead in ensuring equality for women in all fields of communication, and all they were getting was "hot shit."

Because of our long life in our trade and in the Guild, we knew and worked on Guild matters with Perlik and Dale. Lisa knew Chuck Dale both in Vancouver and from her time in San Francisco, where he was based.

Lisa explained the women's history in the eternal "man's world" as if in a lecture hall in academia. The men listened intently in a genuine attempt to understand the women's reaction.

Then President Perlik stated, "We have an immediate – and major – problem. It is going to blow up in a couple hours."

At 7 a.m., he told us, the other three women on the drafting committee planned to release a statement to United Press International (UPI), the Associated Press (AP) and any newspaper reporters they found in the hotel, declaring the Guild executive "Our Oppressors."

Lisa and I found ourselves the unofficial liaison between these men and the younger women. We were ambivalent about intervening. However, we were certain that such a press release could cause a major setback, not only for women in the newspaper business, but for women in all male-dominated jobs. We immediately set out to convince the other members of our committee and their colleagues that the final report was in our hands, that we had the power to bring important change for women in the workplace. The goal was to make the recommendations strong enough to tackle and permanently resolve grievances, as well to implement whatever changes were necessary to ensure career quality and opportunity both for women in the newspaper business and those in other trades, industry, even in academia.

The five of us on the drafting committee thought the ANG executive might get their knickers in a twist over our demands, but we agreed we could not let this possibility deter from the justice of those demands. We reminded the executive that the recommendations we produced would be published not only for our local memberships but for the entire Guild, the publishers and departmental managers.

The conference report ended with more than 60 recommendations. Like the other delegates, Lisa and I presented a report to our local (Local 115) which in turn went to the publishers. Our report noted:

"Within the Guild itself, members have shared in – and supported – management's discriminatory practices. Today there are both brother and sister Guild members who openly resent the fact that a convention was called to study and correct inequities based on sex discrimination. Perhaps it is fear of the unknown … Or is it the belief that the superficial reporting on the women's rights movement as a bra-throwing exercise is accurate?"

Although I had served as vice president of the Guild and the only woman up to that time on the contract negotiating committee, the Guild executive secretary and the local executive – even Chuck Dale, the western troubleshooter – were only amused when I told them of the discrimination I was experiencing.

Further into our report, Lisa and I wrote:

"While hiring and job opportunity problems exist for editorial women at Pacific Press (then the parent company of both *The Sun* and *The Province*), the major areas of concern are primarily in advertising and clerical positions."

The 60-plus recommendations passed unanimously. The first was that a women's rights committee must be established to continue the work started at the conference, with an interim coordinator to be appointed immediately to select and set up the committee, following up on as many of the recommendations as possible. The report also recommended that the Guild be ready as soon as possible to undertake legal action where discriminatory behaviour and wage practices exist.

No doubt the convention with its massive recommendations was a shock to some of the men in the business who had never had to compete with the other half of the population for job opportunities, salaries and advancement in their jobs.

However, the most outspoken critic of the convention results and Lisa's and my report was a woman. Like so many women she did not care how many before her made it possible for her to be accepted and rise to a celebrated byline reporter. She expressed her contempt when told that we – with the convention – were concerned over the huge gap in income of the women on phones who solicited and sold the ads, compared with the salesmen who picked them up and received healthy commissions. Her *sotto voce* sneer at us at a Guild executive meeting was that we were "silly women libbers." But she was a minority of one. Guildsmen and women with that single exception were supportive, even praised our report and the "remarkable advances" made for women in Chicago.

The incident with that contemptuous female reporter was a reminder that some women who rise to management and power over others can be worse bullies than any man, and all too often it is women they target.

And there are some women who would do and say anything to please men in power. I was proud of the fact that I could spend hours alone with men, and never did I have to defend myself in word and action from their advances. I have the memory of my book publisher, Jack McClelland, who was impressed with my record of work and the research contained in my books. While relaxing over a late-night drink, Jack said I got the masses of information on my back.

I snapped at him, "I can't type on my back."

12

Scrapbook Selections

My scrapbooks tell the stories of my city, my country and what has become known as a time and place that has no equal or comparison in the history of this world. Endless numbers of books and articles carry titles and heads that declare it "The Fabulous 20th Century." There are many clippings in the scrapbooks and lying scattered and loose through boxes and file drawers (none in file folders!) as the number of stories ran to three, four or many more each day. They were published too fast and too numerous for me to waste time and energy keeping track of them, for it would have kept me from what I wanted to do beyond all else – find, write and tell as many people as possible the stories I found.

Today, as I search my old scrapbooks, I find that from the first day on the job, I recorded the evidence that I was a reporter, practising the profession which I had long dreamed and hoped I could enter.

My first scrapbook reflects the excitement and awe of a young girl reporter at the start of the career of her childhood fantasies. That cover of that first book is marbled red with the simple title "*SCRAPS.*" As I recall, I bought it for 15 cents at the five-and-dime-store called Woolworths. It was a big investment, given that I had about $10 left from *The Sun* travel advance. That was even less than my family gave me through my years at university ($50 a month, $25 for rent and the rest for bus and expenses). I used the entire first page to pen in large girlish script: "Vancouver Sun Nov. 1–January 3."

That first scrapbook not only provided a record of the time, place and people of the city, the province and the country but, on a personal level, it reminded me that I had the best and most devoted teachers any cub reporter could have dreamed possible. Those teachers gave me the best training any cub reporter anywhere in the world could have received.

Most of the clippings pasted in that red scrapbook were the biographies of those servicemen (and a few women) on the casualty lists provided overnight by the Department of National Defence, the first document on my desk early every morning when I arrived at work. The casualty lists gave simply the ranks, names, ages, some minimum detail, and whether missing, wounded, killed in action or prisoners of war, or occasionally the good news I loved – a missing soldier found safe.

Parents and family members, no matter how deep their sorrow and pain, always were anxious to share reflections and memories of the lives of their children, brothers and sisters in the service. There were very rare occasions that families did not share their thoughts, invariably proud that their loved ones served so the rest of us could be free. And it was not a cliché so often used about those who give their lives in war. We all knew that this war was against a tyrant.

Hitler's march through Europe seemed to be fulfillment of his declared plan in his book *Mein Kampf,* an undisguised blueprint for his ultimate goal to become the Fuehrer of the World and have it populated only by a pure Aryan race. In every country he occupied, his extermination camps were fired up in the first methodical "ethnic cleansing" – mass slaughter of Jews, gypsies, communists, homosexuals, the old, the infirm, all whom he and his Nazi cohorts hated.

There was never any doubt among my friends and my own family that this was a war for the survival of freedom and democracy. My parents – who reminded us so often that they "fled from the pogroms of the Ukraine and Russia to North America to be free" – taught us how fragile freedom is, and when war came to the world they, like most parents of that time, talked of the "family duty" to serve wherever we were needed. My mother worked all her free time and at home for the Red Cross. My Dad, though legally blind, did whatever community work was requested of him. All four of my brothers of military age enlisted.

Mortie, the oldest of the Milner eight, enlisted in the army. Leo joined first in the army before Canada went to war in September, 1939, then transferred to the Royal Canadian Air Force. He rose in both services to the rank of sergeant and was kept in Canada as a training officer.[1] After the war he continued his service for a year or more in the Reserves. Macey was at Queen's University Medical School on a scholarship when the war began, and was immediately put on accelerated course to speed his qualification for service where doctors were most urgently needed – in the front lines in Europe. My brother Arthur, a chemist living in the United States, tried to enlist, but was in what was called "essential service" – the leader of a team of about 30 scientists searching for an alternative to rubber on which the military machine would roll. That research led to the discovery of plastics.

On the first virgin page of my first scrapbook – what would have been Page 3 if numbered – I carefully clipped and pasted in the first story I wrote. It was dated November 2, 1944, obviously written the day before, my first day on the job. It is carefully squared to the left-hand top corner of that page. It was set in one column, little more than a filler, two inches long, a picture slightly larger than a postage stamp inset in the text, under the head:

"Pte. R. A. Armstrong wounded second time"

The next day's story was a half-inch larger, published November 3, 1944. Like Russell Armstrong, the second person I recorded as a casualty – Cpl. Richard P. Kelton, age 19 – was a member of the Seaforth Highlanders. When the picture arrived from his family I thought the soldier looked like a pubescent boy. His parents assured me that the age National Defence gave was accurate. His mother told me he was wounded in February, but returned to duty

---

1 Despite his long service, enlisting even before war was declared on September 3, right to the end of his life Leo was refused the designation of "veteran" for the benefits he needed in his last years. It seems one Alberta bureaucrat declared that, as he had not served overseas, was not wounded in action, had never claimed injuries or sought benefits until near the end of his life, therefore – by some strange logic – he was not a "war veteran." He was actually refused admission to the new Col. Belcher veterans' facility in Calgary. It was only when Alberta Premier Ralph Klein intervened that Leo was admitted. Even then, he was told that if a "real veteran" needed his space he would be evicted. He paid the same rate as a civilian. (Some civilians were accepted into the facility before he was.) His family and I were told that if he had claimed injuries or "veteran's benefits" he could have received the benefits he needed in the last few years of his life. We were even told that "he has no claim; he did not serve overseas" – as if a soldier has the right to decide his assignment. His was a training officer for thousands of Canadians who did serve overseas.

and was wounded a second time, returning home to his family in Vancouver, with his right leg amputated below the knee.

On that page of the scrapbook there are nine separate stories, each slightly bigger than the one before. At the bottom is the picture of Pte. George Edward Hayes, 19, accompanied by a full column with the details in almost two inches in cut-line form. The search for details from his parents was the most difficult up to that time. A family member spoke with pride of his service with the Loyal Edmonton Regiment. He was killed two weeks earlier, on October 22.

Each search for the stories of the people on those casualty lists had to be done with sensitivity and compassion. I always knew, however, that each family I called wanted the news in the paper, and years later I was told by some of them how they kept and treasured the stories of their loved ones and friends.

A significant piece of history, though it probably did not register as such at the time, was the story published November 9, 1944 under the head:

"12 City Firemen to Return Home"

The story reveals that the Canadian Firefighters Overseas Civilian Corps was being demobilized, the last of Vancouver's 12 were listed in my small story as homeward bound.

Upon turning to the other side of that first page, it was evident I was growing in the job. The head on the next story was large print two lines:

"2 B.C. Fliers prisoners
In Germany; 2 missing"

Three pictures were inset in the story that ran across two columns. The story read:

"Reports of missing men now reported in Prisoner of War camps removed a shadow of doubt from the homes of two of the five British Columbia men posted in RCAF casualty list –1053 released today by Ottawa.

"PO Ralph Strang Downing, Vernon, and Flt. Lt. George Percy Edington, Vancouver, who were previously reported missing on active service, now are known to be prisoners of war in Germany.

"Two other British Columbia airmen – PO Henry Raymond English, Nanaimo, and PO Victor Gilbert Buchan Valentine, Vancouver – are listed missing on active service after air operation. PO John Raymond Mayo, previously reported missing on active service, for official purposes is presumed dead.

"On the last lap of a tour of operations overseas, PO Ralph Strang Downing, 22, was reported missing in September. Immediately upon completion of his junior matriculation in Vernon, June 1942, he enlisted and went overseas the same year ..."Flt. Lt Edington, 23, whose wife and one-year-old son live at 2720 Windsor, won his commission two years ago and went overseas October 1943. He attended King Edward High School.

"PO Valentine, 21, whose father was British Naval Intelligence Officer in Shanghai and now is interned there ... (He is the only son) of Mrs. G.J.W. Valentine ..."

And it went on in detail about the different men on this casualty list. What it revealed was that I was learning how to find biographical information and write it. And it seemed no matter what was written was published.

Hal Straight encouraged the use of names. When he asked me to do the first woman's sports column – a sideline to the full-time job – he told me that the more there were names in a story, the more people would read it. Then he added, "If we printed pages of names in the telephone directory, people would read it."

By the third page of my scrapbook, the stories were generally three columns wide with pictures at the top of each column. Soon it was apparent from the calls and letters the paper and I received that these stories were well read.

This page has a carefully pasted clipping at the top left-hand corner. "Nanaimo Ace Prisoner; 5 B.C. Men Presumed Dead; 2 killed." In wartime then, details of the locations of service and servicemen were never given. We could not reveal exact time or place of an event. The most we were told and could report was names and generalized locations such as "somewhere in Italy" or "downed over Belgium" or "in Germany." Billboards and military leaders warned, "Walls have ears," or "We cannot assist the enemy with published information." In war today, not only is every detail of the military machinery given to the whole world in the competition by reporters for their own personal attention, but the contemporary reporters cannot wait for the story to happen; they tell what is expected to happen.

On April 12, 1945, was the story of the local tribute by 500 people on the death of Franklin Delano Roosevelt. Rev. Hugh M. Rae, in a special service in St. Andrew's–Wesley United Church in downtown Vancouver, said:

> "'To all the citizens of the United States with whom we are bound together in one language, in the comradeship of arms, in ideals and aspirations for democratic freedom, to you as brothers we offer sympathy in your distinctive loss.
>
> "'The debt mankind owes him can only be discharged as the nations rise to the ideals of brotherhood that dignified his speech and actions.
>
> "'Nothing can distract from the insight of his statesmanship and his daring effort to enlarge the life of the common man.'
>
> "Another prominent Vancouver clergyman, Rev. Dr. O. W. S. McCall, referred to FDR as 'the laughing cavalier' who 'came in smiling during the Depression' but the laugh 'hesitated … when Italy stabbed France in the back … and vanished completely (December 7, 1941) when Pearl Harbour was attacked.'"

I thought the war and my writing of casualties was over when I wrote beside story May 8/1945 VE Day:

"33,266 Canadians Died for Victory"[2]

---

2   Over 44,000 Canadians perished in World War II.

Soldiers reading *The Maple Leaf*.

The story has those first statistics under my lead:

"With the ending of the war in Europe, the world today is counting the cost of victory."

But it wasn't yet over. There was still the war in the Pacific.

When the war did finally end there were stories of those held as prisoners of war by the Japanese.

My scrapbook reminds me of my involvement in what became a national story and brought calls from all parts of the western world to the managing editor and publisher for more information, for our pictures, and any additional detail we could provide.

It began for me with a tip I received in early 1946 about a man named Reg McPhee, who returned to Vancouver in October aboard a hospital ship with a large group of starved and dying men who were found in Japanese Prisoner of War camps in Hong Kong. They had been moved without public notice on stretchers, barely conscious in many cases, all of them depleted of their normal weight by half or more. The range of their weight was 68 to 75 pounds. In my first of two stories Reg McPhee told me he weighed 88 pounds, having lost half his original weight through starvation and disease. He told me – and the medical staff verified – that he had been depleted of almost all his natural body vitamins. I learned that he had the ultimate of malnutrition and in his words "every tropical disease known to man."

The story of Reg McPhee began with what he called his "Ballad of the Pills."

> "Great pills, small pills, lean pills, brawny pills.
> Brown pills, black pills, grey pills, tawny pills
> sulpha, quadrine, and vitamin pills."

His long slow recovery required as many as 142 pills a day.

He told me, "Thursday night I went to the show and I cried."

It was not because of the action on the screen, he said, but because "my feet are electrified" 24 hours every day.

"Yesterday," the story continues in McPhee's words, "I put my feet in water too hot for my hands. I bet you can't do that."

But despite perpetual pain and the fact that he was about to have all his teeth pulled the next day, the story goes on to describe his remarkable display of courage, as told to me by his nurse so simply: "He has not lost the smile habit."

I recall one of the days that I visited Reg. As usual, lounging against a pile of pillows in his hospital bed, he began to laugh – and as I wrote it afterwards:

"… his smile developed into a laugh when I asked about his weight:

"'Oh, I weigh 130 pounds now. Of course, I am kidding myself. I only really weigh 128. But I put on the kimono and so today, I am a man.

"'Reminiscently, the days of the camp seem funny now … they were pretty horrible then. We were so hungry we would eat anything …(I) saved recipes in order to keep from forgetting there was food in the outside world.

"'The worst thing I ever ate in my life was boiled chrysanthemums … long dead ones at that. It gags you as it goes down, and you can taste it even the next day. Marigolds boiled down taste almost as bad.

"'When I got back (to Vancouver) I walked like a duck.' (Actually he came home on a stretcher.) 'Now I can dance. However, I don't jive. If I jitterbug or waltz slowly I find I fall over.

"'And these,' he continued, swallowing a couple of pills, 'and this' (swallowing some more pills he explained were hydrochloric acid) 'should give me strength and appetite.'"

I remember Himie Koshevoy and Hal Straight telling me of calls they received from news reporters from around the world for more information and pictures by our photographers. Though I had long forgotten it, I found the clipping from the official Canadian military magazine, *The Maple Leaf*, in its April 11, 1946 edition, with the head: "Gets 142 Pills Daily for 'Electric Feet.'" The left top tag line was "Hong Kong Vet loses 62 pounds." The tag over on the right side was: "Reg has all tropical diseases."

At *The Sun*, the original story was followed March 27, 1946 by a four-column photograph of five of the recovering former POWs surrounding a guitar-playing survivor. It topped a two-column picture on one side of the star of the medical miracle, their doctor, Major R.H. Fraser, the head of the hospital's parasitology section. The head beside his picture read:

"TROPICAL DISEASES BEING FOUGHT HERE

Military hospital making History
On Treating Ex-Captives of Japs"

The story begins:

"War has brought tropical diseases and parasites to Vancouver.

"For the past five months teams of doctors and lab technicians in Vancouver Military Hospital have made medical history in their treatment of ex-prisoners of war who have bought practically every type of disease back with them to Canada.

"There have been instances of malaria, typhoid, pellagra, diphtheria, jaundice, dysentery, bacillary dysentery, scrub typhus, beriberi and 12 different types of worms.

"Army doctors are as concerned with the social danger of the condition – that is preventing spread among the civilian population – as they are with saving the lives of the ex-prisoners.

"When prisoners-of-war in Japan began to pour into Vancouver last fall, there were 30 doctors and lab technicians engaged in tracking down diseases and parasites. Today there are still seven on the job under Major R.H. Fraser, Pacific Command Hygiene Officer."

Reference to another story I wrote earlier is reprised here. In retrospect I have to think the hospital had kept the full story a secret to avoid panic over a major epidemic in the city, if not throughout the continent, if the news got out before Dr. Fraser and his team could assure the public that the many tropical diseases brought back from the Hong Kong prisons were eliminated and the threat of epidemic was over. The big release of the story and pictures March 27 – on my 24th birthday – grew out of my first meeting with Reg McPhee and Bill Goddard. The new story revised the Goddard case:

> "A case unique in medical history, described in *The Vancouver Sun* January 14, is that of Bill Goddard, the soldier who lost 90 pounds … weighed only 57 when found in the camp in the Orient.

> "He arrived in Vancouver unconscious, suffering from malaria, pellagra beriberi, amoebic dysentery, and to top all this he contracted pneumonia aboard ship. He also lost the power of speech, and his ability to walk. His pulse rate was almost doubled.

> "Today doctors and the lab crew report 'miraculous recovery.' The first prisoner of the group to survive a condition such as this. He has partially regained the power of speech and his ability to walk, weighs 123 pounds (33 pounds less than his normal weight, and – unusual for a POW – he has an appetite.

> "'In tropical medicine, the microscope practically replaces the stethoscope,' explained Morley Kare, head of the hospital's laboratories … 'Very few of the POWs missed out on beriberi, the disease of Vitamin B-1 deficiency. It struck the men so severely that sensation completely left their limbs, giving them a painfully "tingling" numbness.'

> "To find out if they really had beriberi and deserved medical treatment, the Japs would put red-hot irons to the afflicted parts. If the prisoner did not feel the burn, they got medical treatment.

> "'Diphtheria histories are very common among the ex-prisoners. Vancouver Military Hospital has no active cases (at this time) but there are carriers there … one of our main worries,' said Major Fraser.

> "'Another worry is amoebic dysentery as occurred in a Chicago epidemic during the World's Fair there.'"

Two years later I moved on to another series that told of the power – or magic – of a tiny pill. Now the pill became very personal, and in retrospect I view that long-gone past in the tired cliché of moving from the sublime (life saving) to the ridiculous. That is, from saving the lives of nearly-dead men and preventing a continent-wide epidemic to the ultimate in vanity of the mid-20th century – a pill to lose weight and be fashionably thin.

On April 10, 1948, one-third of the front page in every edition carried the story that I was going on a diet – using pills to fight fat. I always thought that I was overweight, even though I had the desired measurement for a 26-year-old female: 36-26-35. But there it is, taking a full page of the larger of my scrapbooks, with half the clipping hanging over the bottom of the page, the big announcement: **"Science Joins Fight Against Fat for Simma Milner."**

And there I am in three columns on *The Sun* front page, laid out on a bed with a huge bundle of tubes sprouting from a mask over my mouth and nose. Sitting on the edge of the bed beside the pillow surrounding my head is a white-uniformed nurse named Margaret David, a former photographer's model, administering some sort of medical measurement.

Below that there is a picture of me setting out on what was dubbed "Pill Power," preparing to drop the first of my daily regimen of three pills a day towards the goal of becoming glamorously thin. The head for the second picture is: **"Pills Prescribed for Avoirdupois."**

The story began:

"I had my last square meal – rounded off with calorie-packed trimmings – Friday night.

"Now I am on a reducing diet.

"I've gone on diets before. Many of them. But each time my will took a beating and I succumbed to my passion for food.

"Now I have found a doctor who has the newest thing in diets … three little pills."

I experienced the terrible pressures of lost privacy for the first time in my life. I got mash notes from male readers, even marriage proposals. Strangers would walk up to me in restaurants as I was eating, look into my plate, point a finger and say loud enough for all within a radius of 30 feet to hear, "Simma will never get slimma on that …" or "That is a pretty heavy calorie count for

The rigours and anxiety of dieting.

slimmin' Simma." It was pickup on the tag line used in one of the daily progress reports on my diet.

My weight loss was fast and significant, though total strangers said, "We cannot see it" or "You looked slim enough before ..."

In a few days the impact was more significant than the weight loss. I began to feel like my brain was exploding in hysteria, literally screaming in what seemed like a tight cinch holding me together. Through a feeling of excessive mental and physical energy, I felt terrible fatigue, tension that I feared would blow up in my life in public. Nights were sleepless. It was easy to stay up all night and write the daily report of my pill-popping diet. But I knew I was losing my self-control in body and mind.

Two weeks after it began, I stopped "cold turkey." The crash was horrendous. I could barely move. I did not know that the pill I was on would one day be recognized as dangerous, deadly methamphetamine.

New fad diets changed almost as fast and frequently as their clients enthused and then returned to their bad eating habits. It seemed there was always a new diet featured in a magazine, newspaper or book touted by the print media. It was the eve of Weight Watchers, Jenny Craig, NutriSystem, and others that proliferated en masse into the 21st century throughout North America.

The next one *The Sun* wanted to introduce as a feature was the Fat Boy diet. This time I used local and national celebrities who agreed to allow public exposure of their "need" and progress in losing weight. The most memorable in this series was the beautiful blond "bombshell" radio and nightclub soloist of the Big Band era, "Our Pet" Juliette. *Sun* photographer Charlie Warner and I went to her apartment. Like Juliette herself, it was bright and stunning – all white furniture, rugs, appliances and wall cover. Juliette, always obliging and with a love of fun, agreed to pose with a towel wrapped around her nude body – standing on the scale. I could hardly get Charlie out of there. He wanted to return to get a few more shots "just to be sure." He said he feared he failed to get the best in the potential "art."

Though there were attractive women in our Edith Adams (home-making) department, as well as in the Women or Society and Fashion departments, I presume it was because I was the only girl in the newsroom that I became the model for stories. The fact that that I was used as a model so often should have dispelled my negative self-image. Even those pictures and compliments did not convince me then. Too late, I wish I had enjoyed it, and wish I could convince the beautiful young women of today that they do not need to pierce their noses or eyebrows, or streak their hair in purple and green, or expose their navels or blow up their boobs to the size of cows' udders.

Once I even did a story, with illustrations, of how a woman can get into a car gracefully. And when Leon and I hosted a spaghetti party (the only meal I felt safe to prepare successfully for visitors), with our famous cellist friend Barton Frank providing dinner music, the pictures of that night were spread large across the top of a feature page of *The Sun*. My spaghetti recipe was printed in a sidebar box.

On the night of that dinner party, Mrs. Rennie, my neighbour across the hall (who, incidentally, I thought of as an "old lady" – perhaps no more than 60) knocked lightly on my door. When I answered, there she was in all her gentleness, saying, "Dear, I love having you as a neighbour and love to see your joy in life … but could you ask the violist not to play his music so loud?"

Even after I left my job beside the police radio, I seemed to be able to hear a story breaking no matter where I was in the City Room. On February 26, 1947, as I was working at my desk, then about 30 feet from the radio, I heard a bank holdup call, Commercial Street and First Avenue. Minutes later I heard a call for ambulances to False Creek … foot of Glen Drive. A bank holdup was a potential headline story, and as Hal Straight came towards the City Desk I also went to Himie and said, "Something big is happening there," noting the call for ambulances to the same general area. Photographer Art Jones was among the very few people in Vancouver at that time – certainly in the newspaper business – who had a two-way radio in his car. He was the type of newshound I admired most, always mobile, always looking for and finding stories. That morning he had heard the bank holdup call and was moving towards First and Commercial when he was told ambulances were headed for False Creek. That day Art Jones earned the name "On-the-spot Jones." He arrived as a gun battle was going on. Two policemen, Constables Oliver

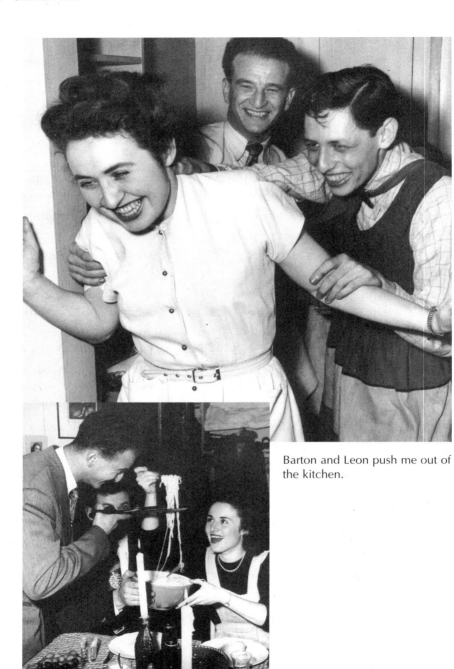

Barton and Leon push me out of the kitchen.

Leon cuts the spaghetti for Tova.

Ledingham and Charles Boyes, as well as one of the bank robbers, were killed. Another officer, Detective Alan Hoare, who had just been wounded, was still firing his gun when Art arrived and got the whole scene. A copy boy was sent out to get his film and bring replacement while he kept recording the scene.

My involvement did not end in that day taking dictation and helping to put the stories together from the reporters on the scene. A police officer friend tipped me that Madeline Medos, wife of the leader of the bank robbery gang, was going to give evidence for the Crown in the trials of her husband and others. I found her in the first floor of the Stratford Hotel, actually one floor over the stores at street level on Granville Street in downtown Vancouver. Her room was directly across from the hotel registration desk. I was not sure whether the men sitting around in the small lobby watching her door were plainclothes policemen or underworld friends of her husband; they all seem to look alike. Madeline and I were both uneasy as we talked together in her room.

I was just starting on the detail I sought for background, asking when she would make her first appearance in court, when there was a heavy knock on the door.[3] I opened it an inch and immediately recognized Gar Macpherson, a long-time police reporter for *The Sun,* very much trusted by and connected with the police force. He told me that I must return to the office immediately, suggesting Madeline and I were both in danger as long as we were together. That was the last time I saw Madeline until she gave the testimony that no doubt led to her husband's conviction for multiple murder. She was taken out of the city, I later learned, and was hidden out in Victoria.

On January 1, 1948 I joined one of the first Polar Bear Club swims to start the new year. The photographer, Harry Filion, who felt the same Pacific coast winter chill as I did even though he was in a heavy coat and hat, agreed we would fake the swim.

It was raining. He thought I should protect against the rain with an umbrella and he could take the picture from water's edge on his well-rounded

---

3 Unlike the Americans, British and Canadian reporters would be charged with contempt of court to use evidence against an accused – virtual trial by the press – prior to the evidence being given in court before a judge and jury.

belly. But the whole management staff turned up to watch the show and our plan ended there. I had to go in. The water was about 58 degrees Fahrenheit, the sandy floor of the ocean was, I was sure, solid ice – and the only way to get my feet off the ground was to swim. Hell was never cold but this sure was hell.

I was sure I would die of shock.

My story, called "I Swam with the Polar Brrrs", took a two-column-wide centre page, with picture topped by the head: **"POLAR BEAR SWIM OK – IF YOU LIKE IT"**

Relegated to one column at the bottom left-hand corner of the page was the heading: **"PHYSICIAN FLYING TO SICK WAR LEADER ...** *in Morocco***"**

I heard from an old boyfriend from back in my Vegreville school days. He wrote, "I am not surprised that you my old friend would crowd Winston Churchill, who might be dying, off Page One."

The byline in those first scrapbooks was "Simma Milner." After my marriage May 29, 1949, when I informed the management my name was now "Simma Holt," I was told that my byline would remain unchanged, that it had been built up by *The Sun* and it would stay as it was. I dared to argue that they had rarely if ever assigned stories to me, that I took the initiative in finding and writing my own stories. I argued that I did not want Leon to be mistaken for "Mr. Milner."

Finally I agreed to their compromise. I would use the byline "Simma Milner Holt." I later changed it to Simma Holt, my name for life ever since.

On June 17, 1958, the Second Narrows Bridge, under construction, suddenly collapsed and two spans stood on their sides like a parallelogram, in tangled steel and blood. Nineteen people died. That day we literally walked in blood. Highways Minister "Flying Phil" Gaglardi was one of the most colourful and revolutionary cabinet ministers in the Social Credit government of Premier W.A.C. Bennett. When Phil arrived to officially see for himself the catastrophe of the collapsed bridge and the tragedy of lost lives, I suggested he might want to go to the hospital (Lions Gate Hospital in North Vancouver) to talk with survivors. "Good idea, Simma," he said. He got into his car, I jumped into the back seat and pushed down all the locks on the doors. When the opposition reporter tried to get in, Phil said, "There is no one around; let's go." My photographer followed me. At the hospital the Highways Minister stopped at every bed, with me standing taking notes unobtrusively behind him while the photographer snapped pictures. At the last bed, Gaglardi whispered, "Have you got all you want here, Simma?" I nodded and went back to the office with my photographer. I had a page of exclusive pictures of all the survivors, and the Minister of Highways got his face in the layout.

Another favourite Flying Phil story for me goes back to the historic maiden voyage of the first ferry in the new B.C. Ferry system between the mainland and Vancouver Island. During that first crossing on the new service, "Flying Phil" was at the helm, either at the wheel or beside it. When we reached the Vancouver Island terminal, the new vessel suffered a minor fender-bender as it crashed into the pylons of the dock of Sidney (Swartz Bay). On our return, with the great North Shore mountains appearing straight ahead as we neared the Mainland Terminal at Tsawwassen, Gaglardi whispered to me, "How would you like me to race this up that hill?"

One day there was an important meeting of shipping executives in the exclusive Terminal City Club. Women were only allowed in as guests of male members in the dining room. I was on my way through the front door to the boardroom for the meeting, when I was told I could not pass. Finally I was taken in through the kitchen and the entrance from the kitchen to the meeting room. To add insult to injury, it was a divided Dutch door; I had to bend under the top half to get into the room, in front of all those male executives seated there. They were smiling at me, which I interpreted as amusement at my embarrassment. I was angry, and when I got back to the office I went straight to the managing editor and told him what happened. I vowed I would never cover an assignment again when insulted that way. "And," I added, "you can fire me but never again …" He replied, "If you ever do it again that way, you ARE fired."

In 1959 I was assigned the waterfront beat. The decision by Managing Editor Erwin Swangard seemed to go against all tradition. This had always been an exclusively man's domain. When I was assigned this beat, I became one of only two women in recorded journalism history who had worked the waterfront. The other was in Hawaii.

On the waterfront

My assignment shocked and angered some of the male reporters. It was a beat they wanted. It may have been perversity, but I suspected Erwin was seeking a new perspective. He financed the wardrobe I needed to be warm and safe on the waterfront, including an expensive lambswool-lined canvas parka and boots that would never slide on slippery gangplanks and docks.

I would work among the stevedores loading and unloading cargo, attend meetings of shipping executives, and interview people around the waterfront. When a freighter or cruiser was about to enter Vancouver Harbour, I boarded at Ogden Point off Vancouver Island with the pilot, who took control of navigation of the ship in the Harbour. Shipping agents and customs officers would board at the same time.

There were many firsts for women on that beat – first to go to the bottom of the sea in a submarine, first on the biggest aircraft carrier in the world, and more.

I was aboard for a Christmas run on the small freighter of Northland Navigation, the *Northern Princess,* taking gifts and winter supplies into small coastal villages. The locals, mostly natives, without any docking facilities, had to come out to the ship in rowboats and dugouts to collect supplies lowered into their boats down the side of the ship. The routine in the last run before Christmas was to hoist an evergreen to the top of the mast before returning to Vancouver Harbour. On that trip there was a wild Pacific winter storm that carried us miles out to sea. When we finally got back into sheltered waters, the ship was still heeling and the men did not want to bother with the tree. I agreed to be hoisted to the top of the mast and lash the tree there. It made good art and copy, and fear never inhibited me from going after a story.

The biggest ship ever to sail under the Lions Gate Bridge into the Harbour was the United States aircraft carrier, the *Coral Sea.* As we neared the bridge, I was on the ship's bridge beside the captain. The entire company of seamen and officers were lined up the full length of the main deck below. Leading west coast navigation specialists, having done careful measurements, were confident the *Coral Sea* mast at its highest point would pass safely under the bridge. The captain suddenly asked me to leave the ship's bridge, because of the old sea superstition that it was bad luck to have preachers and women aboard ship. (I openly called this a "superstition of convenience." It allowed men to have their fun with neither women nor clergy to inhibit them.) The captain, know-ing my scepticism, explained, "If the mast is torn off and falls and injures even one of them, you will be blamed." Though I knew the experts who cleared the passage for the *Coral Sea,* I knew even an unrelated incident would be a prob-lem for me.

They used to say that they could not hire women because they could not inter-view a man in the men's room. (Seemingly that is where big business besides the routine goes on between men.) So one day I proved this was wrong, and when I had the evidence I walked into Hal Straight's office. Both he and Himie were there. I announced as I walked in, "It's not true a woman reporter can-not interview a man in the men's can."

"Oh yeah?" Hal said it as a query.

"Well I interviewed a man in the men's washroom," I told them. It was at a Police Commission hearing held at City Hall. After it ended I needed some information from Commission Counsel Vic Dryer. He went through a door I thought led to the Mayor's private elevator. But it turned out to be the Mayor's tiny biffy.

I asked my bosses, "Do you want to know what he said in the interview?" I didn't wait for a response. "Vic said, 'Ooops,' and with motions, moving his arms backwards, as though he might like me to interview him a few minutes later and in another place."

On the job there were advantages to being female especially when a reporter was required to go out to interview women alone. One night there was a call that "the madman of Penetanguishene" facility for the criminally insane had been discovered living, working and married openly for several years out of his home in the heart of Vancouver. The call indicated that police were on their way to arrest him. I only had the name he was using, no address. I found his name simply listed in the telephone directory, the neighbours' names in my research bible, the City Directory. When I arrived in the neigh-bourhood, the home where he lived was sealed off. But the neighbours had their lights out or were peeking out of the windows. They were not answering their doors. When I turned up, the women opened the doors immediately and swept me in, admitting they were afraid of the men that came to their doors.

Another time, a man survived a plane crash. There were reporters and cameramen on the street in front of the house waiting for the survivor, who was under sedation or simply in a deep sleep from extreme fatigue, to wake up. Bill Dennett, my cameraman, parked his car in a lane about two blocks from the house. We sneaked down the lane and crawled on our stomachs across the open space between the houses (visible to the crowd of opposition reporters and photographers crowded at the front of the home). When we knocked at the door, it was opened by a woman who recognized me and said the man was asleep, but asked to be awakened by about 10:30 or 11:00 a.m. If we came back then, they would bring us in to interview him at the back door. We returned later that morning, got pictures and story, and bellied back the way we came. It was my first story with an "Exclusive" banner on it.

A murder/suicide was reported in a Chinese family home fairly near the office. The two children, ages about seven and eight, came home for lunch from school. When they tried to open the door they could barely get it open wide enough to squeeze through. They found their mother lying bloody and dead against the door. The police found the young parents both dead. By the time I arrived, there were all of the top city male reporters on the scene. The police and coroner were all male. As soon as I arrived I noticed two children huddled in a corner almost out of sight behind the porch. When I started towards them they raced to me. The little girl ran into my arms, crying and telling me her mother and father were dead and she could not open the door.

Here are a few more memories from my many scrapbooks and clippings:

My policewoman friend, Audrey Kirk, tipped me that there was a baby born in Vancouver General Hospital (VGH) to a drug-addicted mother. Medical teams were working around the clock to save the newborn infant's life. The tiny baby was wracked in the agony of withdrawal and convulsion of drug addiction. When the nurses brought the newborn to the mother, she responded, "So what! I go through this all the time." It was a small story on Page One. The administrator of VGH wrote a letter to the editor denying the truth of the story. However, wanting to maintain the good professional relationship we had had, he called to explain and apologized. He said, in effect,

"We are doing research in these cases, and if you can hold back for a while, I promise we will give you the exclusive when our work is completed." I knew, and said it: he wanted to break the story himself in the medical or hospital journals. The addict was released back to the street, I presume, and the baby taken into care. Neither Officer Kirk nor I could do any follow-up. But I never forgot it, as babies born addicted are now being saved routinely.

Miriam Mylaneimi, a 14-year-old Jehovah's Witness who had nephritis, had blood transfusion forced on her while a patient in St. Paul's Hospital. She phoned to ask me to visit her. She told me that she had begged them not to "destroy her soul and her right to eternal life" by forcing her to receive blood into her body.

Miriam said that the hospital lawyers had taken her case into closed Juvenile and Family Court in order to become her legal guardians. According to Miriam and her mother, the hospital wanted to keep her alive for a year because she was a perfect case for an upcoming experiment in kidney transplant that the hospital hoped to undertake. (St. Paul's today is a leader in vascular and heart surgery, and its blood research, its specialization, is widely recognized.)

One dark night, shortly after we met, Miriam phoned me from a pay phone outside the hospital. She asked me to meet her and tell no one where she would be. I met her. She was preparing for final flight from Canada to where Jehovah's Witness doctors, who used blood substitutes both in dialysis and heart repair, were waiting to care for her. I have never heard from or seen her since, though I was informed that she was alive at least five years later.

In the late 1950s *The Vancouver Sun* raised money for Ronnie Richardson, age 11, who could not live through early puberty if the holes in his heart were not repaired. It was the time of the earliest open heart surgery – when doctors stopped the heart to repair it and then packed the patient in ice to control fever.

We raised $7,650 – all the money needed for his travel to the Mayo Clinic in Rochester, Minnesota, for medical care and surgery there, and then for his return to the mainstream. My first trip with Ronnie and his mother, Dorothy Richardson, was for diagnosis by five or six teams of medical specialists to determine whether the surgery could be done and the boy's life saved.

The second trip, for the surgery, was Christmas week, when the hospital was at its quietest. It was as though the whole of British Columbia was involved in Ronnie's life-and-death struggle. Flowers and telegrams poured in literally by the hundreds during the protracted crisis when we did not know whether he would live or die. Everyone from the Premier and Mayor down sent telegrams, cards, gifts. Not only did Ronnie live into adulthood, but the money that continued to pour in for him made it possible for him to start a small gift and card shop.

Edna Achtymichuk was a beautiful university student, in coma for 96 days following a car accident. She was en route by ambulance from VGH to the mental hospital, diagnosed as incurable. The prognosis: an unconscious "vegetable" for the rest of her life. Her mother diverted her from the transfer, loaded her on a baggage car on a train and sat with her all the way to the Mayo Clinic. There, and later in Edna's Rochester hospital room, the mother talked to her daughter, believing that Edna heard and understood. The mother set up ways to message her daughter by touch and eye contact, and reprimanded nurses and other staff who talked beside her bed about her as though she did not hear. The mother told them – and I learned later she was correct – that Edna heard much of what they said. The mother kept Edna warm in love and communication. Suddenly, one day Edna spoke. Today she is a woman of about age 60. She worked to get her mobility and improve her speech to the maximum possible. I worked with her to help her as she struggled through to complete the education interrupted by the accident. She married, too late realizing that it was her money, her home ownership and perhaps the publicity she had received, that had led to the proposal. The marriage ended quickly. She has remained self-sufficient though obviously crippled.

In time, I found more stories than I could ever write myself. One day James Clavell[4], author of some of the world's biggest bestsellers, came into the office I shared with several columnists. As soon as we were introduced, he told me, "If I had all the stories you have I would never have to leave home to find subjects for my books." He urged me to adapt my stories to fiction. When I told him of my block in fiction writing, he said, "Just start by typing 'The' and keep writing … If you get stuck, I'll help you finish it – in fiction."

In my search for the people who lived in that period of my life I found a "kid reporter" I determined to help train. He was Fred Cawsey who came on staff, along with two other young men barely out of their teens, for summer relief. If they were sent out on assignment, nobody helped them with the ways to get stories or even details of deadlines. They did not have the kind of support and training that I had when I came on the City Desk. I saw they were virtually on their own in the big indifferent city newsroom. I had seniority then and suggested that I would go on the job as night editor to help train them.

We barely got to know each other when one of the biggest stories in Vancouver crime history broke. A family of four, including two small children, were murdered in their home. The kid reporters all went to the scene and stayed connected with me by land phone. As I worked the city directory and found people who might have information I gave the young men names and addresses, and told them the questions they might ask. The next morning the headline story by the young men contained every detail possible, and won the praise of the highest levels of management right up to the publisher and the circulation manager.

Fred Cawsey more than any others at that time gave me the final freedom from my bonds with *The Sun*. Fred, raised by a single-parent mother,

---

4   James Clavell often stayed and worked in West Vancouver. When I felt I was slipping professionally and could not go on, I could trace him through the local residence. He was mostly in Paris. Only two or three times, when I had no professional in this area I knew, I would call him. No matter where he was he always called back, and encouraged me. I was lucky in the great professionals who believed I had something special for books. Besides James Clavell, Himie Koshevoy, Bill Short, Hal Straight, and publisher Don Cromie, there were Toronto journalist and author Peter Worthington, U.S. author Mike Schumacher, scholar and concert cellist Barton Frank, and my best friend and husband, Leon, who pleaded with me: "Just write your own stories as you have done through the years – in a book."

A big story on Page One of an EXTRA edition.

Tom Norris was a very famous and powerful Vancouver lawyer, a friend who fed me many great stories. Ray Munro was a flamboyant photographer for a tabloid called *Flash*. The incident that set off this story was the suicide of Deputy Chief Harry Whalen, a wonderful, decent policeman, in no way part of the scandal supposedly surrounding Chief Walter Mulligan and Deputy Chief Gordon Ambrose.

I don't know why I am wearing glasses in this picture. I never needed them. I guess some doctor must have said I should have them.

admitted he was a street fighter and could battle as well as any of the bullies of the newsroom. One day he came to my desk, self-assured now, though still not yet in his 20s, and told me, "Those ... #@#% are cutting up your copy and laughing at the mess they will make ... Do you want me to go up and beat the sh-- out of them?"

I never had a greater moment of affection for a colleague than I had at that moment. I told him, however, it had been going on for years and it really did not matter.

At one point I said to Leon that I could not longer take the "stuff" that was going on at *The Sun*. I loved good editing, but it was no secret that the tampering with mine and others' copy was vindictive. Though it may only have happened to comparatively few of my thousands of stories, Fred Cawsey witnessed it, and other friends had described it.

It was several weeks later that I left the job late at night and suddenly found myself in my car at the US–Canada border, not remembering how or why I went there. The next day I took leave of absence for a few months and went to see a contact friend, psychiatrist Ernie Wong. He told me to consider him "a professional friend ... your favourite shrink." I had already published books, won awards, had constant requests for my work for newspapers and magazines. But I still believed the few bullies attacking my writing skills.

When I was about to return to work, I saw Ernie and he had a short and simple piece of advice. "The next time anyone tells you that you can't write, tell them to 'Fuck off.'"

I had never used that word, nor do I now, even though I know its derivation is totally respectable in old law books[5]

I was uneasy about my return. I had barely reached my desk when the fat redheaded labour reporter, Bryce Williams, accosted me and said in a loud voice for all to hear, "Hey ... the has-been is back."

"Better a has-been than a never-was, Bryce ... so fuck off."

There were as many stories at that time – both personal and public – as there were contacts and people who entered my life. It is not a stretch to estimate

---

5 In old English law books it derived from For Unlawful Carnal Knowledge.

that I wrote and published tens of thousands of stories in my career. Even in simple arithmetic, only counting the 29 years and six months at *The Sun* (November 1, 1944 to May 1, 1974), if I did only one story a day 365 days a year it would add up to about 10,770. That would not count the fact that I could find and write three, four, five stories a day, and does not count the stories I did as a stringer for *Chatelaine*, the old *Liberty Magazine*, *Style Fortnightly*, *The Toronto Star*, *The Toronto Sun*, *Reader's Digest*, and *Fair Lady* (South Africa). I even did one assignment for *Cosmopolitan*. It was a story on Men Who Fake Orgasm, and how they achieved fooling their wives after their extracurricular exploits. The story was assigned by the magazine at the suggestion of Editor Helen Gurley Brown. The story was rejected. The excuse, I recall, was that it contained too much research, too much detail. All of it, of course, was as told to me by men I knew and worked with. I was, incidentally, dubbed the "sexless wonder of Canadian journalism." I didn't know what vibes I sent out but I was untouchable. Both of these characteristics of my style and work were a matter of pride for me and the basis, I believe, for the awards I won.

Years later in Ottawa the truth came out when *Sun* parliamentary correspondent Alex Young was assigned by the managing editor to rent a tux and escort me to receive an award at the Bowater-Parliamentary Award dinner in Ottawa. When he escorted me to the hotel room, Alex made a pass at me, and I broke up laughing. He told me then that there was a pool at *The Sun* for the first to get me into bed. When Alex and I were long retired I reminded him of this event; he denied it. He knew it would turn up some day in a story by Holt and probably did not want his grandchildren to know that sort of stuff about him.

Never did I use sex for advantage on a story or on the job. Except for that one incident I was never propositioned openly by a colleague. I could spend an entire night in a room talking with male contacts and friends, never once having to deal with improper suggestions. My sexy girl friends said there was "only one thing a man wants," and I responded that they send out vibes that invite this. Obviously the vibes I sent off were "Do not touch."

My favourite story of all was contained in single column, about six inches long without a byline on Page One. It may not even be in my scrapbooks. But I will

Dressed for an award in Ottawa by the famous fashion editor of *The Sun,* later *The Toronto Star,* Marie Moreau.

When *The Sun* was notified that I won the Bowater Award of Merit for my series on the new teen-age morality, and that I would be sent to Ottawa for the presentation, I said I would not go. *The Sun* management said, "You are going and you are going to receive that award in Ottawa." Marie had a budget to get the clothes for me and the day I was to leave she arranged for my hair to be set. She ordered me to "have a comb-out before the dinner." The Ottawa reporter, Alex Young, was told to rent a tuxedo and be my escort. He looked great – except I noticed a major hole in the sole of his shoe.

never forget the moment. Never in my entire career was I assigned to a royal tour. However, my first of a few meetings with the Queen and Prince Philip was the essence of a favoured memory and story. Prince Philip was hardly my favourite person, and grew more dislikeable with each meeting. His wife and Prince Charles, however, had the personal warmth and kindness that I saw and admired.

In the first royal visit to Vancouver, Elizabeth and Philip toured Shaughnessy Military Hospital. Before they arrived, I met the padre. He told me of a dying man alone in a single room, who had only one last wish. His wish was to live long enough to see the Queen. The Queen and Prince Philip arrived, signed the hospital guest book, and talked and visited with the ambulatory veterans in the auditorium. Then she began a tour of the wards. Philip was behind, stopping in rooms or talking with patients and staff. I followed as closely behind the Queen as was allowed. After she passed the room I had been to earlier, the chaplain came out and told me, "God gave him his wish. He saw the Queen. She turned, looked in, smiled. Her heel had barely disappeared when he died."

Later, as a Member of Parliament, I would meet with the royal couple twice, able to share briefly the fascinating relationship, with laughter and humour, between the Prime Minister and the Queen.

I met Charles only once. It was at a reception for him with the MPs. My leg was in a cast for a broken ankle, when he came over to talk with me. He was very anxious to know what had happened. He seemed not to be engaged in mere polite concern. Several times he came over to see if I was all right, or if he could help me. We chatted about Vancouver and the fact that I was one of only three women in Parliament from the west in Canada's entire history to that time. Today, when I hear the talk of the "cold" Prince Charles, I want to shout, "They know not of what they speak." I admired Charles and the Queen (and even Prince Philip, though a social jerk) for doing their job with such dedication and remarkable patience. It must be the toughest public relations job in the world.

Peter Worthington (on the left), Knowlton Nash and I, when we were inducted into the Canadian News Hall of Fame in May, 1996.

With my good friend Michael Schumacher, on the night I was inducted into the Canadian News Hall of Fame.

13

The Accidental Friend

Jack Webster came to *The Vancouver Sun,* in 1947 with distinguished creden-tials. Though still very young, his was a well-established reputation in Glasgow and on London's famous Fleet Street before he immigrated to Canada. One of his claims to established fame was that he shared a desk on Fleet Street with Ian Fleming, the creator of fictional spy James Bond.

He also had the depth of a foreign correspondent in Palestine. He was what today would be called an "embedded" reporter inside the battles between the Jews and the British when Palestinian Jews smuggled refugees from the European holocaust into Palestine. The British barred this immigration and, when they could catch them, turned the refugees back. It was a bloody fight of the Hagana, the core of what became the Israel Defense Force, and those called terrorists, the *Irgun Tsvai Leumi.*

Jack achieved fame in Canada because of his self-confidence and massive ego. He did not pretend humility; he knew the truth of his character. He called himself an "ambitious extrovert." In Canada's west he was most respected and held in awe for his fearless assault on injustice of any type, taking on the pow-erful, whether corporate giants, kings, queens or prime ministers.

At *The Sun* we teamed on many stories, exposing wrongdoing. We also were of one mind – and mood (angry and ready to fight) – in uncovering injustice and abuse of the weak. And when he moved on to the electronic world of radio and television, I was a frequent guest on his show, especially when I got a big news or feature story for the paper or magazines, or when he needed to use the background in the subjects of my books. His promotion of my appearances on his show were as "trouble" or warnings of a steamy session

I was often a guest on Jack Webster's radio show.

of "Terror in the name of Simma" (taking off the title of my first book after the publication of *Terror in the Name of God* in 1964).

He always controlled his shows, was challenging but soft and kind to the subjects who were weaker than he. He enjoyed being provocative and no matter how he might have been beaten in a debate with a strong guest (especially political and corporate leaders) he always assured me that he won over the famous guest. He never pretended; he was blatant – to the last days of his career – that he needed attention and centre stage.

In August through September 1968 I became the substitute host for him on CKNW Radio. At that time, Jack was reputed to be the highest-paid anchor and open-line personality in North America. He described his timing and reporting as *"Precise."* Testimony to this was that his facts and judgment on major issues were rarely challenged or found flawed. Throughout almost 50 years as a star in both the local and national media his reputation for accuracy and professionalism never diminished.

He claimed his three-hour morning show and one-hour early evening show netted him an income of one million dollars a year. At that time the average "good" salary in our business ranged from $25,000 to a high of about $55,000. Advertisers knew the four hours five days a week for Webster were worth every cent paid. Jack's was a unique loud and fearless voice, authoritative, and with a Scottish accent – which he retained with scrupulous care, improving it with the passage of his time in Canada. There was no way the gruff voice of Webster could be mistaken.

Thus when asked to do his show while he went home to Scotland for six weeks, it was a challenge I could not resist. Of course, I was afraid, since I had never before handled the switches and buttons of a radio console – and machines have a paralytic effect on me.

At the beginning of my open line substitution job, two major stories broke. On August 20, 1968, the armies of the Soviet bloc invaded Czechoslovakia. The big local and national story was that Pierre Elliott Trudeau was making his first major appearances in Vancouver as Canada's new prime minister. Across the continent, "from sea to shiny sea," a national hysteria had exploded around this man who seemed to come out of nowhere to be the leader of the nation. It was called "Trudeaumania," and just as it would be impossible for an open-line host to ignore the news from Czechoslovakia, I would have to cover and comment on the Trudeau visit.

The one that interested me most was Czechoslovakia. I knew a Czechoslovakian political science professor at the University of British Columbia who, with a compatriot, was closely connected to the leaders in his homeland. They agreed to come to the studio immediately and help me report the sensational and fearsome story of the invasion of their homeland by the Russians. By the time I went on air for the evening show, they had connected with New York friends who had a direct line to insiders involved in the resistance and virtual eyewitnesses to the invasion. Thus CKNW had the story of the quiet but resolute fight going on inside against the invaders. We reported that the Czech people were very cool in their movement of street signs to confuse the invading armies that might have been depending on maps to move their tanks and troops in the takeover. We were told of the humour in tragedy as the invading armies got lost, and of roads blocked by cars and tractors. Our listeners heard that the popular young Czech leader, Alexander Dubcek, had been arrested by the Soviet military. However, he was serving as the nation's leader in absentia. We were being told probably more Dubcek banners were raised then, during the invasion, than were used during an election campaign. CKNW had the first story of how the citizens of Czechoslovakia were fighting back in ways that made fools of the invading armies, even though they could not – and did not – win.

And then when Trudeau was to be in the Hotel Vancouver in the early morning, I had no choice but to record the event even though I held a strong dislike of the man. It was in those first days of Perrier and rose buds – that ever-present red rose bud in his lapel and the drink – if he had any drink – of Perrier water.

He was the one celebrity that I least wanted to know and report. No doubt it was partly because the media was going mad over him and the newspapers, magazines, television and radio were jammed with the excitement this man had aroused across the nation. Actually, in my 30 years in journalism, there were few celebrities that I would cross the road to see if it were not my job. The two I wanted to meet were Eleanor Roosevelt and Adlai Stevenson. Ironically, both had been guests of the Canadian Women's Press Club at different times, and I missed both because I was away on assignment.

Despite my total lack of interest in seeing or meeting Pierre Trudeau that day – four months after he was sworn in as the new prime minister – as Webster's surrogate I had to do what he would have done for his CKNW Radio audience. And so early that warm summer morning I left Jack's studio in the heart of downtown Vancouver, in a corner of the mezzanine floor of the Georgia Hotel, and went to the Hotel Vancouver, there to join the mob of Trudeaumaniacs in the hotel ballroom. Despite wall-to-wall people of all ages, shapes and colour, Pierre Trudeau was easy to find. It did not happen in the characteristic Trudeau way – at the eye of the hurricane of swirling, squealing humanity. That morning the promoter staged it so it would be impossible to miss the Prime Minister upon first entry into the crowd.

He was beside the stage, surrounded by eight or ten pretty young girls terraced at different levels on the steps up to the stage and arranged in a frame around him like a Hollywood production. They were smiling, gushing, hugging and setting him off in a mini-skirted border of red and white (Liberal Party colours).

My resentment was heightened by the fact that these young women, several apparently pubescent girls whose legs were not yet fully shaped, were being used to promote a phony image of Canada's newest sex god, age 48. It was reminiscent of the bobby-sox hysteria aroused by the young Frank Sinatra years before Trudeaumania.

I simply intended to watch, listen, perhaps have brief interviews with members of the crowd – some of national fame – to use as material in my introductory editorial, on my return to Jack's studio for the 9 a.m. to 12 noon "Talk Back to Webster" show.

I was totally absorbed in the staging for the curious and the sycophants, looking away only to scribble a few notes of the scene and various dialogue I heard in my eaves- dropping effort. All of sudden someone had hold of my arm and a familiar voice was saying, "Simma I am so glad you could make it here today. Come, meet the Prime Minister."

It was the Honourable Art Laing, the senior cabinet minister for the west, host for the Prime Minister's visit. Art Laing was a political leader I genuinely liked and admired most for his integrity and the good works he had done for the West. I saw him as the paragon of liberalism; he cared for social justice and human need without compromise. He was one who would always stop to rescue the stranger at the side of the road.

Art drew me out of the milling crowd, turned me into a line-crasher for his introduction: "Mr. Prime Minister, I want you to meet a very special lady, one of the great ladies of the west."

It was neither the time nor the place to change the text. It was a rare moment that I did not want to put my best lip forward in this, the first meeting with the Prime Minister of Canada. Art Laing was giving him a thumbnail sketch of me. Canada's Darling was abstract, smiled politely, but with obvious boredom. We shook hands, saying the polite platitude: "Glad to meet you," which was a lie for both of us. He was obviously as unimpressed with me as I was with him.

I came away disliking him and Trudeaumania equally. I went back to the station and started the Webster show with the editorial on my view of Canada's new prime minister. I began by briefly describing the scene in the Hotel Vancouver ballroom across the road, went on to express my lack of understanding of how women – young, middle-aged and old – were so turned on by this short, wiry man with a face with bumpy skin that was hardly Hollywood gorgeous.

"I am baffled by this Trudeaumania, why he is seen as a macho sex symbol, supposedly turning women on across Canada," I said (or something like that) over the CKNW airways.

I questioned my own sanity, aloud, since I admitted I felt nothing but dislike for Canada's newest icon. I was nervous; I knew I risked letting loose an explosion of angry response. I was certain the outrage would end my six-week contract before it even got off to a full start. So be it! I took this job simply as a new experience. I still had my full-time job as a general reporter at *The Sun*, had magazine assignments coming at me almost weekly, and in my arrogance of being at the prime of my career did not really care whether or not I got knocked off the air my first day on the job.

Every light on the panel in front of me was on. I went to the commercial break on the advice of the technician working in the adjacent room. When I opened the lines – almost in panic – instead of anger there was relief and gratitude. The callers, mostly women and a few men, were saying, in essence: "Thank goodness, Simma! I was afraid something was wrong with me; it appeared that the whole female population of Canada adores him, while I can't stand the man." Another expressed gratitude: "reassured ... I'm not alone."

That day the obvious question was: "Who voted for him? How did he get elected?"

Nonetheless, then and throughout the 20 years he led the country – and long after he was off the main stage – there was an obsessive interest and curiosity about Pierre Elliott Trudeau. To the time of this writing, people wanted to talk to me and hear my many stories and insights into the man who became my best friend in my subsequent career in his Government in Ottawa. It seemed to accelerate after his death, and one poll at the beginning of the new millennium named him the most famous, the most interesting, the greatest Canadian of the 20th century. People wanted to talk about him. They talked of their one or two personal experiences, even the tiniest contact like "I saw him on the street in Montreal" or "I was there when he spoke at ..." or even told stories that were the "incident of a family member or friend who met Pierre Elliott Trudeau."

Rarely did a day pass that Pierre Trudeau, whether as Prime Minister or later out of politics, did not make the news.

On March 4, 1971, a new Trudeau surprise trumped them all. In a secret ceremony Pierre Trudeau married Margaret Sinclair, the beautiful 22-year-old daughter of Jimmy Sinclair of West Vancouver, a prominent former cabinet minister in the Liberal Government of Louis St. Laurent.

By the end of a week I thought the media had exhausted the story. Anything about the newlyweds would be simply fillers, I hoped.

But that was an error in my fantasy.

It was my friend Doris Anderson, editor of *Chatelaine,* who brought me back into the life of Pierre Elliott Trudeau. She phoned to ask me to do a story on Margaret as the hippie bride of the Prime Minister of Canada. I knew the father of the bride, Jimmy Sinclair, from the time that he was Fisheries Minister in the St. Laurent cabinet and I was the waterfront reporter for *The Sun.* I was confident that Jimmy Sinclair and his wife Kathleen would give me all the information I needed to start me off. Not so.

The velvet curtain had been tightly closed. The ever-helpful and friendly Sinclairs were silent. There was no way the family would be interviewed.

Kay Alsop was a *Province* star feature writer, a colleague and friend I admired for her writing and reporting skills. She had the only in-depth interview with the family after the surprise marriage. I asked Kay if she would care to work with me on the *Chatelaine* story. She agreed.

There had been literally thousands of news and feature stories written about the Trudeaus and their wedding before the blackout. We set out to go beyond those stories to find the information that was still hidden and unknown. Both of us had no interest in scalping the writings of others, other than to get the basic pegs of what was then part of the biography in the Trudeau history.

We got everything available in biographical material, personality and pictures – some going back to Margaret as a baby in the bathtub, to her life as a charter student and activist at the new Simon Fraser University (SFU), known as "Berkeley North," right up to those involved in the creation of her hippie wedding gown, wardrobe and lifestyle. Margaret's beautiful young face filled the *Chatelaine* cover to its edges.

Shortly after, on the request of the South African magazine *Fair Lady* we expanded the story of the hippie bride, flower child, and student rebel. Even the courageous Doris Anderson was loath to publish full details for home consumption. However, we did fill in details as requested by the South African editor. Further, by then Margaret had already made shock news abroad in Cuba and the Soviet Union. This added new angles and insight into the young beauty who had suddenly become the first lady of Canada.

Many who knew Margaret talked freely about the beautiful rich girl who participated in SFU's weak attempts at civil disobedience and then took off overseas with other rebels – including the primary leader, Martin Loney – turning up in France and Morocco – at one point in a hospital, allegedly "freaking out" on drugs.

I still had not any personal, professional or political interest in Pierre Trudeau. And I had little fondness for the man. I recognized his newsworthiness as the most controversial personality in Canada, an enigma in our plodding, dull, unimaginative but rich and wholesome society.

Then a bridge appeared that led me out of my 30-year-career at *The Vancouver Sun* onto the main stage of Canadian politics, to share Pierre's day job.

In 1974 I began a campaign in my column and in the news pages to get police-women back on the streets. Despite their costly training in police work (identical to what the men on the force obtained) Chief John Fisk had relegated them to escort duty of female prisoners from lock-up to court, and to desk duty that any lowest-level clerk could do.

It was a time when women were needed on the streets of Vancouver. Wandering children – some as young as 12 and 13 – seeking easy climate for their street life, poured into Vancouver from all parts of the continent. Harvard Professor Timothy Leary was becoming their guru in response to the preaching of his gospel according to his mind-altering love of drugs, primarily LSD and hashish, and with his famous cry to the young to "Turn on, Tune in and Drop Out." An older man who wanted what he wanted when he wanted it– a hedonist – he taught the young about the wonder of "free love." The girls on the street were sleeping with boys and men whose names they did not know. Some of these girls and young boys came into my life and into my home, needing shelter, freaking out and having to be treated in hospital for various forms of hepatitis and emotional breakdown. In this period, I received a call from Constable Mary Fraser, a woman I admired as a dedicated and courageous street cop. She told me that the wandering children through the back streets of Vancouver were in serious trouble, being exploited by older men and in need of rescue and care. At this very moment of crisis for the young in Vancouver, when women were desperately needed to save and protect these young people, the policewomen were being taken off the streets.

It started my newest crusade against a terrible and stupid act in so-called city leadership.

My column and news stories focused on the tragedies on the streets of Vancouver, including a story on a man playing Messiah to the young. I later recognized him as Charles Manson. He and one of his girls, Linda Kasabian, were giving out flowers on the West End streets, and inviting children to their pad off Kitsilano Beach. It was becoming a time when the Outlaw Bikers found a huge source of young girls for their gross sexual parties.

I exposed the costs and the waste of valuable well-trained women personnel in the city's law enforcement budget. I compared the cost of their training and pay against that of a clerical worker. Suddenly the male officers began phoning me to say that they too were doing menial jobs that could be done by those with less costly training and experience. It became a virtual revolt against the police chief's policies. My stories mobilized great public support for my position. I applied and was invited to appear before Vancouver City Council. The day I appeared, the gallery was full of women and some men. I was nervous because there was a group of older, stern-looking women representing the National Council of Women. I feared they might be critical of me as "one of those dreadful feminists." But within minutes it was apparent that they were on my side and formed perhaps the strongest support I have ever had in my fights for equal opportunity and justice for women in the community and the workplace.

The reaction from the Mayor and Council was positive. Only one, a famous left-wing lawyer-alderman, Harry Rankin, challenged the majority of speakers. But we knew we had won.

Suddenly Chief Fisk resigned.

At the Oakridge police substation a sign went up: "Simma Holt for Chief."

That set off a chain of action I never foresaw. At that moment my vow never to enter real politics weakened.

I thought, "Not a bad idea."

I had no intention of leaving the career I loved most. But I decided to apply for the chief's job to see how I would fare in the competition. Also I wanted to let women know that when a management job opens in the man's world, go for it.

I prepared and entered my application for the job of Chief of Police of Vancouver. I listed my qualifications in bulleted points. I sent it special delivery registered mail to Mayor Art Phillips. No reply. I decided to take my fight to the air on Jack Webster's show. There I talked of the blatant sexism of Mayor Art Phillips. I charged that he did not even have the courtesy to acknowledge my letter, but was determined to pretend I did not exist. There were 21 other applicants, all male.

Jack thought my application for the job was hilarious. I showed it to him with the list of qualifications. He put on his thickest Scottish accent to tell his audience, "Migawd … she *is* qualified." He treated the dialogue seriously. Positive support poured in over the line. Several callers said something like: "If the chief was chosen by election, I would vote for you."

Mayor Phillips held his position – safe and mute. I sent a second registered letter, phoned – and still no response. It was my cause *célèbre* of the month.

About the same time, I was in correspondence with Marc Lalonde, a Trudeau friend and confidante. Marc had been Primary Secretary to Prime Minister Lester Pearson. He was in the portfolio of Health and Welfare when I first met him and enjoyed his amusement when I dubbed him "the Grey Eminence of the Liberal Party of Canada." He did not demur or deny it. I interviewed him in his office in the House of Commons and wrote several columns as a result. Subsequently, at his request, I did a confidential research project for him. It arose out of repeated attacks by Jack Webster on federal government grants to two middle-aged women who had set up a "drug treatment home." I charged him only the cost of a ferry trip to the site of the investigation and the meals for myself and a witness (photographer for my books, Jane Sloan of Sidney on Vancouver Island). The cost, as I recall, was $89.

In a phone call, Marc and I chatted and I told him of my plan – not yet formed or even serious – to run for Mayor of Vancouver, as an independent. I said my bumper sticker would read, "Vancouver needs a jolt from Holt."

His response: "Why not a bumper sticker that reads: 'Ottawa needs a jolt from Holt.'"

It began as a joke but some niggling seed seemed to be germinating out of my control. Leon and I talked about the possibility that I might do the unthinkable – enter politics.

Before I could even think about the Vancouver November municipal election, Pierre Trudeau prorogued Parliament and set the election date for July 8, 1974.

For several years through several general elections and by-elections I was approached by all three political parties – New Democratic, Liberal and Conservative – to enter as their candidate. I knew if I did declare myself it would be as a Liberal. It would allow me to act in what I realized was my style – freewheeling with the best of the political spectrum – free enterprise with social policies that put people first; I would be able to speak from and for the large flexible 85 per cent centre span of the political spectrum. As a journalist I avoided any labels that marked a prejudice or bias towards a social, economic or political issue. I knew that if the day ever came that I had to choose my place in politics, it would have to be where I could act with broad strokes sociologically and economically on issues and problems.

I came close at one time when a by-election was called for a vacated seat in the provincial Legislature. Dr. Pat McGeer, then Liberal leader, phoned and told me that he had a poll taken in the riding and found that "Simma Holt could win the seat easily." I sought advice from a former colleague and long-time friend, Hal Dornan, then a primary advisor to Prime Minister Lester Pearson. His response was negative. "Politics is a mean and dirty business ... they will tear you to shreds." His wife Mickey phoned that night, near tears, pleading with me not to do it, saying, "It will destroy you ... you care too much." That settled that one.

Now years later, stronger and surer of my ground, I was vacillating. But beyond that memory there was the pull of my first and eternal love – journalism. I knew if I was going to make a career change it had to be then, or not at all. I was 52 and tempted by a new "story" I could see and live on the inside. I saw it for a moment the way we did as young journalists when we went into a seedy hotel to live for a while to write about the life of those who had no other choice – or had a doctor bind our eyes in order to know the life of the blind. It was a huge step – a drastic change in career. I expected new experiences and new perspectives. A small chink had opened in my intransigence towards politics.

The appointment of a senior police officer I admired and liked – Don Winterton – was the ending of the momentary police chief hiatus. That was the end of one phase, but there was a sort of tidal wave roiling over me. Within days I received a call from a candidate recruiter asking me to run for alderman on Vancouver City Council on the Non-Partisan Association (NPA) ticket. My reply was instant and unequivocal.

"No ... I will only run for Mayor – and against Art Phillips ... if necessary as an independent. (I had offers of substantial support and I let the caller know that.) If I win, I will head the Police Commission so never again will a male chief or an Art Phillips discriminate against a woman either for the top job or for equal opportunity on any city job."

Through all this Marc Lalonde was on the line periodically to encourage me, and even offered to come west to support me in my campaign if I decided to run in Vancouver.

Leon and I, like most people in Canada, knew the reality: any candidate running with Trudeau had a good chance of winning.

On May 9, l974, when the Prime Minister called the election for the 30th Parliament, I watched and listened to his dissolution speech on television in *The Vancouver Sun* editorial room. My colleagues, some of whom pretended superior political wisdom under the guise of "pundits," predicted he was too disliked to win the election. I bet them that he would be returned as prime minister. Had I recorded those bets and collected I would have had a rich base on which to start an election campaign, which at that time was as remote and impossible in my life as my scaling Mount Everest.

Barely two weeks later Senator Ray Perrault, for whom I always had great respect, asked me to run for the Liberals in Vancouver–Kingsway. Incumbent Grace MacInnis was retiring because of ill health. She was royalty of the social-ist party of Canada, the New Democratic Party (NDP), being the widow of Angus MacInnis (former east side member) and daughter of J. S. Woodsworth, founder of the CCF (later NDP).

I told Ray, "I really do dislike Trudeau. It would be impossible for me to work with him amicably."

Ray persuaded me to attend the picture-taking session for the candidates' campaign publicity in Trudeau's Hotel Vancouver suite, and make the deci-sion after that. I assured him it was a waste of time.

My dearest friend, Tova Snider, convinced me to attend. Tova was an intransigent politically. She was NDP, and close personal friends with the lead-ers and their wives, from Premier Dave Barrett and Human Resources Minister Norman Levi down. When I told her my dilemma – whether to meet with Pierre Trudeau and have campaign pictures taken – she admitted to me that, her NDP loyalty notwithstanding, she "adored" Trudeau. She wanted me to participate in the session, and said, "You must take me with you … I have to meet Pierre Trudeau."

I snorted, "Trudeaumaniac!" and she agreed. I told her there was "no way I will join his team."

And so it happened. Tova and I went up to that Trudeau suite. Actually I knew that my never-satisfied "nose for news" could have influenced my deci-sion. It was a newsworthy "Happening" and I was curious about the people who would enter the political fray with Trudeau. However, posing for pictures was not my choice of entertainment – especially demeaning, I thought, to pose with celebrities I did not know personally. It made me feel like an underdeveloped groupie.

When my turn before the camera came, I knew I was on the brink of a complete reversal in my life. I kept thinking "I am at a crossroads." My ambivalence seemed like a backward tow. But the debate within me continued; if I did not do it now, it would be too late to get inside the nation's management team. I had shouted in print and on the lecture platform about the problems of the nation, the province, the city and the streets. If I continued to sit outside, see wrongs, criticize and hope to correct those wrongs simply by writing I could never achieve the changes that I saw as necessary. One thing was a certainty: whatever my decision, I knew Leon would support me as he did in everything, with his cool judgment and unconditional love.

On that day I came face to face with Canada's prime minister for the second time in our lives. This was not the same as our first meeting. Then I was simply a reporter doing a radio show, the meeting with Trudeau just another story. This meeting was potentially an end of one career and the beginning of another. We shook hands, and I thought, "You come out gloves poised, in case of a fight." But this time his demeanour was different. The indifference and boredom on our first meeting were substituted with a genuine smile from the *great man*. No doubt he had been briefed by my ever-enthusiastic friend Senator Perrault. Ray probably told Trudeau what he had said to me, that "Simma is a very attractive candidate" who with her biography (he was sure) would win.

As we stood facing each other, getting prepared for the camera being focused on us, I tried a dialogue opener.

"I hate this."

He said, "Me too."

"I wish we were dropping into The Bugaboos for skiing instead of standing here like a pair of oafs posing for pictures."

He chuckled and agreed that the pictures would be improved tremendously in the natural mountain setting. Now I saw small signs of warmth and the charm that fired Trudeaumania. Trudeau was a great athlete. I knew my Bugaboo reference was dumb, but it was all I could think of to say, and I always fill sound gaps when I am uneasy. It was silly, I knew, because we both were aware that I would never jump from a helicopter into deep unbroken snow. I could never navigate it, and would probably have to wait till spring melt to get out.

But it worked; it was a starter towards my view of the man who would change the direction of my life and turn me into a political junkie.

Again trying to make conversation, I asked, "What did you think of the story of Margaret in *Chatelaine*?"

"That one with the beautiful picture on the cover?"

"Never mind the picture. What did you think of the story?"

He said, "How did those people get all that information?"

"No bloody thanks to you. Those people were me. You pulled that velvet curtain when my friend and I tried to get the story."

"Oh no ... not me ... it was Margaret."

"Don't give me that stuff. It was you." (I am not sure the word "stuff" was the preferred one, but I was on my good behaviour.) He burst out laughing. At that moment, I knew I could work with him; if he could put up with that, I would not have to be a hypocrite or walk on egg shells in the job. It could be, I thought, another way to continue to serve the public interest.

After the picture session, I told Ray I could run with this man, and would seek the nomination in the riding the Party had selected for me. However, I told Ray that I would never ask anyone for money, and if the Whip tried to control my positions on issues that adversely affected those I represented, he would get the whiplash. In fact, never once when I voted against my party, did Trudeau criticize or reprimand me.

It was a rare opportunity to work inside the national and international news with this leading headliner. The man was a puzzle and an obsession for journalists in Canada and around the world. Syndicated columnist Joseph Kraft, in his *Washington Post* column, described Pierre Trudeau as "perhaps the world's most gifted leader."

The complexity of his character was fascinating. At times I was sure I knew the man and could predict what he would say before he said it. Then I realized that he could only be defined in anecdotes, that probably he himself could not analyze what and who he really was.

I do know that he was perverse, was amused by actions that annoyed others, did what some considered outrageous, and encouraged and was amused by those who acted out of pattern. In fact, he praised me in my fight against a government bill[1] (one of several I refused to support). Over lunch in that period he told me, "You know, I love people who swim against the current."

I suspected for some time that he was amused by Margaret's publicly criticized behaviour, and accepted it until it got too embarrassing for him. I saw it over and over with various Members and cabinet ministers.

My decision to go with him not only began the move to a chain of several new careers, but also let me know the man – and receive his remarkable and supportive friendship – as few others could.

And I got there despite what started out as probably the worst campaign in Canadian history.

---

1   Bill C58, the Time-Reader's Digest bill, that would end tax deductions for advertisers who used foreign owned magazines published in Canada. *Time* and *Reader's Digest* became the main targets of the bill. I fought against it. It meant bureaucrats would measure in inches the Canadian content of a magazine to allow advertisers to qualify for tax discount. The bill passed in February 1976.

14
A Campaign Run by a Loser

I had absolutely no knowledge about politics, what the job entailed. The only political experience I had was interviewing and writing about national and international leaders. I had no interest in politics, not even how the people got there. My major interest was the human story and the only time I got involved with a politician was to seek help in a social problem or to write a feature story on the personality. It is hard to believe now, as a political junkie who never stops searching for every angle on a political situation, that I did not even get interested then in political scandals unless I was assigned to investigate them. Election night was the one night I joined my colleagues and the public as we watched results being written on big boards inside the editorial room and on the outside of the Sun Tower for the public.

But now I was the focus of the process, in what was a high-profile riding. I did not even know or seek to know what the job entailed if I got elected. I thought – with the same superficial knowledge of the public – that I would simply go to Ottawa periodically, and in between the periods spent doing whatever one does as a Member of Parliament, I would use the rest of the time to work in the famous Parliamentary Library and Archives doing research and writing.

What I did not know was that it was a very big, full-time job, difficult because I had to commute 16 to 18 hours every weekend, crossing three times zones, living with perpetual jet lag, working at a job in two Canadian cities – 2,200 or more miles apart. It meant my first duty was to the citizens of the riding. Some weekends my time with Leon was little more than in the drive from the airport to whatever duties I had in the riding. But what was most remarkable for this political neophyte was the realization after the fact that the whole process in which I was nominated as the candidate for the Liberal Party in Vancouver–Kingsway, and the events that followed, were unique.

It all happened without my doing anything. I was nominated unanimously without challenge by a small group of voters of the Kingsway Liberal Riding Association. The campaign chairman and headquarters for the campaign were chosen for me.

In being introduced to the campaign chairman, Ed Bodnarachuk, I was told he had "excellent" political experience, and that although he did not live in the riding, he knew it well. Bodnarachuk had served as campaign manager for Jack Austin, who lost. He then was a candidate himself for this riding in the previous federal election, and lost. Naturally, all the losers could explain it by the reality that no one could win against Grace MacInnis.

In hindsight it was obvious that with Grace out of the running Ed Bodnarachuk might believe there would be a chance for him to win. When I realized how much he wanted the seat, I suggested, "Let him have it." But the response of Party insiders was cool and definite: "Not a hope in hell."

It did not take long for me, even as a political neophyte, to realize the campaign manager was worse than incompetent; he was dedicated to my defeat. It became apparent within a week or ten days. People who had come into the office to work as volunteers were turned away (if Leon and I were not around). Leon started to hear some of this "strange" information – as he described it – from students and colleagues in the staff room at school. My own sister, Hannah, told me that she was informed she could not work – or even be seen – in my campaign headquarters because she was not a Canadian citizen. Though she lived most of her life in Canada, she had been married and divorced from an American. She was told that my nomination would be nullified if she were found working on my campaign.

Ben Wosk, a multi-millionaire British Columbia furniture and appliance chain store owner, decided one day to drop in on my campaign headquarters.[1] He had bought most of the candy and treats in the little grocery store next door for the young people he expected to find in my campaign offices. He found

---

1   The Wosk story was of the old Horatio Alger genre – struggling upwards from nothing. I wrote it for *Reader's Digest* – "The Golden Rule of Ben Wosk" – and it was reprinted in many foreign countries from Holland to Japan.

the place empty except, as he told me, for that big heavy man sitting alone behind a long table, reading. He said that when he asked the "campaign manager" where the candidate was, the man said he was not sure, but supposed I was somewhere in the riding. When Ben asked why there were no workers there, Bodnarachuk told him that he was "having trouble getting volunteers for Simma Holt."

Ben sensed something was amiss. He decided to cruise through the riding to check on the number of lawn signs. That night he contacted me and told me of his tour of the riding and that if there were any signs they were obviously homemade.

"Something is wrong," he said, referring to the "empty office" and his dialogue with Ed Bodnarachuk. He told me he sent several of his staff in to offer to work on the campaign. Returning, they reported, "The man said we were not needed."

Ben Wosk said, "You are in trouble. If you cannot run a respectable campaign you should not be in it at all. This is not worthy of you."

My reply: "I'm out … don't want or need this."

When *Sun* publisher Stu Keate heard I was returning to my job and the reason why – the final straw being the failure of the manager to provide lawn signs to friends and supporters who requested them – he responded, "Your signs have been up in Vancouver for 30 years … Don't quit … you'll win."

Ray Perrault acted speedily when I told him to find another candidate for Vancouver–Kingsway. He asked several of his staff to go to my campaign office and offer to work for me. They verified what Ben Wosk suspected: they were being told they were not needed in my campaign.

Once Ray and Ben were on it, the campaign went on fast track.

Leon and our close skiing and motorhoming friends, Mike and Ingrid Blomfield, came in and became the "Sign Brigade," arranging for sign locations and enlisting the help of students and other volunteers to do the silkscreen production of the signs, then to deliver and plant them on lawns throughout the riding.

The Liberal Party put up billboards after I told them I would no longer run. I think they'd had them ready but Bodnarachuk had not done anything about it.

Within two or three days the riding was dotted with my red and white signs.

The circus came to Vancouver and I topped an elephant as it left its railway car for service in Canada, mid 1970s.

Campaigning with Pierre Trudeau

Trudeau and I put our heads together.

Margaret Trudeau assisted B.C. candidates with our campaigns.

A lifelong resident of the riding, a very bright and feisty Shirley Phillips appeared in the campaign headquarters – a return visit she said, having earlier been turned away several times. She and her family became a team that seemed ready to do everything – from baking cakes and cookies for volunteers to building lists of supporters to setting up door-knocking teams.

She knew the people, the community and its needs. She knew and cared about the neglect of the east side of the city and was, as she said, at last able to do something to correct it.

Shirley was strong, tough and loyal as few women I have ever known, and I have had many good strong friends. She was a whirlwind in her strength and relentless determination to see me win that election. It seemed there was never a time that there were not at least two members of the Phillips family working on the campaign. But Shirley was there from early morning to late night.

Kory Palmer and Audrey M. "Corky" Clark joined Shirley and her husband, Peter. They also knew most of the people in the riding – customers and friends in their small but busy stationery-general store near my campaign office on Kingsway. They turned my office into a place people came into to see what was new. They created coloured paper dioramas and humorous signs, some of the "projects" filled with candy, usually jelly beans. When the campaign manager criticized it as "all silliness" or "clutter," they ignored him; as they put it, "We pretended he doesn't exist ... and it's easy." Kory and Corky neither sought nor needed favours. My friendship with them lasted as long as they lived.

No doubt it was because these people were not born with the silver spoon and privilege that they were sensitive and understanding of the real human problems that came to the office. They knew that when a citizen came to government – or a journalist – with a problem, it was often the citizen's only hope, and it should be treated as if it came from one's own family.

As this was all happening, I heard from Jennifer Lloyd, a young woman who had joined the *The Sun* City Room staff during my last years there. She was a slim, attractive former airline stewardess who did executive-style organization of the City Desk. Jennifer reminded me that she had told me if I ever ran for political office she would work on my campaign.[2]

---

2   As mentioned in Chapter 10, Jennifer Lloyd was married to Bruce Larsen.

She wasted no time taking over *de facto* leadership, though Ed Bodnarachuk had the title. She came in after work every day and then left for her duties at home. Shirley and she were a high-powered team that must have frustrated Ed Bodnarachuk. They kept detailed records of donors and donations. They organized the teams to handle phones, to prepare literature for distribution, and for door-knocking.

The place was always full of teenagers and children. Perhaps some came in for Ben Wosk's huge supply of goodies and the many displays made by Kory and Corky. I realized once I had parliamentary experience that these young people would understand the system and be well prepared to deal with politics if they decided to work at the top or within the system. They would know what I failed to learn in my first 52 years – how the political system works, how to use it when needed. I finally knew that these were important lessons for life, that all life is politics, whether it is in the home, in the trade union, in executive offices or corporate boardrooms.

Door-knocking is a major campaign technique. Once my signs were up to tell the community I was a candidate for election, it became a lovefest. People actually stopped their cars to call out through the windows – and in several cases got out and ran over to meet me and declare their support.

When Leon and I went out together, Leon often caused the most excitement, especially when the knock on a door was responded to by a Gladstone student, past or present – a teenager or a parent. I was of lesser interest, though many knew me from my involvement with Leon in school functions, or as a speaker at Parent-Teacher or other community events. But I often thought Leon would have been a shoo-in to win if he had been the candidate.

Margaret Trudeau came door-knocking with me, noting mine was the first campaign in which she was involved since her marriage to Pierre.

Margaret and I set out together in mid-afternoon. It is normal for the companion to introduce the candidate and quickly outline the reasons why people should vote for the candidate. This time, I introduced Margaret. Needless to say, the candidate was irrelevant. When our knock on one door was answered by a man slightly younger than Margaret, I barely uttered the name of my beautiful young companion before the young man let out a yell: "Hey come … Margaret Trudeau is at our door." A voice from inside the house

With Leon, on the campaign trail.

responded, "Yeah, Margaret Trudeau and Queen Elizabeth!" Nonetheless five or six young people strolled to the door, and instantly their mouths literally dropped open. All at once there was animated dialogue between the Prime Minister's bride and the crowd in the little hall at the door. They begged her to come in and have a beer and pretzels with them. As we were leaving, Margaret said, "If you can vote, vote for Simma ... and if you are not yet old enough, tell your parents to vote for her."

Margaret, a very kind and caring woman, saw elderly women looking out the window of a retirement home. They may have heard that she was in the neighbourhood. We went in and visited almost every resident there. If I had brought Pierre or Queen Elizabeth, the residents could not have been happier, as Margaret held their hands and chatted with them.

My good friend Tova, wife of Leon's best friend Mitchell Snider, was one of my most loyal supporters, which would not be remarkable except for the fact that she was lifelong NDP, as though it began in the womb. Her mother, Pauline Robb, was even deeper in left-wing politics than Tova.

Often the four of us – Mitchell, Leon, Tova and I – worked together both in the office and knocking on doors. It was not unusual to be welcomed at the door with someone vitriolic about the NDP and making comments such as: "Maybe now we can get rid of the damn NDP." And to my surprise Tova responded, "You're right. And the only way you can get rid of them is to vote for Simma."

The first time it happened, when we had moved away from that door, I said to her, "No greater love hath my friend than to accept that without punching them in the nose." Her reply: "I couldn't punch them because I had my fingers crossed behind my back ... but I heard their garbage."

I had become closely involved with the large Chinese Canadian community from my earliest arrival in Vancouver, through my friendship with the owners of the Lotus Gardens Lounge and Hotel across from *The Sun* building. The partners, Sammy Kee and Lila Chen, openly supported the Liberal Party. They were my advisors and worked with me to serve those who came to Canada as refugees from Vietnam, Korea and Taiwan. Not only did Lila and Sammy provide temporary housing for such people in their hotel, but also helped them with translation, preparation and delivery of legal papers, finding homes, explaining legal documents, banking, and initiating the process for landed immigrant status. For example, when Lila and Sammy learned that Taiwan immigrants with briefcases full of cash negotiated the purchase of a house – often on the front porch of a house for sale – Lila vetoed this style of doing business in North America and taught them the importance of having legal records of purchase.

When I told Sammy and Lila I was accepting the nomination of the Liberal Party in Vancouver–Kingsway, they immediately linked me with other leaders of the entire Chinese community. After my campaign finally got going, not only did the large and vital school population of Chinese young people become supporters, but also their parents were strong supporters, inviting me to speak to their many social and business gatherings.

One man I will never forget. He was about 77 years old. He did not speak English and I did not speak Chinese. We communicated with gestures, an informal sort of sign language. It was a cold day, with frost or a dusting of snow on the ground. He wore a thin shirt, sleeves rolled up, and his totally bald head bared to the elements. He walked into Chinese homes without waiting for anyone to answer his knock, and introduced me. I learned later he "ordered" those inside to vote for me.

I was invited to every Chinese function – weddings and celebrations of births – and was introduced as the candidate at every major event.[3]

The Chinese community at the time I was at *The Sun* and in the House of Commons were National *Kuomintang,* connected to Taiwan. There was minimal immigration from Mainland/Communist China. Thus I linked and worked closely with the Chinese Benevolent Association and the Chinatown Merchants Association.[4]

---

3 After I was elected I was contacted by Chinese from every part of Canada, and let my western friends know that I appeared to be the representative for the Chinese Canadians. The only letter Pierre Trudeau did not answer from me was one that I wrote scolding him for his barring the Taiwan athletes from participating in the 1976 Summer Olympics in Montreal.

4 Though my association with the Canadian Chinese and those who came to British Columbia to escape communist tyranny continued, the long support and connection I had from and gave to the Chinese Benevolent Association and the Chinatown Merchants Association of Vancouver was broken when their support moved from the nationalist Chinese of Taiwan to Mainland People's Republic of China.

Near the end of the campaign a group of Ismailis came to my office to tell me that the Aga Khan "love Trudeau" and they had been told that they had to get out and work for every Liberal candidate. The little grocery store next door was run by a Somali. He put up my "Vote Simma" sign and I was invited to every function of their organization throughout the city, mostly on the east side. I had met many of them when I called at their doors to introduce myself. They never failed to invite me in for tea and told me of their life and their escape from Idi Amin in Uganda.

Cabinet ministers and other luminaries of the Liberal Party came to support me in my campaign. Among them were Marc Lalonde, André Ouellet, and Francis Fox.

Suddenly, as my signs seemed to dominate the riding, trouble began. Cars were driven over lawns and flower gardens, crushing the signs. One home owner who had placed a big sign on what was a highly visible and desirable location – an intersection of two main roads in the riding – came into the office admitting he was "terrified." The sign was set afire and he said he feared for his home and family. He was apologetic, telling me he did not dare to replace the sign. I assured him I understood, however if political thugs could do this in a campaign to silence him and the candidate he chose to support, he would have more to fear if these same people got power through the candidate they supported. He raised a new sign. It survived through to the election.

At 8 p.m. on July 8, 1974, when the polls closed we already knew that if I won this seat I would be in the Government of Canada. Trudeau and his Liberals had swept to victory. So far the only province with a blank for the Liberals was Conservative Alberta.

The results started coming up, posted on a large blackboard in my campaign office. I was leading in almost every poll. The room was jammed with supporters and it was soon apparent that I would win. A huge bouquet of red roses appeared in my arms, and the packed room vibrated with cheers.

I heard voices saying, "Simma is our Member of Parliament … the Liberals won."

Then I heard the voice of my campaign manager. "I'm going home where women know their place. I guarantee you will never again win an election." Ed Bodnarachuk left and that was the last time I saw him.

After we celebrated together in our own headquarters we all piled into cars and vans for the Hotel Georgia where the Liberals were holding the post-election party. When we arrived the ballroom exploded in cheers. It was spoken of as a momentous piece of history – the first time the Liberals won a seat in Vancouver–Kingsway. We were mobbed and I was rushed onto the stage with the other local victors.

The next morning when I turned up at the campaign office to work on thank-you notes to the volunteers and others who had helped me, I found my supporters crowded outside a locked door. They told me the campaign manager had changed the lock and cancelled the phone lines.

Leon and I – exhausted and stressed out – had plans to get away for a week of R&R. Instead, Ray Perrault and the sophisticated campaigners advised us that we should go directly – as quickly as possible – to Ottawa. There I would have to be sworn in by the Clerk of the House, Alistair Fraser, and attend to establishing offices, furnishing them, and recruiting staff in the capital and in Vancouver–Kingsway.

Thus, within days after the huge "hurrah" in the Hotel Georgia, Leon and I were at work – in Ottawa.

Marian Bruce, who worked at *The Sun* before moving east to do magazine writing, did a feature for *Weekend* magazine and described my move from news writing to politics as simply "a change of venue."

15
A Change of Venue

The oath of office was short. It was only 19 words in one sentence:

> "I Simma Holt do swear that I will be faithful and bear true allegiance to her Majesty Queen Elizabeth."

I was now a Member of the Parliament. An office was assigned to me – Room 568-CB on the fifth floor of the Confederation Building. I would be sharing it with an Ontario Liberal named Ross Milne. The divider for the two offices was a double row of filing cabinets. Later, as it turned out, this provided an easy way for two longtime friends – Mary Kennedy and Shirley Strean – to communicate and continue their friendship and shared knowledge of The Hill without leaving their desks or using telephones.

Alistair Fraser, the Clerk of the House, told Leon and me that the most important immediate job we had was to set up two offices, one in Ottawa and the other in the riding. He assured me that if I could find an experienced executive secretary/office manager who knew The Hill, the crisis of lock-down of the campaign office in Vancouver could be resolved, allowing Leon and me to take off on our planned trip away from news and crises in the post-election period.

It was all happening so fast it became a thick mass without defining lines or identities, a jumbled blur. Leon and I had barely found chairs in the sparsely furnished Ottawa office when the first applicant for the executive secretary job arrived, mysteriously. She was a tall plain brunette woman whom I estimated to be at least 40 or 45 years old.

With Alistair Fraser, signing the Members registry.

I told Leon her unimpressive appearance, her age and her knowledge of The Hill suited my perception of my need. Leon simply said, "I think you should check a few more before you decide."

Shortly afterward, a gorgeous slim Hollywood-style blond arrived. Her makeup was perfect in every detail. She was dressed in what I suspected was a high-end suit with almost underplayed accessories, right down to shoes and hosiery. She looked like a young Angie Dickenson. My first impression was that her features were even more perfect. She had 11 years' experience with two Members, one Conservative and the other Liberal, and I would soon learn she was respected by the public service and House staff, able to get any services and supplies she requested.

I liked her obvious knowledge of The Hill and the people. But I was uneasy – she was too attractive. She let me know she was not ready to make a decision, that she had other appointments with other Members.

At some point I managed to tell Leon privately that she was too attractive, that I would be safer with the plain woman.

Leon said he was surprised. "Why would you even think that way?" he asked me. "One of your closest friends at *The Sun* is Marie Moreau.[1] She is one of the most beautiful women in the west. Why should you worry about this woman?"

He was right and I agreed. I would let her know I was interested in hiring her. She was Shirley (Claman) Strean, divorced mother of a 17-year-old daughter, living with her parents, and needed the job. I indicated to her that I was interested in having her head up my staff. However, I urged her to carry through on her other job interviews.

At the door, as she was about to leave, she turned and asked a question that chilled me, made my stomach feel like it tipped over. She inquired, "Are you Jewish?"

"Yes I am," I responded. "Does that make a difference?"

"I was not sure. I heard you were the first Jewish woman elected to the House ... in Canada. There was talk that you made history." Then she clinched the partnership that has lasted to the day of this writing. She said, "I am Jewish too."

---

1   Marie Moreau was fashion editor at *The Vancouver Sun*, later at *The Toronto Star*.

At that moment she cancelled her other appointments. She explained, "My ego had to know how many job offers I would get." Without equivocation she added, "I want the job with you."

Shirley Strean was everything in my new life – office manager, executive secretary, appointment secretary, wardrobe mistress – and, above all, my totally loyal lifelong friend and sober second thought. (For those who believe in the influence of the stars and timing of birth, Shirley, like Leon, was born in early September, Shirley on the 5th and Leon on September 10th.) Regardless of the astrological description of these two Virgos, they were both cool, thoughtful and, most of all, perfectionists.

Shirley's first job was to hire two secretarial-clerical assistants for the Ottawa office and an office manager-secretary in Vancouver. She had to arrange budget, furniture and supplies for the two offices. In the Vancouver–Kingsway office I wanted to be sure that there was a workplace for staff and a comfortable small living-room-like reception area for the constituents who would come in for help or simply to socialize or meet with me and Shirley Phillips, the well-known and well-liked community person who had already offered to take the job, even as a non-paid volunteer. Neither of us knew then that it would be a salaried job. We didn't understand enough about the system to know that the government financed both offices and staff.

At that time I was told the number of staff for the Ottawa office was based on the amount of mail the Member received. Three was the maximum. My mail was very heavy, flooding in within a week or ten days after I was elected.

From the start, Vancouver Shirley told me she had "read everything (I) had ever written, admired the work I had done as a reporter, and would be happy to share in my future work" for the constituency in which she and her family lived throughout their life.

This big warm woman was truly a soulmate; like me she despised social injustice, was ready to take on the whole world to help another person, always ready to rescue and nurture the abused and dispossessed in her community.

We became a united front, working to begin improvement and development of community resources and to seek ways to correct the deficiencies of long neglect, in places such as the nearly dead Trout Lake at the heart of the riding.[2]

The precipitous closure of my Vancouver campaign office turned out to be a blessing in disguise. It forced me to establish new offices within a week of the election and get a staff to begin all the work other Members might not start until weeks later. Vancouver–Kingsway had a full active team working for them on two sides of the continent even before I had any clue as to what my own job was.

When the two Shirleys took over my life, and I knew there was little I had to do immediately, despite the number of calls and requests for my intervention already piling up, Leon and I took off for much needed R&R.

Shirley told me she would respond with what she called "diplomat letters" to acknowledge letters received, promising that the Member would deal with it when she returned to Ottawa or to the riding.

She produced a telephone calling card, with my Member code. It would allow staff and me to maintain phone contact wherever Leon and I were. It also meant that staff in the two offices could always have links.

By the time we returned to Ottawa, everything was in place both there and in Vancouver. Shirley Phillips had found a constituency office at the heart of the riding, and hanging on the corner, visible seemingly from all directions, was a neon lighted sign that showed the flag of Canada with "Simma Holt MP" across the bottom. The sign was donated by Neonex, one of the companies of the growing Jim Pattison corporation.

The next bit of education for the Vancouver–Kingsway MP from the "veteran of The Hill" in charge of 568-CB was the "Idiot Card." Every morning Shirley Strean handed me the card with time, place, name of the person or persons I had to meet, the committees (times, subject matter and people who

---

2   Pierre Trudeau encouraged us to see to the needs of the Vancouver–Kingsway riding. There was $7 million left from Habitat in Vancouver the previous year, and it could be allocated for this purpose. Trudeau had a personal interest in the section of the riding that included Trout Lake and the Grandview Community Centre, long neglected and in need of restoration and revitalization. At an event in the park beside the lake and community centre, his picture was taken in somersault on a trampoline. The picture was put on the front page of *The Sun* and was picked up by newspapers and magazines throughout the continent and abroad.

might be there as witnesses), speeches in the House when required, the social and business events. And even at these events she accompanied me; if there was a follow-up or an appointment required she would write it on a cigarette pack. (In those days it was still chic to smoke.) She would note protocol if titles were required, or style of address of ambassadors or other dignitaries.

She even scheduled my dates with my husband, sadly forced into secondary priority to those on the Idiot Card in Ottawa and in the constituency. On occasion the Idiot Card would note meetings with other Members in their ridings across Canada. All the B.C. Liberal Members and senators travelled to every riding in British Columbia to learn about community problems and to return with those problems to our caucus and cabinet. Our position was that since we were Members of the Government of Canada we had a duty to learn and assess the needs and problems of all B.C. citizens.

Shirley Strean told me that my reputation for persistence and even going public if I could not get what was needed and wanted in order to resolve a problem had "filtered through" to Ottawa. She said that was making it easy for her to get things done. She told me that she only had to say, "Mrs. Holt needs …" or "Mrs. Holt would like …" and it happened. I argued that it was the respect and admiration of my Ottawa office manager, a beautiful charmer, that got us everything we needed. Shirley Strean knew and seemed able to get support and friendship from some of the most intransigent bureaucrats.

Now with four women tenants of Room 568-CB, there were three sets of eyes that watched over everything I did, protected me from all and any critics, championed me as the "best boss on The Hill," and dealt with problems they could handle with the other staff in ministers' or department offices. Whenever they could not get a solution I would take the lead, often getting the minister in the relevant department to intervene. But no matter who solved the problem, the two Shirleys made sure that the message was "Simma did it." Occasionally I would hear stories in the riding of what I had done. In all honesty I had to tell them that one or both of the two Shirleys had taken care of it. It did not matter to the people in the riding; it was our office that solved a problem. For some, their problems had previously been neglected for months and years.

But beyond the clerical and business duties, the three women became my wardrobe advisers and dressers for the House of Commons and Committees. It was almost routine to have one or all of them order me: "Straighten your seams ... you skirt is creased ... no don't wear that jewellery ... your lipstick clashes with your dress ... comb your hair ..."

It is unlikely they would have been surprised if I told them that my former boss, Himie, periodically called me "Little Dupe" because there was frequently a smudge of carbon paper on my chin.

Wednesday was caucus day. The provincial caucuses were from 9 to 10 a.m. and the national from 10 a.m. till 12 noon. The Government (Liberal) Caucus was where legislation was revealed and discussed and constituency problems were raised before the prime minister and cabinet. Our caucus room, obviously, was the largest of the four parties in the House. (The other parties were the Progressive Conservative, the NDP and Social Credit.)

At the first caucus meeting there was cheering, joy and euphoria over the victory in the election. The cabinet members sat at the long front table, with the prime minister in the centre. The PM could barely restrain his pleasure that the election had made him the leader of a "truly national party" with representation from the Atlantic to the Pacific. The room exploded with applause and cheers when he noted that a historic record had been created in B.C. with eight Liberals elected – the largest contingent of the Party in years.

I had taken a private vow of silence for this first caucus. All of us from B.C., except for our one cabinet minister, Ron Basford, were huddled around Ray Perrault. Four sat in front of him, two on each side of him, and the rest of us behind them. I sat directly behind Ray. There was a roll call of all the Members and senators in the room. Each one in turn gave his or her name and riding.

The co-chairmen of the national campaign – Marc Lalonde, the French chair, and Senator Keith Davey, the anglophone chair – each made their "rah-rah" speech, detailing their organization and the ways they achieved their national victory. First to speak was Keith Davey, known as "The Rainmaker." In addition to this one, he had co-chaired two previous successful campaigns. He praised the senators from every section of the country, except for Ray Perrault. Remarkably, he praised the Calgary senator, from the one province that did not have a Liberal member elected. I knew my vow of silence would have to be broken if I did not act quickly. I worked my way from the back of the room to the far end of the cabinet table, to Marc Lalonde. I knew he would speak next. I told him that Senator Davey had neglected to credit Ray for our victory in B.C. I asked him to correct the omission. He smiled and all but patted my head to comfort me.

Nonetheless, during his speech he made no mention of Ray or our victory. Back in my seat behind Ray I saw him slump down into his seat, the back of his neck so red I thought he might have a stroke. I sent a note up to the caucus chairman asking him to put my name on the list of speakers. I had had personal welcome from many of the Members so I knew I had friends in the House. When my turn came I announced that none of us would be here if it were not for Ray Perrault. I recall looking directly at the Prime Minister and telling him, in essence, that Ray was "the godfather" in the recruitment of candidates in every B.C. riding and the reason so many of us were elected. When I sat down I saw Pierre Trudeau lean over, whispering to House Leader Allan MacEachen.

Keith Davey was to have been named leader in the Senate. It did not happen. Senator Perrault got the job and thus became the only senator in the Trudeau cabinet.

Another appointment I know I was responsible for was the senior cabinet minister for the west. There was talk that Trudeau had negative feelings for Ron Basford, and that Ron was likely to be ousted from even his minor role as Revenue Minister. I expressed my concern to Art Lee, who was chairman of the B.C. caucus, and to Ray Perrault. We agreed that it was important to have a Member in a senior cabinet position, and Ron was well respected for his work in his riding of Vancouver Centre, as well as throughout the city and province. I cornered the Prime Minister in the lobby and expressed my concern that British Columbia lacked a Member with a senior cabinet portfolio. The Prime Minister seemed to put on a cynical grin. "And who would you suggest?" he asked.

We had only one senior Member, Ron Basford.

"And what portfolio do you suggest?"

"Justice or Transport."

Basford was named Justice Minister in the new cabinet.

Never in my adult life could I sit in a room where people were speaking or in dialogue without taking notes. It did not take long, in caucus, for about three veteran Members to descend on me to tell me that I was breaking rules by writing in my Day-timer. I replied, "How can I quote The Boss (Trudeau) accurately if I don't get his words down as they are said?" There were no other challenges of my habit.

I thought the House was a silly place. I am not sure I ever changed my opinion that it was a stage for those who loved attention, and would have their words – petty or profound – recorded for posterity in the parliamentary record, *Hansard*. It did not take long for me to learn that real work of Parliament was done in standing committees. It became the one part of my new career that had meaning for me and challenged my versatility in research, perhaps a degree of leadership or initiative in writing policy and law that might improve the lot and life of Canadian citizens.

My first choice was the standing committee on Justice and Legal Affairs. I saw it as an extension of my primary career interest – crime, corrections, courts, prisons and on the streets where human conflicts and pain could occur and be ignored unless society noticed and cared.

The House and the committees were dominated by lawyers. Thus, when each of us around the large square of committee tables introduced ourselves, with the label of our profession or trade, most were lawyers. When my turn came, I revealed that, though my career was not law, I probably spent more time on lawyers' turf than many lawyers, since when I covered courts I would work in three or four courtrooms and in the registry where civil actions begin. As well, I had worked in police stations, studying the blotter where all the arrests and charges are recorded, and then following those cases through the courts. Beyond that, I worked on the streets where those who were the players in some of the most important and poignant dramas unfold.

At that first meeting, I announced that the reason I was on the committee was to edit the bad copy – rules, regulations and law that is so convoluted and ambiguous that its obvious purpose is to force every citizen to have a lawyer at his or her side constantly, just to exist in society. John Crosbie – whom the media loved because his corny sense of humour made good 20-second clips or fillers in newspapers – was on the committee. He used to say, "Law is a growth industry; I am glad my sons are in the business."

Art Lee, Vancouver East, also expressed his pleasure at the very quality of the writing of the law, as it meant that he, comparatively fresh out of law school, would be sure of a profitable future after leaving Parliament.

The other major committee I chose was one the media ignored. It was Regulations and Statutory Instruments, where new laws are defined by rules and regulations. This important committee was chaired by two of the most distinguished parliamentarians – the veteran Conservative Member Jeb Baldwin and the highly respected constitutional authority, Liberal Senator Eugene Forsey. I was amazed that I rarely, if ever, saw the media at the committee's meetings. Important stories were legion. Most significant in the area of scandals was the blatant contempt of bureaucrats to respond to requests for information from the committee. Presumably there were those who resented the committee because it could limit their power.

It was at the request of Finance Minister John Turner that I went on the Committee on Finance, Trade and Industry. I told him I suspected the reason he suggested I would be "useful" there was that he "valued the input" from "a simple housewife" who could not manage even a simple budget.

There I had my first significant chauvinist moment. It was a day that verified the fact that our world was run by men, especially where the obvious money was controlled. It was said that there were many rich widows and whatever power they might have was not apparent in the world in which I had operated.

If there was any doubt of this it did not show on the day that the head of the Royal Bank of Canada was the chief witness before our Finance Committee. Behind him and in the chairs along the three other walls of the committee room were men – what some would call "Suits." They were, no doubt, all bankers, either managers or senior staff. When my turn came to question the chief witness I made an obvious sweep of the room with my eyes and asked, "Where are the women?"

I cannot remember if there was a pause. His reply was something on the order of "Women are not interested in these jobs."

When the story hit the paper, the whole thing hit the fan.[3]

Just as I was leaving the committee room, barely outside the door, I heard Minister of State for Small Business Tony Abbott say, "Hell hath no fury like a woman scorned."

I came right back and confronted him with the group of bankers around him: "And Hell hath no fury like a woman who catches men in the false belief that keeps them in power, that their brains are at the top of their body."

In the House of Commons I rose on a point of order when I was called by George Hees an "Honourable Lady."[4] I wanted the record corrected.

"I am not an Honourable Lady; I am an Honourable Member."

The next day the papers had box stories headed: "Simma is no Lady."

A wonderful man in the Opposition front row named Lincoln Alexander, whom I learned was the first black Member in the history of Canada's Parliament, came over to my back bench seat four rows behind Prime Minister Trudeau and said, "I have been here six years and I have yet to get as much ink in the newspapers as you have received in a few weeks."

I suppose I told him I did not realize how easily this happens, but the good thing was that I met Lincoln Alexander early in my new career. He was a warm friend. There were times that I felt I could be seated anywhere in that House; I was comfortable with so many of them as friends, and certainly my convictions were not like those who believe their vote must always be "my party right or wrong."

From the start I made it clear; my priorities in actions and voting were first my constituents, then the country, and last the Party. I made my decision, my statements and votes on the basis of what I believed was moral and right on all debates and votes. I was lucky that Pierre Trudeau was the boss and him-

---

3   About a year later, I walked into a Royal Bank near where I lived in Arbutus Village in Vancouver and the place seemed to be women only. I decided to convert a small amount of bonds there to start a new bank account. I almost lost my investment through mess-up of the transaction. I argued with myself that "women were new in the executive positions there." Since then, as women moved into management and other responsible jobs in the banks – CIBC and the B.C. Credit Union are the ones I know best – there has been for me no repetition of the foul-up I experienced at that all-women-managed Royal Bank in the late 1970s.

4   George Hees was a Progressive Conservative Member of Parliament from 1950 to 1988.

self independent in his political morality. If I had had Jean Chrétien or Brian Mulroney as my leader I would have been thrown out of their caucus

The Liberal whip, Charles Caccia, Member for a Toronto riding, tried his best to change my positions. When the pressure did not let up, I told Trudeau that I would quit the House before I would go against the will of my constituents or in wrongful Party policy. I said that if Caccia did not get off my case, I would go home to Vancouver and have someone build a machine to pound my desk as required.

He asked me, "Can you get re-elected?"

In my arrogance and belief of support in Vancouver, I replied, "Of course."

Trudeau said, "Then you do not have to worry about Caccia."

The heart of the Government of Canada was not immune to the immaturity of male gossip when they notice a man and woman enjoying each other's company. One of my first and best of my new friends in the House was the Liberal Member from St. Catharines, Gibby Parent. He had been through a terrible tragedy, and somehow my knowledge of it and his kindness to me as a stranger brought us common ground for association. We would visit together in the Government lobby and sometimes in the dining room. Soon I heard snide remarks about the "Gold dust twins," and the suggestion that we were becoming "an item." I hated gossip and certainly had no interest in telling them that I was "untouchable." Until they knew me better I denied myself the nice friendship, but only for a while. Gibby, his wife, my husband and I became good friends, to the extent that I went to his riding to speak to various groups, including the Jewish community of St. Catharines, on his behalf.[5]

It may have been because I was an unknown from a far-off riding, outgoing in manner and one of only two females from the west, that speculation rising to gossip occurred. The other woman from west of Ontario, also from B.C., Iona Campagnolo from the riding of Skeena, escaped the type of talk that surrounded me. Though she was unknown, she was tall, cool, elegant, perhaps seen as too private and aloof for speculation by the simple-minded.

---

5   Gilbert (Gibby) Parent was a Member of Parliament from 1974 to 1984 and again from 1988 to 2001. He was Speaker of the House, from 1994 to 2001.

The first break from my weekly Vancouver–Ottawa commute came in the Easter Break. Leon left from Vancouver with our skiing friends in their motorhome, and I flew to Denver from Ottawa to meet them for a holiday at Vail, Colorado.

At the end of that break, Leon took me to the plane as usual for my return to Ottawa on the red-eye flight. Back in the capital, I showered, rested for a while on one of the cots in the Members' Lounge, then went into the House.

Within the first hour a page came up with a note from Shirley Strean: "URGENT. Come to the office immediately."

I raced outside and caught the little green shuttle bus back to the office. When I came in Shirley said as carefully as possible, "I have your ticket ready … You have to go home. Leon is in hospital … had a heart attack."

"How bad?"

Shirley, a very sensitive woman, was careful in her response. "Shirley (Phillips) said you must return as quickly as possible."

"He's dying?"

"She says it serious – a major infarction."

Shirley Phillips was waiting when the plane arrived. I was rushed to the Intensive Care Unit at Vancouver General Hospital. Leon, lying pale, looked up and smiled that wonderful smile I loved so much. I looked at the intravenous in his arm, the oxygen pumping into his lungs and thought if he survived this I would never again leave for Ottawa alone.

Two days later I had gone home for some sleep and barely got through the door when I received a call. The doctor told me to return to the hospital immediately; Leon had an embolism, a blood clot had struck his brain.

When I arrived on the ward, the head nurse greeted me, tried to ease my fear, but admitted it was serious. She said that Ben Wosk had been in to see him, and noticed "something wrong." They were able to give him medication to dissolve the embolism. It had struck the speech part of his brain.

Ben was on the hospital board of directors and was around the hospital often. If he had not made one of his frequent visits to the room, Leon would have died.

Leon did recover and returned with me to Ottawa. We got an apartment together and he began spending time in the Members' Gallery, having his meals with me in the parliamentary dining room. Though he told me he hated politics, his favourite time in the House was when Trudeau and Donald Macdonald spoke or responded to questions.

His strength returned gradually and when the House recessed we returned to Vancouver. There he began speech therapy. Though he thought he would never be able to teach again, every day I noticed his speech improved and by September he was back at Gladstone. He was sure that he had an impediment in his speech, having trouble finding words, but it was not evident to me or any of his associates.

After his first heart attack Leon decided to enjoy a hobby, got a piano and took piano lessons.

He had a second massive infarction some years later in Santa Ana, California. Again the doctors told me to get the family there if they wanted to see him, that this one probably would be fatal. But again he recovered.

My first speech in the House was given July 4, 1975. It was on the budget presented by John Turner, Finance Minister. I knew John from my earlier career when he was Justice Minister and I was concerned about the wandering children of Canada who were on the streets using drugs and being used by older men. I had great respect for John Turner, for his intellect and what I saw as his selfless service to Canada. His great sensitivity caused him to know I was hardly joyous in my new career. I especially hated wasting time with the silliness of Members who speak in the chamber when it is empty except for a few table officers and a fill-in Speaker, just to get their statements in *Hansard* so they can send them home to their constituents and make it seem as though they are doing something to better the lives of the people and the nation.

John came over to me one day and said, "I feel you are not too happy here. Any time you get discouraged come up to my office, put your feet on the coffee table, and have a Scotch with me ... we can talk it out."

In the budget debates a Member can speak on any subject. I remember making my speech and then being stopped by John as I passed through the lobby. He said, "That was quite a speech you made in there."

I could never forget the intensity in his eyes. I decided in writing this memoir to look up that speech. I could not believe it. It was totally relevant to what is happening in the new 21st century. By the summer of 2008 oil prices climbed

Pinning a button on Pierre Trudeau. The words on the button, as I recall, were: "I'm going to work for Canada today."

to unprecedented levels above $100 a barrel, and gasoline at the pump reached $1.40 a litre in Canada, despite Canada having, in northern Alberta, one of the largest oil reserves in the world. In the United States the crisis caused President George W. Bush to demean his once-great nation by begging his long-time family friends, the Saudi Arabian Royals, to release more oil to America. They refused bluntly, without any polite rationalization.

Now as I reread my speech in the House, with the entire economy of the western world going belly up, I can hardly believe what I foretold that day in the House. I began by voicing my respect for the Finance Minister:

> "During his three years in this portfolio, he (the Minister) took important steps to spare Canadians the impact of the international economic crisis that has so shaken our long-time friends and neighbours, the United States, Britain, and ... Japan. Compared to the hyperinflation they have been experiencing we seem untouched by (that) inflation and recession ... Canada has weathered these troubled times so far with less pain and discomfort ... thanks to our Minister of Finance.

> "Economic and political problems which were impossible to foresee have been forced on us by unsophisticated nations, which have suddenly achieved wealth of a magnitude never before seen in this world.

> "... Perhaps the most sobering event in the life of all people in the industrial society is the shift of power that has come with the contrived 1974 international energy crisis. Small nations dominated and controlled by a few people established cartels to control the life-blood of industry and economy, and the world's money."

Moving into the "current history" and the cause of the "massive shift of power" I zeroed in on the base of the shift – *oil.*

> "Oil prices (have) quadrupled and the Group of 13 (members of OPEC) virtually took control of the money and the economy in months, if not weeks."

On that July day in 1975, in the House, I noted the price of a barrel of oil was $1 at the start of the 1970s, $3.44 by the end of 1973, and $10 a year later; on the day of my speech it was $12.

Not missing a chance to lighten the heavy stuff I was throwing into the debate, I pointed out,

> "There are intelligent people on the other side of the House. I do not like to go to extremes and say they are overly endowed …"

A voice from the Conservative benches is recorded in *Hansard* with a brief:

"Thanks."

Further on in that speech I noted:

> "In the West we believed there would be human progress and material growth indefinitely. The hope crashed around us when the wealth of the world shifted and the industrial nations in North America, Europe and Japan became dependent on the oil rich countries of the Middle East. In 1974 old powers, old alliances, and old allies declined, and we saw the rise of the new ones. The greatest and swiftest transfer of wealth in all history occurred in 1974 .

> "The OPEC countries earned $112 billion from the rest of the world. They could not spend it all and they ran up payment surpluses of $60 billion. The fragile structure of the international financial system cracked under the strain, and Honourable Members Opposite expect Canada to survive all this without feeling it.

> "In 1974 Saudi Arabia alone earned $28.9 billion by selling nearly one-fifth of all the oil consumed by non-Communist countries … that country, practically owned by less than a dozen princes, had a surplus of $60 billion in 1974, and (it was predicted that the Saudi Royals) would take in $164 million more each day, and $6.8 million more each hour than they currently spend."

I told the House that day that, according to *The Economist of London,* at the rate of accumulation of OPEC money, the cartel could buy out all companies on the major world stock exchanges in 15.6 years, all companies on the New York Stock Exchange in 6.2 years, all central banks' gold (at $170 an ounce) in 3.2 years, all U.S. direct investments abroad in 1.8 years, all companies quoted on the stock exchanges of Britain, France and West Germany in 1.7 years, all IBM stock in 143 days, all Exxon stock in 79 days, the Rockefeller family wealth in six days, and 14 per cent of Germany's Daimler-Benz in two days.

I went on to say:

"… Compare: Canada's oil reserve, nine billion barrels for a population of 22 million people; little Kuwait, 64 billion barrels for a population of 880,000; Iraq 31.5 billion barrels for a population of 10 million; United Arab Emirates, 24 billion barrels for a population of 210,000; Qatar, 6.5billion barrels for a population of 113,000; Nigeria, 10 billion barrels for 79 million people."

In December 1975, my second year in the House of Commons, Leon and I decided to take a vacation in Israel. The Israeli ambassador arranged my visit with the Canadian Government Secretary of State. On December 27, we visited Golda Meir at her office and she was ready to go out to lunch with us but her grandson arrived just as we were ready to leave.

I have a wonderful poster picture I got in my first foray into a women's conference, "NOW" (National Organization for Women) in Seattle. The poster is a picture of Golda, and written under it is: "But can she type?" When Leon and I knocked at her door, she came to meet us and I said, "It is the same wonderful face I have in my office." I told her about the poster. She smiled.

I brought my copy of the book *My Life* by Golda Meir, published the year before by Weidenfeld and Nicolson, London. She autographed it: "To Simma and Leon Holt. In friendship and admiration, Golda Meir Dec. 27, 1976."

As we were leaving, she said, "By the way, Simma, I can't type."

Incidentally, that picture used to hang behind my desk in Ottawa. When people came into my office and asked where my picture of the prime minister was (meaning of course PET – Pierre Elliott Trudeau) I would point to Golda. "There she is." I did not have any problem with the censure in the eyes of the Liberal hacks, but then I noticed my constituents who had worked on my campaign were not amused. Into my third year, I hung a picture of

Trudeau. Funny, I got away without hanging one of the Queen – even though I do like and admire her. But that was a Conservative thing.

There was some so-called "poetry" produced by a group that used the publishing name "blewointment press." Having worked in a man's world in wartime, with newspapermen, soldiers and police friends, I learned a great deal of male language and many of their secrets. I knew what use men had for blue ointment.

What the blue ointment producers called "poetry" was done in typewriting, the lines formed in different size to create shapes such as a sharp-angled hourglass, triangles joined, short lines angled like cars parallel parked, etc., the publishers obviously struggling to be clever and different.

I produced this government-subsidized poetry at the first B.C. and Yukon caucus after I obtained the "work."

That morning I read some of the "poetry" from the blewointment booklet to our MPs and senators. Someone dared me to read it in national caucus. It was an easy dare.

I booked the allotted three minutes for a Member to speak. The minister responsible for these "cultural" grants, Minister of State for Small Business Tony Abbott, was sitting about three places to the right of the prime minister (who was always centre in caucus and in the House).

I started out by reporting the public anger we were receiving because of the government grant to blewointment press in B.C. "And I am sure all the men at the front of this room know what blue ointment is. Every soldier knows what it is. Even I know…"

I did not have to lip-read to know what Trudeau was asking when he leaned over to whisper first to Secretary of State for External Affairs Allan MacEachen on one side and then House Leader Mitchell Sharp on the other side. Though a most sophisticated man, there were naïvetés he revealed that always surprised me.

So I said, "Mr. Prime Minister, if you do not know the use for blue ointment there are many in this room who can tell you."

It was a rare person in that large caucus room that did not watch for Trudeau reaction. That was all that mattered.

Then I began to read a few lines from several poems: "I need a warm place to shit... I need a warm place to shit ..."

Trudeau asked for an explanation from Tony Abbott for the whole caucus.

When he came into the House that afternoon, he stopped at my desk, and asked, "Any more dirty poetry for me?"

"Lots ... a whole $7,500 worth."

And then came the most astounding – and treasured – words from a man I respected and liked so much: "It did not sound dirty – because you are so highly principled."

At another time I took on a senior bureaucrat in the office of Health and Welfare, Dr. Alex Morrison, in the House and in caucus over the ban of saccharine and the obvious protection of a monopoly sugar company in Quebec. André Ouellet, then Minister of Consumer and Corporate Affairs, was on side with me on this.

I challenged that it would take about 50 bottles of Diet Coke a day to get the dangerous quantity of saccharine. By then one would drown. Chocolate was more dangerous than the sugar substitute.

In the midst of this issue André Ouellet was in trouble in the House. It was a three-day assault by the Opposition in Question Period because he "talked to a judge" during some legal proceeding in Quebec. André was a good friend right through my time in Parliament. He came out to the west several times, went to Leon's school to talk to students, and visited with our family in our home. (He got into serious trouble long after this as Postmaster General and the media vultures never once talked of the good works he did as Minister of Consumer and Corporate Affairs, Housing, and his many other portfolios.)

I went to his desk to talk to him about something – I had served on consumer and housing committees and he had come to my riding to help those in cooperative housing over problems with Central Mortgage and Housing. As we were talking, Trudeau came by and said, "Don't get him into any more trouble than he is in now, Simma."

Some of the most insightful times with Trudeau were in national caucus and in one-on-one dialogue.

I doubt that there is a single person, including his most intimate friends, who would dare to say: "I know him." Trudeau probably did not know himself fully.

To avoid inaccuracies in analysis, most will explain Trudeau by anecdote, suggestive of the man but not conclusive. I, also, can best explain him from my personal experiences. Often small incidents best revealed the man.

I saw how he would push others into unacceptable behaviour which he could not bring himself to do, despite episodic unorthodox acts.

One hot, humid Ottawa summer day in national caucus, Roger Young, the Member for Niagara Falls (Judy LaMarsh's former riding), came dressed in a flowing brown-and-black African-patterned kaftan over his heavy frame. He made his statement regarding a concern to him and his constituents, using the three minutes allotted to those who have asked to speak. After all have spoken, including explanatory reports by Cabinet Ministers, the Prime Minister has the last word.

When he responded to Roger Young, his only comment was: "Roger, I would give anything if you would wear your kaftan into the House today." He knew that Roger would be ordered out by the Speaker to get appropriately dressed.

Even then I wondered if Trudeau did not get a vicarious pleasure out of Margaret's public displays of rebellion and non-conformity, if some of it was not her way of amusing her husband. But it was no secret; that once she humiliated him personally he would never forgive her.

One day when we were talking together at a party at Harrington Lake, I noted her picture still on the piano even though the marriage was over. As he talked about her his love for her was apparent. At one point he said, "I cannot understand why the media is so cruel to her. She is such a good person."

I wonder if this was naïveté, an act for me as a former professional journalist, or another of those quick, and quickly-lost, moments of truth of Pierre Trudeau?

He would go through intensive harassment from the Opposition in the House, handling most of it with the traditional shrug of a clever one-liner or with enviable cool. But some days, they would touch a tender nerve. I sat directly behind him, in the back row. I could feel his impatience, anger or frustration developing.

Sometimes I would send him a note or a quotation of significance. I would write "Mash Note" across the top of it and add some ridiculous four-number figure, such as 3306, indicating a list much longer than the reality.

On occasion I wrote them to him when he made an impressive speech or responded to my questions in a way that pleased me. I believed the word "mash" was well known to his and my generation.

One Wednesday after national caucus, I was one of four or five Government Members invited to 24 Sussex for lunch with the Prime Minister. When we got into the limousine, he sat beside me, and the debonair, sophisticated world traveller whispered, "What is a mash note, Simma?"

I was stunned. "You're kidding."

"No, honestly. I really would like to know."

"It is a sort of love note." "Oh," he said, as light dawned. "I thought it had something to do with that television show, you know the one about the army medical men, called 'MASH.'"

One bad day in the House, I sent him pictures of Vail, a favorite ski area for Leon and me. I attached a note saying, "Relax and dream about powder snow."

He started going to Vail. Once on his return, he asked me, "Where were you and Leon? I thought you were going to Vail this year, but we could not find you. President Ford's staff looked all over the Hill for you."

He wrote me a note one day, on his return to the House after a ski vacation, telling me he would always be grateful for my introducing him to Vail.

He was known for not being exactly generous with money, in fact was considered unbelievably penurious. I recall a saying from earlier times about his type: "They would pinch the nickel till the buffalo bellowed."

In Ottawa the Liberals, as the Government Party, were responsible for Quorum – 20 Members in the House – or risk the embarrassment of a sudden vote being called by the Opposition and losing it because they did not have the majority. This was, in my mind, one of several silly games played in this Old Boys' Club, having nothing to do with running a country.

The whip established a Friday Club as a way to keep as many backbenchers around the building as possible, when the bells sounded at 2 p.m. to call Members to the House. Unless we had Friday night business in our ridings we could delay our return to the constituency to a 6 p.m. flight after the House closed.

The Friday Club was a rather poor imitation of a Lions Club luncheon, with its tail-twister collection of money – usually 25 cents to $1, for such transgressions as making a bad speech, or coming late to caucus, or not passing the coffee.

One day the Prime Minister came to lunch with us. He found himself charged 25 cents, possibly because he liked Keith Davey, whom most of the caucus disliked and distrusted; or because they did not like something he said in a recent speech.

He paid his 25 cents on the first round, but when they found another cause the ante was upped to $1. He did not have it. The Members demanded an IOU. On the flap of a Member's DuMaurier cigarette package, he wrote: "IOU $1, P.E. Trudeau."

As we met in the lobby and were walking into the House together, he said to me, "I didn't know you people charged so much at your Friday Club."

"Don't worry, Mr. Prime Minister," I reassured him. "You could end up rich. They probably can sell that little piece of cardboard for $1,000 or more."

"Oh you are fooling!" he said and I looked to see if he was serious in his surprise. He was.

"No. It is almost priceless. But remember, if they do sell it, to let them have only $1. If they sell it for $1,000, you should expect $999 of it."

He appeared genuinely surprised that his writing was worth anything. I told him that John Diefenbaker used to say to me, "You wrote your note by hand and I will give you a handwritten reply in return. John Diefenbaker knows the value of his handwriting. You could take a lesson from him."

I also knew Trudeau's kindness and sensitivity, but saw it juxtaposed by cold rejection, including the cruel and illogical attempt to prevent me from participating in the Leadership convention of 1984. Perverse.[6]

Glaring inconsistency showed in his verbalizing his admiration for the challenges I put to him in the House, and events that happened subsequently. He told me he "loved people" who swim against the tide, after I fought the cabinet and most of the caucus on a bill pushed through the House in hot and angry debate. Yet, when we met in the lobby after I lost my seat, and I noted the backbenchers were "very inactive and dull," doing little to challenge him, he said, "Don't try to change them. I like it this way."

My mother, then living in Edmonton, had some trees planted for his children in Israel and sent him the certificate. He was pleased and wanted to know everything he could about the location. He wrote her a beautiful letter of thanks. He spoke of her gift and about her frequently, and when she visited me in Ottawa he invited her to his office, showed her pictures of his children. That was shortly after his third son, Michel, was born.

"But Mrs. Milner, this must appear rather silly. You had eight children and I am talking so much about my new one."

She replied, "Mr. Prime Minister, it does not matter if you have one child or eight or ten; you love them all. And I can tell you, if you lose one it does not matter whether it is three or eight, it is as though a piece of your body has been cut away."

She had lost a daughter at age 17. He said, "I cannot even think about it."

There was a letter that came to me with Trudeau's editing marks. It was about two women who had come before our Justice and Legal Affairs Committee

---

6   The 1984 leadership convention chose a successor to Trudeau. It proved to me that Trudeau thought I had more influence on others than I had. I was sure I had no influence. In any event, I felt that Turner had the brains, charm and dignity to be a respected leader. Trudeau and he had had a quarrel and Trudeau wanted to get me out of the Turner team. I was not a Member of Parliament then, but on a Government Agency, the National Parole Board. I was cornered by Judy Erola, Resource Minister, and Bob Kaplan, Solicitor General, after a cabinet meeting. Judy, in the washroom, warned me to step away from my support of Turner. Later Kaplan told me that my activity for Turner was noted by the Prime Minister, and Trudeau had asked Kaplan (who, as Solicitor General, was my boss) to get me to withdraw. Ignoring all dignity and bitch that I am, I paraded my sign for Turner more blatantly.

PRIME MINISTER · PREMIER MINISTRE

O T T A W A, KIA 0A6
November 19, 1975

Dear Mrs. Milner,

　　　　Margaret and I were both very touched
to receive the certificate that tells us 18
trees are growing in Israel as a tribute to
our three young sons. What a thoughtful
gesture for you to make.

　　　　I enjoyed our visit in Ottawa and only
regret there are so many activities going on
around the House of Commons that these meetings
are never long enough. I have told Simma she
must bring you to see me again when you come
back to Ottawa. She is a fine girl and we value
her highly, as I know you do.

　　　　I hope you remain in good spirits and
the best of health.

　　　　　　　　　　Sincerely,

Mrs. Nassa R. Milner
　　302, 11610 100 Avenue
　　Edmonton, Alberta

The letter of thanks Trudeau sent to my mother .

(of which I was then deputy chairman) in our special study on pornography. I had written to the Prime Minister to ask him to hire them to do some more work for us on the definition and details of law.

His correspondence secretary, Hellie Wilson, had written the letter. Just before I left for Washington, I told him, "I am probably the only person in the world who has a letter with a Prime Minister's editing carved into it ... I was impressed how well you know me. When Hellie wrote that you would have your 'officials work on it' you underlined it and wrote, 'Simma will never accept this.'"

"Oh," he said, "that is the letter about using Lewis and Clark to help you with the pornography bill."

"Migawd, you remember the actual letter!"

A twinkle came into his eye. He said, "Simma, write me a letter asking why you had not received a reply to your request for this help for the committee. And I will ask Hellie what happened to that letter in reply ... Give it to me in the House so I am sure to get it."

I went back to my office, dictated the letter and took it to him at his seat. His response, as usual when he was pleased with his mischief: "Oh super ..."

I had to leave on a trip to Washington, D.C. That was the last time Prime Minister Trudeau and I met officially in Ottawa.

Leon was with me in Washington. It was a historic moment. Menachem Begin and Anwar Sadat were meeting there for the signing of the Israel–Egypt Peace Treaty. We were invited up to the floor on which the entire Israeli delegation and staff were settled. While I was chatting with Begin's Chief of Staff and waiting for Begin to finish his meeting so we could join him for a brief break, Leon disappeared. Suddenly I saw him coming back down the hall, virtually at gunpoint. He was grinning and the Israeli soldier accompanying him was himself obviously amused. He left Leon, telling him it is not safe for him to wander in "the territory."

This was the second time I met with Begin. The first time was in Ottawa when I was a guest at the embassy with a group of leading Jewish women. We were barely seated and at ease when a maid came in and said, "The Prime Minister of Canada wants to talk with Simma Holt." When I went to the phone Trudeau was all apologies, telling me, "I am so sorry ... I am sending a car to

This was one of many moments of happiness I shared with my mother, Nassa Milner.

I first met Menachem Begin in Ottawa.

Menachem Begin and Pierre Trudeau at the gathering in Ottawa. There I am, to the left of Begin.

pick you up and bring you here. All the Jewish Members of Parliament have been invited to meet with Prime Minister Begin and his staff … someone goofed …" He seemed embarrassed and I laughed.

Our Committee of Regulations and Statutory Instruments was in Washington for a meeting with our American counterparts on Rules and Regulations. We were suddenly recalled. Parliament had prorogued and we had to return to Canada immediately. We were no longer legally able to act in our parliamentary role.

We were rushed to the airport and held in a VIP lounge, a special Canadian aircraft already parked on the tarmac to take us home. Lined up with it was an Egyptian plane which, we learned, was there to take Anwar Sadat and his party back from the peace conference with Begin. We were informed we would have to wait until Sadat's plane got safely into the air before we could go out to our aircraft. "The security," we were told, "is very tight."

We were all talking and full of the reality that we would have to face an election. I looked around and could not see Leon anywhere. I was sure he would find a place and a person with whom to socialize. I watched the Egyptian party stream out to the aircraft, and there, on and around the steps, say their farewell. Leon appeared, smiling, and walked over to me. As casually as if he were telling me he had been out for a breath of air, he said, "That was very interesting. I was with the Egyptian delegation. They offered me drinks and food. I didn't think it was right to accept it."

I asked if he "posed Egyptian." He only smiled some more and said they were most cordial; no one asked him any questions but they included him totally in their group.

When I caught my breath at the wonder of it, I asked, "Why didn't you go with them to the plane to see Sadat off?"

He said, "I knew I should get back because your group would be leaving next."

I always marvelled that this gentle man, so unlike me, could have such *chutzpah*. No matter how curious or compulsive I was when it came to getting a story, unless I could identify myself as a reporter seeking information I could not do what my seemingly quiet husband did with such cool.

We watched the Egyptians leave and we were in flight north about an hour later.

The Prime Minister had gone to see the Governor General to close the 30th Parliament.[7] We all headed to our ridings to campaign for the 31st Parliament of Canada.

When the NDP candidate, Ian Waddell, set out to contest my seat he could not attack my record of service in Kingsway or me personally without getting a political whiplash even from members of his own party. The gains I made for the riding were well known and years later Ian admitted he could not touch the subject. What he did do was simply point out that I had made a good friend of Pierre Elliott Trudeau. It played into the fact that the West was hysterically anti-Trudeau.

Instead of denying that friendship, I ran a huge cover picture of Trudeau and me on my campaign newspaper. I welcomed Trudeau to my riding, making sure – almost as a perversity equal to Trudeau's own – to have my pictures with him all over the place. There were issues we disagreed on, and my constituents knew about the times I voted against my own party and its leader. They also knew Trudeau accepted dissension in the caucus.

In the 1979 campaign, I thought if I lose my election because of honesty and loyalty to a man I had grown to respect and admire, so be it. I could live with myself in victory or defeat. I would know I had not become what is commonplace today in politics since the Trudeau years – especially with the little man named Jean Chrétien who nurtured pandering opportunists.

And the government of Pierre Trudeau was defeated, with the west wiped out of all but three Liberal members – two in Manitoba and one in British Columbia. I lost to Ian Waddell, and had two weeks to empty my Ottawa and Vancouver offices.

---

7   Members of the 30th Parliament included many well-known Canadians. Among them were: Lincoln Alexander, Warren Allmand, Harvie Andre, Perrin Beatty, Monique Bégin, Ed Broadbent, Iona Campagnolo, Jean Chrétien, Joe Clark, John Crosbie, John Diefenbaker, Tommy Douglas, Jake Epp, Francis Fox, Ralph Goodale, Herb Gray, George Hees, Ray Hnatyshyn, Donald Jamieson, Otto Jelinek, Serge Joyal, Stanley Knowles, Marc Lalonde, Charles Lapointe, Roch La Salle, Roméo LeBlanc, Flora MacDonald, Allan MacEachen, Elmer MacKay, Heath MacQuarrie, Don Mazankowski, John Munro, Erik Nielsen, André Ouellet, Jeanne Sauvé, Robert Stanfield, Sinclair Stevens, Pierre Trudeau, John Turner, and Eugene Whelan.

PRIME MINISTER · PREMIER MINISTRE

O T T A W A, KIA 0A6
May 29, 1979

My dear Simma,

What will I do without Simma? Who will keep me honest and who will make me laugh?

I can't tell you how sad I was when I received the word that you would not be coming back to our Caucus this time around. It seemed as though a spark went out.

You are such a good person and felt your role as member so strongly that your successor will have to be pretty special to satisfy the people of Vancouver Kingsway.

I hope you will stay active and help us rebuild in B.C., and I hope you will be back in Parliament in spite of all the frustrations that beset a journalist trying to work with the system.

We have had so many good times in the past five years, and none more so than when you brought your Mother to visit me. What a kind and marvellous lady. Please give her my very best wishes.

And for you, take care of yourself and keep fighting for what you believe. I certainly will be doing that myself. *your warm letter of last week gave me added strength and hope. Be happy, and let us keep in touch.*

Affectionately,

Pierre

Mrs. Simma Holt
Room 568 CB
House of Commons
Ottawa, Ontario

Mike Blomfield worked with me in Vancouver over two days. We took the signs to the city dump the first day; and all the rest of the garbage the next day. When we returned with that final load, I had my last Party political laugh.

The sea gulls were wall to wall over the dump. The only place they were absent was a circle of about 25 to 30 feet in diameter where the pieces of Liberal signs lay – the distinctive red and white mulched into large confetti-like pieces. The best the gulls did in recognition of the Liberal Party of Canada colours was drop more waste from high places as they flew over.

It was truly the end.

Happily I would be back home permanently with Leon and return to the career I loved – searching and researching stories to be written. And there were books …

16

Inside the Bush Power Drive

No moment in my life, except for the day of my birth in March 1922, was more important in determining my future than was November 26, 1985. That day my beloved friend and partner of thirty-seven-and-a-half years died.

Widowed and alone, without children or responsibilities for any other person, I was able to move on to a totally new arena in my professional career. It was into a place and time that any journalist would envy; it was at ringside at the pinnacle of American power while history was in the making – the rise of the Bush dynasty, and that family's role in the decline and fall of America from its height as the world's richest and most respected nation in the 20th century.

It began while Leon was still alive. Some time in early spring 1985 a gentleman named Bill Wead arrived in Vancouver. He was an American writer. We met on what seemed to be a short-notice invitation to luncheon with Judge Patsy Byrne, a former colleague at *The Sun.* She wanted me to meet the brother of her "very good friend." She herself was meeting him for the first time and, for reasons she did not explain on the phone, was anxious for him to meet me as well.

When we met, Bill was 42 years old, with big ambitions as an author and entrepreneur. He had already initiated the legal process for starting a book publishing company out of Vancouver. However, the first dialogue was Bill updating Patsy on her friend Jim. I learned that Jim and Bill were the two oldest of four sons of one of the most powerful leaders in the Assemblies of God in the United States. Jim was 44, two years older than Bill. A third brother, Doug, was 40. All three were writers and ordained in the faith of their father.

The youngest, Tim, then 23, also put his hand to writing with his brothers, when required, but was primarily an actor in Los Angeles.

Bill appeared to me as a very sensitive man, with facial features fine and delicate like those of an attractive young woman. He had a kind and gentle personality that immediately endeared him to me. There was no doubt, from the start, that Bill wanted my help and asked at that first meeting if I would become a director of his company, Rostrum Publishing. The manuscript for its first book was ready for publication once the company completed the various requirements of the province. It was hoped the company would meet the criteria for listing on the Vancouver Stock Exchange, to raise the money for publishing.

Leon and I agreed that I would lend my name to this project. Bill made no secret of the fact that he needed Canadians on his board, and my name was synonymous with writing and publishing.

My husband and I enjoyed Bill's company. Most intriguing was his collection of anecdotes and stories of some famous people – politicians, actors and writers. In table talk and in phone calls he would tell us the latest news, gossip and stories from inside the Washington Beltway, right up to the White House and Oval Office. He had stories that never appeared in the established newspapers, radio and television. We knew how close the Wead brothers were, especially Bill and Doug. We also knew of Doug's close ties to political leaders, philanthropists, high-ranking lawyers, and newsmen.

One night, Bill invited Leon and me to dinner at the downtown club where he was living. It was begun cordially, but all at once Leon became very abrasive with Bill. Never in all our life together had I experienced Leon being openly rude. He was picking on everything Bill said. I tried to stop him, in vain. We finally made a fast departure with thanks. That was the last time the three of us were together.

Within a week or ten days Leon died. When I phoned Bill to tell him, I let him know how sad I was that the last meeting between the two of them had been so hurtful to Bill.

"I am so sorry, Bill," I said on the phone. "I don't know why Leon turned like that."

Bill said there was no need to apologize, and said something to this effect: "I think Leon knew he was leaving you and feared that I might somehow do you harm."

Everything Leon did in the days before he died seemed to be aimed at finishing up and getting our home ready for me to manage alone.

It was Grey Cup Weekend. The B.C. Lions would be playing the Hamilton Tiger-Cats in the Olympic Stadium in Montreal on Sunday afternoon, November 24, 1985. Another major event was also pending about that time. Leon and I had received our tickets, complete with ID, for Expo '86 in Vancouver, and were invited to visit the site to have a preview of the staging and some of the international pavilions that would be expected. Leon, forever the perfectionist, said he would like to wait and see it all when it was finished.

Before the Grey Cup game I suggested that we have a party. As I began to list the friends we could invite, Leon stopped me and said, "I really would like it to be just Mitch and Tova with us."

After we checked with the Sniders and the plan solidified for the Sunday party, Leon began work on the parquet floor he had laid in our townhouse kitchen and entrance hall. The day of the party, he set out to finish the job, setting in the moulding between the floor and the wall. He completed it by early afternoon, then set out to pick up a jacket he had on hold at a local store. Leon never bought excessively in sales. He believed in buying the best in quality. For our wedding he bought the best dark suit he could afford and did not need to buy another dress suit for ten years. He was meticulous in his attire and always looked well-groomed. He had the good fortune to have a neat body that made clothing look good.

For the party, I had enough food on the table for a dozen people, though there were only four of us. We jumped, cheered, high-fived every time the Lions scored or made a good run. We laughed and yelled as if we were in the Olympic Stadium in Montreal. I cannot remember being happier than we were that day. It was a close game. When the cup was presented to the Lions and then filled with champagne, we cheered with the crowd. It was a perfect day.

Then it began to snow.

About 5:00 a.m. Tuesday morning, the television went on suddenly, blasting me awake. I shoved Leon and yelled, "Why in hell did you set the television to go on this early? Your tennis game is not till ten."

Leon did not stir. He continued his sleep in quiet and peace.

When he came down to breakfast I asked, "How come you set the television to go on at 5 a.m.? The damn thing blasted so loud! I shook you and yelled at you and you didn't move."

His ever-ready smile was his only reaction. I went on, "You were so still; you could have died and I would not have known why."

"Second best to dying on the tennis court."

In the doorway as.he was leaving, he asked, "Do you mind that I spent so much on this jacket?"

"You look so good in it … I love it. See you later."

The snow was coming down in blobs and piling up as Leon backed out of our townhouse carport into the Arbutus Village roadway. Turning east, he smiled and waved. That was the last time I saw him alive.

Some time later the club manager called. He told me that Leon had collapsed on the tennis court. My car was in service. I raced out to the main street and stopped the first car that was moving through the wet heavy snow. I told the driver what was happening. He drove me directly to the club. The paramedics were working on Leon, his doctor friends and others standing by in the hallway behind the players' dining room. I watched and did not utter a word. Immediately after I arrived Leon was wheeled out to the ambulance. I told his doctors, "I didn't say a word to him. All those people around us … Maybe if I'd talked to him he would have heard me and lived."

One said, "If he had come back he never would have a life."

When Leon died I was totally incapable of dealing with life and finances. From childhood, there was always someone else to take care of the money and structures of life and to fix things around the house – first my father, then the landlord, and finally a husband. The day I woke up alone, the day after Leon's death, the television was broken and the pilot light on the furnace had gone out. Financially, though, I had the home and would have Leon's pension, which he reduced when he took early retirement; his pension would last until February, 1989. I had savings from my own career, having bought Canada Savings Bonds by payroll deduction throughout my working years. There were small government pensions from my years of service in various capacities (including the Parole Board from 1981 to 1985). I was 64 and did not yet quality for Old Age Security.

I sought the help of an investment manager, a total stranger in Scotia McLeod. He offered to establish an "investment portfolio," taking all my savings and "handling" them for me. He could not tell me where I would get the monthly sums I needed to keep my home and pay my bills. He had no plan for any account from which I could draw cash if I needed good old-fashioned money.

I allowed myself to be locked into grief. Just when I thought I was going mad, a friend told me about a man I could trust. And thus I found Hugh Mitchell, who was also with Scotia McLeod. Hugh recalls when we first met I was "a basket case."

Hugh became my financial adviser, a substitute money manager for Leon. With what I had saved and what I later got from the sale of the townhouse, under Hugh's management I was secure and – most cherished of all – independent for the rest of my life.

Though my entire career was based in Vancouver, I never again wrote for the local newspapers. Nonetheless my writing and publishing career grew and my work became more challenging as I wrote for a larger market with national and international readers.

Then one day in September 1987 Bill Wead phoned. Jim, only 46, had died suddenly. Bill needed to get home to the family in North Dakota as quickly as possible. The plan was obvious; I would drive him to Sea-Tac Airport south of Seattle. In less than 90 minutes he was packed and in the car, headed out of downtown Vancouver.

When he finished all that was needed to be done with and for the family, he went to Washington, D.C. to help his brother Doug. Doug was already working towards the campaign for Vice President George Herbert Walker Bush's election to succeed Ronald Reagan in the Oval Office. Bill did not return to Vancouver, except for a day or two to close off all his affairs there and move whatever was needed to his new base in his brother Doug's organization.

Bill would phone me at least once or twice a week to tell me about his life and the people with whom he and Doug were closely involved. They were some of the most famous names, primarily the movers and shakers operating at the pinnacle of American political power. He was excited not only by what he saw and heard, but by the fact that he could give those stories to his reporter friend "just in case" I could "use it in a column or someday in a book."

He assured me that some of what he told me would never appear in newspapers. Always he said, "I am at the heart of the making of history." Later he would urge me, "Keep a diary; you are watching/hearing history in the making."

It turned out that the so-called "truths" and "facts" I heard were "plants" of information. Bill thought I could write them in Canadian columns, to be picked up by the American journalists who were working in the same areas of my publication – Ottawa and Toronto. Though I knew this was the way of "useful leaks" to advance a political agenda, I would later see it from ringside and not fully recognize the seriousness of what was happening when it happened.

When I saw it in it perspective, that is with all the benefit of hindsight, I would realize that the election victory of the first George Bush in November 1988 against Democratic candidate Michael Dukakis was as contrived and manipulated by backroom power brokers as was the victory of George Bush the Second against Al Gore in November 2000.

In late November or early December 1987 I met Bill's brother Doug for the first time, in Crystal City in Arlington, Virginia. Their luxury home-office in the Waterford Apartments was directly opposite the Washington Capitol and the Ellipse, where all the major monuments of American history stood out as the primary view.

My first move into their household began with a phone call from Bill inviting me, on behalf of his brother, to the "event of the American capital season" – the Washington Charity Dinner and Ball. He told me Doug and his long-time friend, singer Pat Boone, sponsors of the event as a fundraiser for their main philanthropy, Mercy Corps, had reserved a ticket for me to attend. Nancy Reagan was to be the honoree. Her highly-publicized cause as First Lady (every

First Lady has her own cause) was to combat drug use by young people. Her memorable slogan was "Just say 'No.'"

I accepted the invitation. I told Bill I would stay a few weeks and bring my laptop to help him complete the book Doug was producing for release simultaneously with the VP's announcement of his candidacy to succeed Ronald Reagan as President in the November election of 1988. The announcement would probably be in January. The book was entitled *George Bush: Man of Integrity.* I knew Bill was not strong, actually frail, and needed help in the very heavy load he was carrying for his brother. Doug had many responsibilities with his own business abroad, with his work as a motivational lecturer with Amway, and in his own filmmaking and writing.

So many celebrities came to the Washington Charity Dinner that there were two head tables about 40 feet in length on two levels at the front of the huge ballroom. Most of the Bush family was scattered through the crowd. I met George Bush Junior ("Dubya"), who would be the gatekeeper and front man on his Dad's 1988 campaign. Someone took a picture of George, his wife Laura, Bill and me, and it was sent to me while I was in Washington. That was a night of elegance, with a large orchestra playing soft classical music, and many of the rich and famous in attendance. But the honoree – First Lady Nancy Reagan – did not show. Her mother had died a few days earlier and Nancy herself was in hospital.

The first and foremost job Bill and I worked on together was the book on George the First. It was done in the style of the famous television game show Jeopardy. We would excerpt bits and pieces from his speeches, then top it with the appropriate questions as if they were challenges posed by those who wanted to know where he stood on issues. From this base Doug fine-tuned the questions and answers to meet what he knew would be acceptable to voters, religious and those who were part of the "New Right."

I returned to Vancouver after the work on the book was complete, early in January. After that, I talked frequently with Doug and Bill by phone. Then in late April I got a call from Bill, saying, "We desperately need someone with political experience, who has good knowledge of America and of Canada–US relations." He continued listing the needs: a writer, a person who knows Canadian–US-international issues, who knows politics and how to deal with challenges by potential voters.

At the Washington Charity Dinner and Ball in December 1987.

I'm on the right. The others are (left to right) Bill Wead, Laura Bush, and George W. Bush.

I stopped him. "All right, already … What are you trying to tell me?" He said that Doug and he would like me to come to Washington and work with them until the convention in mid-August and the election in November. I could make the decision immediately. When one is alone, every decision is unanimous.

I said I would come there in a few weeks, and stay a month or two, and "see how it works for the three of us." He assured me there was enough room for personal privacy and good work space in several areas, including the patio that stretched about 50 feet across the front of the apartment. He further assured me that everything I needed in living comfort and food would be provided. No financial remuneration was offered, nor did I seek it.

When a columnist broke the story in Vancouver that I was going to Washington to help in the presidential campaign of George Bush, my close friend Barry Broadfoot left a howling vulgar message on my answering machine. He said in effect, "…crazy dumb broad … have you gone insane? How in hell can you work for those bloody a--hole Republicans, you once a Liberal Member of Parliament?" When he finally talked to me in a long-distance call I told him, "Hey old buddy, if you had the chance to work and hear what I am hearing, and declined, you would not be much of a reporter."

At 7:00 a.m. on May 3, 1988 I arrived at Washington International Airport (later Reagan International). It was so close to the Wead apartment that I could see the furniture on their long balcony as we came in for a landing. I was at the apartment at 7:30 a.m. and Bill's first words were: "We have to be at campaign headquarters (downtown Washington) by 9:00 a.m. The Vice President is meeting with a delegation of evangelical leaders."

He did not have to tell me that they were coming to find out his positions in areas of their concern. I showered quickly, unpacked a light summer outfit that was not too creased, dressed and was whisked to the campaign headquarters and into the boardroom minutes before the delegation arrived. A man introduced to me as Stan Walksteader, who was familiar to me from discussions or in phone calls to the Wead home when I was there the previous December, was the leader of the delegation and was seated at the head of the table, the central chair being left for the Vice President. About a dozen others sat around the campaign offices' board table and waited. At 9:00 a.m.

George Bush arrived. But it was not the Vice President; it was his eldest son, "George W."

Clearly he was there as the surrogate for his father. He announced that he was there to speak for his father, to answer their questions on behalf of "the candidate for the Presidency."

He told them at the outset that his father was adamant that there could not be a divided (two nation) Israel, that this was "non-negotiable." (He obviously was briefed by Doug that the evangelicals are intransigent on the belief that Israel should be a Jewish state.)[1]

I listened as Junior respond to questions during the session. Just before it ended, he announced he planned to run for Governor of Texas, and asked them for their support and that of their evangelical friends in his home state.

At the end of the meeting, Stan Walksteader said they would pray for his father, and begin with a "laying on of hands." Bill and I, standing at the side of the room, bowed our heads with the evangelicals and the Vice President's son. I peeked up and saw George W. Bush, his face blood red, shuffling in his place in his discomfort.[2]

When this meeting was over Bill told me we had another meeting a few blocks away. It was in the office of a prominent Washington lawyer, an adviser on the campaign. This lawyer was preparing the list of people whom it would be politically beneficial to have on stage at the convention as speakers before the platform committee. The platform would be the nexus of the convention, next in importance to the official nomination of the GOP (Grand Old Party, the Republican Party) candidate. This was a remarkable moment in the months I spent inside the campaign. It was obvious that morning that the Wead brothers would be totally open with me.

---

1   When I met with Pat Robertson in Virginia Beach in mid-September 1988 I asked for the reason why the evangelicals were so strong in support of Israel being a Jewish state. He told me that the belief of "true Christians" was that the Messiah would not return until all the Jews are in the Promised Land – the promise given by God to Moses on Mount Sinai.

2   After George W. became the 43rd US President, sounding like a hyper Born-Again Christian, I told this story to a Bush family insider and said, "He has no more religion than a snail." The reply was he got religion when Laura told him she would not sleep with him until he "cleaned up his act."

As it later turned out, they even shared inside information from their colleagues and friends in the Republican National Committee, the White House, and campaign headquarters. The main operatives, the most powerful backroom manipulators talked totally openly when I was around. Because I was a Canadian, an "old lady" (then 64), overweight and simply "around" the Wead household and the campaign offices with them, they saw me as little more than a piece of furniture in the Wead household.

There was no doubt in the minds of any of the workers in the campaign and out of the Vice President's office that George Junior would run interference for his father. He was unabashed in telling even campaign workers – the paid ones and the volunteers – that he was in charge, that he was "the eyes and ears for my Dad." He had an office in campaign headquarters directly across from Chairman Lee Atwater. Despite his watchfulness of Atwater and everyone else in the campaign, his mother, Barbara Bush, said her son and Lee "became friends."

Doug Wead recalled his first meeting with George W., Laura and their twin daughters in March, 1987, in Corpus Christi, Texas. W. said, "I've been reading your memorandum. Good stuff, Wead. I'm taking over. You report to me. I'll be your boss."

Nonetheless, messages came directly from George Senior to Wead. Doug was given a direct and private line to the candidate's office. Senior's secretary was advised to put any Doug Wead calls through to the Vice President.

The entire Bush family recognized and needed the deep and full knowledge Doug Wead had of all religions. He was a true religious scholar and a writer who could put his knowledge across with clarity.

Doug wrote reports, analyses and what could be perceived as a training manual of 158 pages for Ronald Reagan that created the foundation for the conversion of the former actor into an icon of the Christian "New Right." He prepared another, eight years later, for George Bush's bid for that large vote. For Bush the training manual was reduced to 53 pages.

George Bush had been comparatively liberal throughout his career. The evangelicals were uneasy and spoke their concern openly. In 1979-80 Bush ran for the presidential nomination against Reagan. At that time there were indications that George and Barbara were pro-choice. There was no doubt that he was more liberal than Reagan, who by then had learned the power of the "New Right" and the magnitude of their vote. Reagan lived and spoke in the style and ways he had learned from the Wead primer, injecting his own distinctive and personal, warm and humorous moments. It was harder for George Bush.

The far-right conservatives distrusted Bush as a *"liberal,"* a character so vile that some Americans will not say the word. At most they will whisper a reference to it as "the L word." In an interview on PBS, on the show entitled "The Jesus Factor," Doug Wead candidly admitted the problem he had getting the VP, who lacked Reagan's acting skills, to say the words that could get the huge vote of that constituency.

Doug explained that he had to teach the presidential candidates the language before George One could "build a relationship with the evangelicals." Doug went on to explain, "Every subculture has its own nomenclature, its own language, its own style. You can be out on the street and a person can put just one word in front of another word and you instantly know where they are from. The same is true of the evangelical subculture."

A bad moment for George One came in a 1980 meeting with a group of evangelical leaders at O'Hare Airport. They asked, "Are you a Born-Again Christian?"

He replied flatly, "No." When pressured, Bush Senior said, "Hey, fellas. You need to talk to my son. He's a real Born-Again Christian."

The PBS interviewer pressed Wead on this dialogue. Doug admitted it happened after the elder Bush had been "well prepped."

Doug reminded the Vice President in one of his memos at the time of the O'Hare meeting, that 36 per cent of the American population was "born again." By the time of the 1988 Bush campaign for President it was up to 46 per cent. In the campaign, when George Junior was the lookout for his father's interests, he would ask Doug, "How did he do? What did he say? What did they think?"

George W. told Doug that when he ran for Governor of Texas he used the lessons provided for his father to win the evangelical vote.

When questioned about George W.'s integrity in his very public pronouncements of faith, Doug answered the PBS interviewer, "There is no question … that the (then second Bush) President's faith is real … genuine, authentic and there's no question it is calculated … That sounds like a contradiction, but that will always be the case for a public figure, regardless of their faith."

Using the great Christian public figure Constantine as an example, Doug pointed out, "Constantine, when accused of being 'calculating,' said, 'How else would (he) keep open the temples to the Greek gods and the Roman gods, and fund some of the temples of the Roman gods?' The Christian community was outraged. Yet he was their hero. He was the first Christian monarch and he had this born-again experience."

Thus, it seemed, Doug Wead, in briefing of the right words and phrases required to win the votes of a huge constituency, showed both Bush generations the way. Bush Senior, whom Doug called the "Man of Integrity," could not do it, and had only one term as President. The son not only won the Texas Governor job but, unlike his father who could not fake it, was elected for a second term as US President, using – as he confessed – the Teachings of Doug Wead.

From May to September I continued to do research for Bill and writing of massive reports on North American issues and considerable political stuff from abroad. It was useful to Bush in campaign ideas. I responded to queries from supporters or potential supporters of Bush on his positions on such topics as abortion, fetal tissue transplant, prayer in schools, etc. This was primarily for the Christian media – the Christian Broadcasters' Association, *Christianity Today, Focus on the Family.*

I was also heavily into what I suspected was the main reason I was there. Doug Wead, a fast book writer, had received a payment on a commissioned book on six second lieutenants, heroes in an unusual inside story of the Vietnam War. They were the First Force Reconnaissance (the Marine counterpart of the Army's Green Berets and the Navy SEALs), a special small force of six Marines operating at the Laos border as collectors of intelligence, including capture of senior officers for interrogation, When the campaign went into high gear, the Weads knew they could not fulfill their commission and asked me to work with the main player in the story, former Lieutenant Bill Peters, who incidentally, like most Marines I met at that time, was deeply religious. He was a spiritual counsellor.

I would go out to a coffee shop every morning to read and write, giving Bill Wead his privacy at the start of his day. One day when I arrived at the suite, Bill was flushed and excited. I barely got through the door when he told me he had received a call from New York, from the leader of an organization fighting for "Justice for Jonathan Pollard." The organization wanted Doug to intervene with the Vice President to save Jonathan.

Bill proceeded to tell me that the caller had explained Pollard was a civilian intelligence officer who had warned that there was a planned attack by terrorist leaders in the Middle East, that there was a buildup of military forces in Syria and Libya to attack Israel. Despite the mutual security pact President Reagan initiated with Israel, the Americans, under then Defense Secretary Caspar Weinberger, were deliberately withholding this information. Pollard went to the Israelis to warn them and was turned away into the waiting arms of the American CIA (Central Intelligence Agency) – and was charged with treason.

I told Bill I would go "immediately" to the Washington, D.C. court registry where the case was first filed, then write a report for the Vice President. I was about to add, "and Doug or the Vice President can deal with it, can use it in his campaign as a matter of correction of injustice." But Bill blurted out, "Oh my God NO! They cannot get involved in something like this in the middle of the campaign … No … no, I just told you about it because I know it might be a big story for you – even a book."

Bill never stopped loading book ideas on me. This was just the latest.

Nonetheless I dressed and went at once to the district court in Judiciary Square in downtown Washington – which, incidentally, was across from the Canadian embassy.

At his appeal hearing in the autumn of 1988, Jonathan Pollard was represented by Theodore (Ted) Olson, a prominent lawyer in the Bush–Wead contact group. It was unsuccessful. Olson went on to become Solicitor General in the first administration of President George W. Bush (from 2001 to 2004), yet did nothing in that office to arrange a pardon or release for Pollard, even though he knew the truth.

Jonathan Pollard is still locked away for life, without parole.

As the convention (scheduled for mid-August in New Orleans) grew closer, the meetings at campaign headquarters increased. Doug and Bill initiated the plan for a Family Values Suite which they would organize and man. All the Bush family, at least one or two at a time, would be present while the convention was on. That would include the Vice President and his wife Barbara, and their children, George W., Jeb, Marvin, Neil and daughter Dorothy.

Every major televangelist and leaders of major congregations throughout the United States would be invited to the Weads' Family Values suite. Among them would be failed GOP presidential candidate Pat Robertson (whom the Weads were wooing to announce support of their candidate).

One time when I was returning to the apartment, Bill could hardly wait to tell me his news. "We got Phyllis Schlafly ... My God, can you believe? We got Phyllis Schlafly."

I responded, "That bitch ... What's the big deal? She hates everything I have fought for all my life ... equality for women ... in business, office, workplace ..." I did not stop in my fury, and I knew I was in serious conflict. I recognized that George the First was a decent man, and I admired the brilliance, writing and integrity of Doug. I wanted to help my friend, Bill; I was concerned over his frail health and the fact that he was on overload. But now Bill was excited at the "coup" of getting Phyllis Schlafly for the Family Values Suite, and I was torn between my beliefs and my desire to help my friends.

From Bill's point of view, no doubt Schlafly was a gold-plated attraction to draw leaders of the "New Right." She had massive credentials: born and raised Catholic, mother of six children, author of more than 23 books ranging from child care to phonics, and heard on radio programs on 460 stations. Her emphasis on the destructive force of radical feminism against women's rights led to the 1980 Supreme Court five-four decision in *Harris vs. McRae* – to provide funding for childbirth, but not for abortion. She founded a powerful lobbying organization, Eagle Forum, in 1972, and led it against every liberal and feminist cause, seeking to influence public policy along the lines of her convictions – including intolerance of homosexuals, even though her eldest son, John, was "outed" as gay by *Queer Week* magazine.

I realized I was in the wrong place, considering the agenda I was supporting. I would have to leave it, though I hoped I could hold the friendship of the Wead brothers on the larger basis of their intellect and character.

I met Lee Atwater when he was only 36. It was when I first entered the Wead campaign from their luxurious backroom in Arlington December 1987. His reputation was well established in phrases that described him as "the most astute campaigner on the Washington scene," simply "a wizard … did magic on the way to victory trail for his candidate."

After the Iowa caucus vote in 1988, Doug Wead hinted that Atwater faked the numbers, giving the victory to George Bush and taking it away from the actual winning candidate, Pat Robertson. When I interviewed Robertson in his offices at Virginia Beach in September of 1988, he was still bitter about it. He blamed the Wead brothers for it; later he would receive a confession and apology from Lee Atwater.

It was one of many appeals for forgiveness that Atwater sought and received as he was dying. It came four years after he used what was called "hard-edged" methods, such as planting fake results of "surveys (by) independent pollsters" which his media contacts would publish as being from a "most reliable source."

Atwater was dying from an aggressive brain tumour. It became public knowledge that he converted to Roman Catholicism and, in an act of final repentance, sought forgiveness from many he had harmed, including those whose political hopes were destroyed by his spread of false information and phoney survey numbers. Pat Robertson told me he was with Lee in his last days, prayed with him, and assured him that he could go in peace "to meet his Maker."

Lee issued a confession and apology to all he damaged in his time as a Republican consultant and as campaign manager for President George Bush the First, the forty-first US President. His confession indicates that the election of President Number 41 was as fraudulent as that of George Bush the Second, President Number 43.

At the end of August, after the convention was over, Bill and Doug did not speak to me. I was treated like a copy girl by snob journalists. I knew then I had to leave, that I would not wait until the November election, even though I had promised to stay. I used the excuse of Doug's son, Scott, needing to stay with his uncle Bill because Doug and his wife, Gloria were breaking up.

On September 15, 1988, I left and never went back. Though I feared for Bill's survival, he knew and I knew that everything in which I was now involved (the extreme right, the Phyllis Schlafly stuff, the Christian extremism, the compromise on morality for victory for Bush) was the antithesis of everything I believed in.

Bill Wead died in Phoenix, Arizona in the spring of 1991. Doug Wead moved there to run for Congress in what was then a "sure" Republican constituency. Doug was peaking, with support from men like John McCain. But at the last minute Doug was scuttled, after the legendary Republican Barry Goldwater called him "a nice young man … but too extreme in his Christian politics."

17

Condominium Calamity

May 3, 1999 was a day of total joy and hope.

Six days later I found myself in a protracted nightmare.

It was on the first day of May that I closed the deal on the purchase of a $110,000 condo. It was clear title, no mortgage hanging over me. It was a perfect home and office. The location could not be better.

My new home was apartment 420, in Heritage Grand on Maude Road in Port Moody. Maude had only one address on it – 301, the number on the five-building, 257-unit Heritage Grand complex. The complex was built against a natural slope of land from sea level rising towards Heritage Mountain and Buntson Lake Park. It was at the eastern end of Greater Vancouver's North Shore, originally the planned terminus of the Canadian Pacific Railway.

The location of the unit I chose was on Heritage Mountain Boulevard, on the east side. The Port Moody recreation and meeting centre, public library, city hall, police station and fire hall were across the road on the south side of the complex. Kitty-corner on the north-east side was the small but complete Newport Village Mall, with a variety of restaurants, grocery stores, clothing stores, a medical centre, services to meet every mood and taste. One block east beyond old-growth trees, on the east side of Heritage Mountain Boulevard, was Eagle Ridge (General) Hospital. (Within two years the old-growth trees were replaced by more townhouses and a palliative care facility, an adjunct to the hospital and medical building in Newport Village.)

Port Moody was one of the Tri-Cities, the others being Port Coquitlam and Coquitlam. All three were carved out of old forest and farms, the centuries-old growth replaced by a forest of high-rises and townhouses, and blocks of business developments. The Tri-Cities were 25 to 30 miles from downtown

Vancouver. The charm of the entire region was the many natural old forest parks with lakes and streams running to the sea.

As I moved into my new condo that sunny warm May 3, I was certain this would be my last move. All was in place for the conclusion of a good life, with my writing career continuing and without having to worry about making money for travel and research.

For the first time in my apartment living I now had more than a ledge for a patio. As soon as I put the deposit on the purchase, I bought a green two-seater swing, matching high metal table with two chairs, and a green outdoor-indoor carpet. My newest fantasy was to sit there reading and correcting manuscripts outdoors in cool comfort and peace year-round in the mild Pacific coast weather.

Friends shopped with me to get more bookshelves for the second small bedroom that would become my library and study. My lounge chair and footstool would sit beside the wall, allowing me to reach out and pull whatever book I felt like reading at the moment. My desk was in front of the window with the view across the road to the huge trees.

My friend Nan Harrison helped me buy a small bed chesterfield that became the divider between the dining and living areas. My dining space was the coffee table in front of the new chesterfield, opposite a new television set I bought.

Three days after I moved in, on May 6, 1999, I had to go to Toronto on business. I was eager to get that done and return to unpack dishes, books, and generally enjoy life in my new home.

When I returned three days later, on May 9, I saw the corner of a sheet of paper sticking out from below my door. I opened the door, picked it up and read my first notice as an owner in Heritage Grand. The strata council management advised that I had an assessment for $31,280, my share for the reconstruction of the leaky condo complex. The first quarter was to be paid by September.

That turned out to be just for starters. By December the figure rose by $9,884 to a total of $40,664 for my 860-square-foot unit. The walls of my new home were riddled with rot and mould and, with all the other 152 units in the building, would have to be torn out and reconstructed. The assessment was my share of a $5- to $7-million reconstruction.

I had been cheated and lied to.

The builders had already walked away and, as I found out later, had immediately re-registered under a new name and number, to begin construction of more and bigger high-rise condos in Vancouver on the money they had taken virtually by fraud.

The unit owners of Heritage Grand soon learned what tens of thousands throughout the Lower Mainland and Vancouver Island had already learned – that the building inspectors in the cities of Vancouver, Victoria and surrounding municipalities had approved rot-and-mould-ridden buildings, and occupancy permits were issued recklessly and without conscience. These were residences in which people would be damaged irreversibly – pushed into bankruptcy and homelessness and their health damaged by deadly spores.

When I decided to buy a home in Heritage Grand I was financially secure, a renter in a luxury condo in Coquitlam on the edge of Burnaby. But I had begun to reflect that my rented condo could at any time be taken from me on short notice by the Hong Kong owner. The British Colony across the Pacific had been returned to Mainland China with the expiration of Britain's 99-year lease. I had moments of unease that if the communist tyranny began in Hong Kong the Chinese capitalists would flee with their huge wealth to North America. The thought never left me that one day the owner of my rented apartment might want his property for his own residence.

In January, 1999, on a walk through Lougheed Mall in Burnaby, I stopped momentarily at a real estate kiosk, looking abstractly, barely registering the details below the picture displays. As I turned to move on towards the east exit door of the mall, I heard a woman's voice ask, "Have you any questions?"

She introduced herself as Ada Van Leeuwen and handed me a card identifying her as an agent for Coronation West of Royal LePage Realtors.

At that moment I made the worst mistake of my life. I told her I was curious to see what was available in a small condo in the range of $100,000 to $120,000. I indicated, "I'm just curious, only slightly interested."

Everything she did and said inspired trust, whether spoken or implied. I told her that if I did decide to buy, she could be sure it would be from her.

Ada Van Leeuwen immediately set up an appointment for lunch "just to talk about it." I assured her that I was not ready to quit the apartment I was in. She said that did not matter; she would not pressure me to buy. But, as was natural for a realtor, during lunch she showed me what was available in the edge cities east of the high-priced real estate of Vancouver. She assured me there were still many choices within my stated price range.

And that day, over lunch, the vague germ of an idea – buying a condo – took on a life of its own. I began to feel like I was sitting outside of myself watching it happen, and helpless to stop it.

When Ada van Leeuwen began her sales pitch, my first question was about the "talk" of "leaky condos." There were no large or significant stories in the newspapers. Obviously, I thought, if it was a major problem, there would be massive media coverage. If there were stories about the situation, they were minimal.

My friendly realtor assured me she would never sell me a leaky condo. She would no more damage my life by selling me a disaster than she would her own mother. There was no hesitation by Ada Van Leeuwen to show me what to look for in identifying a leaky condo. In her education of Simma Holt she drove me many miles, within a radius of 30 or 40 miles of Vancouver. It began with the edge cities of Vancouver we both favoured – Coquitlam, Port Coquitlam and Port Moody. Then she took me into the Fraser Valley. She showed me examples of defective construction. She taught me what to look for – window frames edged with thick black-and-grey muck falling in filthy irregular folds onto mostly stucco walls of the buildings. The stucco, I was told, was often low-quality and thinned with soap. I noted these buildings on her tours had no overhangs from the roofs. Later I learned they did not even have eavestroughs to carry off the water from heavy Pacific coast rainfalls.

I saw block upon block of condos covered with green tarp. These were leaky condos under reconstruction. I wondered how people could live behind those tarps for two or three years. I would all too soon get the answer.

Every time Ada Van Leeuwen and I met or she talked to me on the phone she assured me that she had read and reread the minutes of the strata council of the Heritage Grand complex and I could be confident there were no problems. I also read the minutes, but relied on Ada, an expert in real estate, who would see through and beyond the endless details of a noisy tenant, a tap dripping, a tear in the carpet in the common property area, graffiti on a wall.

She compounded my trust when she, on her own initiative, told me she had negotiated a $10,000 holdback with the previous owner and the primary realtor in case there was a problem within the first year. She said that the money would be held in escrow by her friend – the woman she recommended to handle the conveyance in the sale, Notary Public Rose Miller.

When I decided on the suite in Heritage Grand, Ada assured me that it was only two years old and that the builder, the Richardson Brothers, had an enviable reputation for fine home construction. The appearance of the complex lent truth to her claims. The halls were wide and bright. The two parking spaces that came with the suite were spacious.

Having two underground parking spaces was a great enhancement, though I had only one car. It meant I would have space for guests. When I asked to see the back-door entrance to the parking garage Ada kept saying she had to get a key and make arrangements ahead. It was not until I moved in and went down there myself that I saw water stains on the steps and walls. When the reconstruction started, it was the northern building in the complex and that northern entrance to my building, including my eastern wall, that were the worst. The foreman of reconstruction told me that Heritage Grand was among the worst of the leaky condos in the entire Lower Mainland of B.C.

The statement that the building was only two years old turned out to be false. At the trial of the case, Ada Van Leeuwen kept saying she had yellow-tagged the areas of problems in the strata council minutes, but the few times I had seen them there was not a single mark on them. Rather, she always assured me, "I have read the minutes again … no problems … the question mark beside ingress is insignificant."

Shortly after I got that note from the strata council on May 9, 1999, I contacted a lawyer. I chose one who had been one of my closest professional friends in my years of writing about criminals, crime, courts, and prisons. He was brilliant, always courteous before the court, and highly respected among his peers and his clients. He confirmed that I had a case against Ada van Leeuwen and the unit's former owner, and he agreed to take it.

He immediately filed notice of action, and followed through with his juniors handling the case up through the examination for discovery.

I wanted to go to court to have my purchase of the condo cancelled. I wanted the agreement nullified because it was obtained fraudulently.

A date was set for a hearing before a judge in September. It was postponed to October and then, I was told, February 2000. The hearing never took place. In fact, six years later nothing had happened – and by then the lawyer said it would be too costly for me to go to court. He wanted to settle without a cent for me, and no costs.

But I did not know that in 1999. I immediately began paying $500 a month towards the costs that I knew would pile up if we had to go to court. I kept paying $500 a month for about three years. No one asked me to pay at that time and I did not think to ask for it to be done on a contingency basis, because the lawyer was my friend and I knew that he had to pay disbursements and his corporate costs.

Surrounded by rot and mould, I tried to work at my computer with a mask on, the back of the machine only six inches from the mould being torn out by workmen on the patio in front of me. At night a choking cough kept me from sleep and at times made me feel like I might strangle. There was mould inside the wall at my headboard, within inches of my head.

I was forced to seek a safe place to sleep, staying at a friend's home for long periods. (I had two sets of friends, Nan and Doc Harrison and Erika and Wolfgang Roesner, who had rooms for me.)

I rented an office downtown in a vain attempt to finish my writing assignments. I stayed in hotels, abandoned my apartment for weeks at a time as the walls fell through huge chutes to the dumpsters under my window, throwing choking dust into my apartment. Sometimes I would drive 50 miles to a cottage I had bought in 1987 (when I was still financially secure), south of the border in Washington State, in a development called "Peaceful Valley." I would stay there and commute to Vancouver for my growing medical needs and personal business.

With all this, I saw my life savings dwindling.

For three years I lived with workmen pulling down walls, uncovering the mould around me by cutting the stucco and facing and digging into the walls and pillars above, below and beside me. My books, pictures, bookcases, groceries, bedclothes, patio furniture – everything I owned that once could be placed in cupboards, closets or on walls – were piled into my living space. I had only my bathroom, part of my kitchen and my bed space available.

Once a workman screamed at me when I dared to bend under the wooden bar over the sliding doors to go out on my own patio! He later apologized, explaining that, because the walls were crashing around me and the rails of the patio were insecure, I might be hurt.

Where once I went to doctors rarely, and then only for minor problems or for my annual checkup (which I delayed for months), now I was seeing doctors several times a month. I had previously been so proud of – at times arrogant about – my good health and energy, and how I did not abuse Canada's marvellous universal medical and hospital insurance.

I hated appearing to be a hypochondriac, yet I felt sick often. When I began lying around watching television and sleeping, I knew I was dropping into depression. I felt my life was over.

My physician, Dr. Monte Glanzberg, took it seriously and referred me to a super professional friend, psychiatrist Dr. Barry Segal. Dr. Segal kept me going and even at times put the spark in me to try writing again. When I am not doing my writing I feel that my life is without purpose.

One day I began having double and sometimes triple vision, seeing two or three of the same picture on my television. My ophthalmologist, Dr. Craig Beattie, solved it by prescribing antibiotic drops for the infection from the mould.

Then after the double vision cleared and my eyesight seemed perfect, in late 2003 – two-and-a-half years after I moved into my leaky condo – I began to notice in my daily morning swims that my goggles were rubbing against my eye. Soon the edge of my eyelid felt pinched and I would take off my goggles with the same relief I had when I took off my tight boots after a day of skiing. I could not keep my goggles on for more than five or ten minutes. Then I noticed that there was a black circle, like a large earthworm, at the underside of my eyelid and my right eye was bulging like that of a cod. After several weeks of this, I reluctantly felt I had to check it with Dr. Glanzberg. I told him that maybe plastic surgery would be a solution to get ride of the "worm" and lift the lid of my eye.

Usually patient, this time he seemed a bit annoyed, and said, "Before we talk of plastic surgery I want to know why that eye is protruding." He personally called Dr. Beattie to make the appointment for me – in haste. He said it might be thyroid.

Dr Beattie wasted no time. He referred me on an urgent basis to a specialist, Dr. Peter Dolman. He found a "mass" behind the right eye. Dr. Dolman set the biopsy surgery for June 16, 2004. The biopsy would be done through the upper lid of the eye.

The surgery was done and for three days I was cared for by my friends Erika and Wolfgang Roesner at their home. I was told the results of the biopsy would be known at the first of the following week and I would be advised by Dr. Dolman's office. The appointment to see him was set for three weeks later, upon his return from Spain. Over and over I tried to find out what the diagnosis was. I was not sleeping because there were hints of cancer. Finally I phoned Dr. Glanzberg. Within an hour he was back on the phone telling me they found "low-grade lymphoma," and that it can be controlled though not cured.

The lymphoma started in the lymph gland behind the eye. I had to undergo bone marrow biopsy, x-rays, endless blood tests, CT scans, three different forms of chemotherapy for about eight months, a short period of remission, then a new intravenous chemotherapy for four consecutive Fridays of December 2005. Each series of treatments was followed by medical conferences to see whether the treatment worked. The first tests revealed the cancer cells behind my eye had spread to my bone marrow and near the kidneys.

I was referred to an excellent oncologist, Dr. Katherine Paton, probably one of the best oncologists specializing in ophthalmology. When I told her I feared the loss of my sight, she was impatient in her reply. "You are not going to lose your sight; you simply have lymphoma."

Using laser technology she improved my sight to a sharpness that I had not had in years. She told me I had 20-25 vision, whatever that means.

The amazingly sensitive medical team at the cancer clinic took over my life, dedicated to saving it. I was told I had a good chance of dying of old age before I die of lymphoma. The medical team always had time to answer questions put to them by myself and my support person. They encourage every patient to have a support person present in the medical team conferences. Mine has been my dear friend, Erika Roesner. No sister could have been more devoted.

I feel as strong and healthy as I ever have, with very few side effects from the chemotherapy. Even my blood count has been maintained as good.

While the doctors were dedicated to saving my life, the lawyers were exacerbating my anger, frustration and sense of hopelessness that the damage done to me would ever be paid for.

Six years after the whole catastrophe began, the lawyers still had done nothing to recover the $10,000 hold-back. Then because the lawyers failed to act, the people who had dumped their rot on me claimed the $10,000 for their lawyer and costs.

My lawyer was saying, "Because you did not act in the case they believed you abandoned it and therefore you must pay the costs." And this after telling me over and over that they did not want to mount up huge bills by going to court, or saying "we needed instructions" even after I delivered the instructions repeatedly by e-mail and by hand-delivered letter. Nobody seemed to be reading the files. Then the lawyers said, "You cannot claim twice on one matter." The strata council had an action on behalf of the owners of the complex. No matter how often I stressed that my case was different, the lawyers persisted that I would have to wait until that was settled.

While this was going on, the value of my property was dropping. The government assessment on the apartment when I bought it in 1999 was $111,000 (I paid $110,000 for it.) Three years later the assessed value was $50,000; the land had risen from $20,000 to $25,000. I was in debt for $41,000 for my share of the building's reconstruction.

At the same time – and for the first time in my adult working life – I could not pay my taxes. I believed then that before anything else I had to save my investment in my home and office, so for three years I had to default on my taxes. Though I began to pay down my taxes as soon as I could borrow money, the penalties and interest grew beyond my total tax bill. Even when the basic tax bill was paid, I still owed over $17,000 in penalties and interest – and compounding. I took bank loans to try to keep ahead of this debt.

Besides my personal fees, I was obligated to share in the legal costs of another large law firm retained by the strata council of my building. That law firm pushed us into a settlement of less than 30 cents to the dollar. I received $16,000.

More than seven years and a second law firm after I purchased my Heritage Grand condo unit I was still stuck with the fraudulent agreement. But I ultimately won my case because a judge saw through the crime, despite the fact that I had an amateur in court with me who was too dazzled by the defence counsel and the court itself to allow me to produce evidence I knew to be of value.

What happened to me could be multiplied by 300,000-plus, and many more seriously damaged – including loss of life savings and loss of life itself.

Many young first home buyers who were allowed to invest $5000 to $10,000 to buy a condo chose to walk away rather than pay four and five times that to repair the apartment and live for years behind tarps in the flying dust and mould of reconstruction.

A journalist colleague Larry Rose, who became special assistant to the Port Moody–Coquitlam Member of Parliament Lou Sekora, developed cancer, attributed it to mould in his "new" condo. When released from hospital, in remission, he returned to his home to find it covered with tarps, the place being torn apart "under reconstruction" to clean out the mould. Within a few weeks he was dead. Despite this, Sekora refused to deal with the catastrophe in Ottawa.

And the prime minister of Canada, Jean Chrétien, told his caucus not to get involved with the western catastrophe.

Usually a small public burp leads to a government commission or study just to stop the complaints and get the publicity, and even make a gesture towards solution. Remarkably, to this day the Government of Canada has never once considered setting up a commission and a research team to determine the extent of the disaster. When the outcry of thousands of victims broke in the west, the prime minister remained silent, and ordered caucus representatives from the west "to stay out of the leaky condo issue." In effect they must "let nature take its course."

One day in August 2001, I was suddenly hit by shame and anger, not only at the people who had been my colleagues and friends, but at myself for not trying to do what I had done in my many battles for justice and against crime. I was just sitting back and feeling whipped. I had been writing former colleagues and friends, including media barons and cabinet members right up to the PM of Canada and the premier of British Columbia. I received form letters of official indifference, even contempt that anyone would dare to challenge them and the developers.

Suddenly I knew that not only for the sake of my own survival mentally and emotionally, but also for the sake of others, I had to fight back. Being a "victim" was hardly my lifestyle.

I contacted Dr. James Balderson and John Grasty, founders of COLCO (Coalition of Leaky Condo Owners), to tell them we had to form a delegation and "beard the lion in his den" by taking our case to the Government of Canada in Ottawa.[1]

At an earlier meeting of the strata council in my own building, when we were preparing for legal action against the developer, the engineers, architects and the City of Port Moody, I had agreed to serve on the council's public relations and justice committees. The first assignment I had was to attend a mass meeting of leaky condo owners in the Tri-Cities (Coquitlam, Port Coquitlam, and Port Moody). It was there that I first heard the first series of nightmare stories from victims of the catastrophe. I even heard that day that there were 2,000 leaky condos (estimate 10,000 victims) within two square blocks of Coquitlam City Hall, within easy walking distance of my own leaky condo.

That evening, the room had been packed to capacity with leaky condo owners. Among the many facts we heard that night was that no matter what representative in government was contacted, nothing was done. Only one bit of research and leadership was going on, from the later discredited leader of the provincial New Democratic Party, Glen Clark, who set up the Dave

---

1   John Grasty is a Metropolitan Vancouver realtor who was himself the owner of a leaky condo in 1997. COLCO held its inaugural meeting in Vancouver on September 13, 1999.

Barrett commission to inquire into the cause and extent of, and liability in, the leaky condo crisis. Though he brought in an excellent report, the Royal Canadian Mounted Police, commercial crime division, was stopped from pursuing the crimes uncovered in the New Home Warranty Program, financed by builders, which took money from condo owners and then failed to produce the contractual payments when the trouble started.

"You must go political. That means you have to have enough money to be a threat to the governments and the developers. Without money they will ignore you."[2]

I urged the leaders that night to go flat out politically. To do that they had to have a financial war chest that was sufficient to gain the attention of the politicians and the lawyers. Although they were raising money by sale of leaky condo T-shirts and umbrellas, and through donations at meetings, it was not enough to declare war on the developers and their political friends. I believed that if each of the estimated 100,000 leaky home owners, their family, neighbours and friends gave at least $10 each, we could get action.

That didn't happen. But COLCO did not give up. They set up an Internet website. They gathered repeatedly for demonstrations around new and highly-touted condo complexes, and outside the luxury Westin Bayshore Inn when the elegantly-dressed developers, the media owners, and their friends were entering in limousines for the Georgie Awards night.[3] There was no reporting of one of the most colourful stories in the same hotel – the COLCO-sponsored "PourGee" awards for the developers and their partners in crime who produced the worst and deadliest homes in Canada.

The hotel management had tried to cancel the room booking for the PourGees the afternoon of the event, in response to the Georgie sponsors' complaints. However, after being confronted by a group of us, some with celebrity and power of their own (including one who was the head of a major

---

2 COLCO had sufficient numbers and determination to defeat an MP at the heart of the Tri-City crisis, and almost defeated two cabinet ministers – Herb Dhaliwal (a real estate developer), who refused to deal with the victims or even let any of them into his campaign headquarters, and Dave Anderson, Minister of Fisheries and Environment.

3 The Georgie Awards are presented annually in British Columbia for excellence in various aspects of the home building industry, including planning, design, construction, sales and marketing.

international cosmetics company that often booked conventions and blocks of rooms there), the hotel management not only provided a large room but free coffee and refreshments.

The PourGees were blocks of rotten wood from the worst of the leaky condos, for presentation to winners in the categories of builder, politician, and media mogul. The citations alone were humorous irony.

Being involved in this was cathartic. But it went nowhere. I knew we had to do more.

The public – the noisy – way was the only way I knew. I would use my experience as a reporter, researcher, writer, public speaker – at times what some described as a "motivational lecturer" others called "rabble rousing."

This was the biggest, and probably the last fight I would face in my life. All the resources were in place – a huge constituency of angry, robbed, sick and frustrated people, the strong and well-organized COLCO with its tenacious and uniquely well-informed leaders, and an almost unlimited amount of graphic and shocking evidence.

The media did not want this story, because if told it would cut the profits of the most important part of the newspaper to the owners – the advertising bonanza in this massive real estate boom.

In the fall of 2001, I decided to organize a delegation to go to Ottawa and tackle the media at the heart of government. Even if Canadian reporters would be reluctant to write the story and lose millions of dollars of advertising, there would be reporters from United States and Britain who were free to write the story.

I had already tried to get Prime Minister Jean Chrétien, once a colleague and friend, to come west and see the people and their rotten mouldy homes. He did not bother with the most basic courtesy of acknowledging my call, a basic duty for all public servants. Even if he believed himself too self-important to be bothered, he had staff that should have known their duty to Canadians.

When I phoned Conservative Leader Joe Clark, he came to British Columbia within a week, looking at the rotten buildings in various stages of reconstruction. He met with local mayors and with men, women and children who were in the throes of losing hope and homes.

Meanwhile a group of women formed an ad hoc committee with me to take our case to Ottawa. It was decided we would travel at our own expense. Joe Clark, Opposition Leader Stockwell Day, and the Conservative MP for Port Moody James Moore, assured us of their help, and that we could use their offices and staffs.

I knew cabinet ministers and members of all parties whom we could approach, and hoped perhaps those in Opposition would force the government to investigate and seek solutions to the disaster, and stop the developers and their partners from continuing the crime.

A delegation of eight of us went. As soon as the word was out that there was a delegation various groups held fund-raisers and "Conduit" (the Victoria, B.C. counterpart to COLCO) arranged a community meeting, requesting that I attend and speak to the group. Two members of the provincial legislature turned up and spoke in support of the victims.[4]

I knew the route in Ottawa. We would "storm" the cabinet ministers, their departments and bureaucrats, mainly National Health and Welfare, Consumer Protection, Justice, and Finance.

Our presence was recognized in the House of Commons, the issue raised by the Opposition from the floor. Opposition Leader Stockwell Day of the Alliance Party called his entire caucus together to meet with us.

Prime Minister Jean Chrétien not only refused to see us but ordered his B.C. Liberal caucus not to get involved. David Anderson, then the senior cabinet minister from B.C., refused to talk with the victims of the leaky condo disaster, even in his own riding on Vancouver Island.

Most disturbing was that Chrétien was the primary creator of the catastrophe when he was the cabinet minister with responsibility for national energy. In that portfolio he established the national building codes to conserve energy by sealing building envelopes. He established the same codes for the rainy climate of British Columbia as for the often bone-dry prairies and the totally different weather of Ontario, Quebec and the Atlantic provinces. So for the last 18 years of the 20th century, homes and the forests of condominium complexes soaked by the heavy rains in B.C. began to rot and turn into viru-

---

4   The next day, after the story appeared in the local papers, the two were silenced by Premier Gordon Campbell.

lent mush and mould the moment they were completed.[5] The specialists who call themselves "building scientists" claim the rot and mould grow at the rate of an inch a day.

---

5 Average annual rainfall on the B.C. Lower Mainland and Vancouver Island is 110–250 centimetres (44–100 inches).

18

The Love Child

As part of my activities on behalf of COLCO, I was in Victoria, B.C. to meet with leaky condo victims from that city. Every seat was taken in the large hospitality room of the complex near the Parliament Buildings. After the meeting ended, a young woman who identified herself as Lynn Gray approached me saying she had "some information" she wanted to share with me. Of course, I thought it would be a further scandal in the leaky condo crime. But it could not be farther removed from that.

She began by explaining that she was in the elevator of this complex to visit her mother, a resident there, when she saw the poster announcing I would be in the building to speak about the problem faced by thousands of Victoria condo owners. She said she had a special reason for wanting to meet me. Then she hesitated, and I think she shuffled nervously and said, "I don't know how to tell you."

"Just tell me," I said, never requiring subtlety in dialogue.

"Well, I don't know how to tell you," she continued, and hesitated some more.

"Look," I said finally, "you can call me anything you want, say whatever you want but for goodness sakes tell me what is on your mind – or forget it."

She blurted out, "You have a niece you do not know in Victoria. She is a famous photographer here … the daughter of your brother, Macey." She went on to tell me, "You are her aunt. She learned about you when someone sent her the obituary of her father in a Calgary newspaper."

Lynn Gray handed me a card that identified this niece. Her name was Frances Litman. The picture on the front of the card was that of a child who looked strangely familiar. It gave me a moment of pause. Macey was the brother closest to me in years and shared friendships. He was divorced and estranged from his wife, Cathy, and daughter, Louise Milner, but close to Louise's fraternal twin, Marvin, and devoted to his first-born, Lawrence. When Cathy was first married she admitted to Hannah that she had set out to "hook" Macey, the "the good-looking young doctor, so handsome in his captain's uniform" when he first returned from overseas.

Macey was unbelievably child-like and naïve, despite his overseas experience. Doctors who served with him said, "He was too young … to be in a theatre of war." They also said, "He was compassionate and caring to the point that he would work around the clock there, and later in Calgary, whenever he was free of the post-war stress that dogged him to the end of his life."

When the marriage broke up, Cathy and her parents revealed their deep anti-Semitism, which was picked up by his daughter Louise. She refused to talk to him when he tried to connect with her in a special trip to Vancouver Island, where she lived. She would not even send him a postcard or a note when he was dying.

Lawrence got involved in the pot-and-acid culture at age 17 and ended up with flashbacks and voices in his head. He had become schizophrenic.

Now my informant, Lynn Gray, told me that Frances had only two pieces of background about her father. One was the obituary that told of his family, the other a faded photocopy of the small picture in his university yearbook.

Frances recognized my name because she herself worked for the *Times Colonist* in Victoria as a photojournalist. She not only entered the same avocation as I, but followed in what was my brother Macey's favourite hobby – photography. When she went into her own business as a professional photographer she collected several awards.[1] She was the only Canadian to be asked annually to serve as a resource at the annual international photo seminar in Las Vegas. Her reputation was so great, I was told, that people seek her service, have even changed wedding dates to have her as their photographer.

---

1   Among the awards won by Frances Litman are:
    Canadian Wedding Album of the Year 2002 –
    Professional Photographers Association of Canada
    Kodak Gallery Award of Excellence (2001, 1999)
    Best Wedding Album in B.C. 2002 – Professional Photographers Association of B.C.
    Award of Fellowship 2008 – Professional Photographers Association of Canada
    Fujifilm Canadian Merit Award 1999 & 2000

Following that meeting with Lynn Gray, I phoned the number on the card and spoke for the first time with the "love child" of my brother.

Frances had been born in Calgary and raised in Victoria, B.C. She had always known she was adopted. She had learned the identity of her natural mother, Sally Slifka, from the adoption papers.

When Frances was age 13, her adoptive father, Charles Litman, was in failing health, as was his wife. He contacted Sally, who was clearly listed in the Calgary phone book. Sally declined to meet Frances but offered to write a letter and send photographs to appease Frances' curiosity and explain the reasons for her decision. It wasn't until Frances was 29 that she discovered the letter. The heartfelt sentiment in the letter convinced Frances that she would leave Sally alone. The photos had appeased much of her curiosity.

Now Frances was 40. Her adopted parents were dead. It was thanks to her friend Lynn Gray that Frances began the search for her natural family about half a year prior to my meeting Lynn.

At that time, Frances was out with Lynn and two other friends when a taxicab nearly plowed into them in a crosswalk. Lynn had an appointment booked for herself and Frances to see a psychic the next day. Although traumatic, Frances insisted they not miss the appointment. "When you have a brush of near tragedy like that and feel spared from it, you don't cancel an appointment with a psychic," Frances maintains.

Although the psychic had never met or seen Frances or Lynn before, she went to Frances the moment her front door opened, and insisted on sharing some healing Reiki energy with her. While doing this, the psychic fell into a trance-like state and told Frances that she (Frances) had "just been lifted from the path of danger by her guardian angel," and went on to say that in three months' time Frances would meet a woman who would show her "unconditional love."

Searching the Internet, Lynn turned up Frances' natural mother's obituary. Fearing Frances would be upset, Lynn started to dig further and uncovered a great aunt, Charlotte Slifka, who lived in Stettler, Alberta. Charlotte was close to Frances' mother but never knew of Frances' existence. Frances contacted Charlotte, and from her learned about Maureen (Mo) Parker, Sally's very best friend. It turns out Frances' connection with Mo was the mother-daughter relationship she had always wanted but never had. This was the woman the psychic had told her about.

Mo has since moved from Calgary to be near Frances in Victoria. It was through Mo that Frances learned the details of who her father was, as well as the circumstances relating to her adoption. According to Mo:

> "When (Sally) was a young woman she loved to sing and entertain and was very popular. She became a school teacher, then a speech pathologist. With her usual style and flair she returned to the classroom to finish her career as a master teacher. It was when she was a young teacher at the beginning of her career she met and fell in love with a charming and bright doctor, Macey Milner. Sally and I were living in a house at that time with three other gals. Sally brought Macey to our wee house a few times and introduced him to us. It was that summer (1961) that Sally became pregnant. I had left for Vancouver ... and missed hearing about Sally's predicament. A few years later Sally told me about Frances; she had given her up for adoption. Moving right along to 1980 I moved back to Calgary to share a townhouse with Sally. It must have been in the mid 70s when Sally received a call from Frances' adoptive father ... requesting that she meet with Frances. Sally declined. I learned of this a number of years later. In 1997 Sally and I were living in Carbon (near Drumheller). It was there she had her final heart attack; she died that year, December 23."

Frances and Mo then both learned that Macey, my brother and Frances' biological father, had passed away just three months after Sally. They obtained a copy of the obituary, which gave them the names of Macey's family.

Thus I met the love child of my brother, my beautiful and talented niece, Frances. She has developed into the one person dearest and closest to my heart next to my sister Hannah. And so, in the midst of the condominium trouble, there was this strange and fascinating turn of fortune. Here was this wonderful life that came to me in the last years of my life, when I had no family of my own and only one niece and a nephew I knew or for whom I felt some affection.

Throughout the years I always believed – and really found – that no matter how bad the moment, the next could be better. Perhaps that was the way it

My beloved big sister Hannah, now age 94, and me, 86, in Louis Brier Jewish Home and Hospital in Vancouver.

happened for me because I expected it. Or it could have been that the first of the songs I heard my mother sing imprinted so deeply somewhere in my brain that whenever life seems to dip low I am certain it will change and get better.

My Dad died in 1962. The last days of his life were, in some ways, the richest in our father-daughter relationship. When he came out of long sleep – or perhaps coma – he was lucid in conversation. A few days before his death, using his style of my name in endearment he said, "Simmale. You have no children … The children of the world must be yours."

I have had the experience of knowing that exposure of truth and facts forces action in the real politics of life. Over and over I saw public servants and politicians act because a story in the newspaper told the whole world something was seriously wrong.

I saw every decade of my life as more fulfilling and interesting than the one before. So much has happened. So much has changed. So much was good. And I saw so much evil.

From the start of awareness I wanted – and announced to my family – that I loved living so much that I planned to have three careers in my one life. In the end I had five. The best of all was the first 30 years as a news reporter and broadcaster. I was an author of books, beginning with the publication of my first book, *Terror in the Name of God*, in the fall of 1964, and continuing with *Sex and the Teen-age Revolution* (1967), *The Devil's Butler* (1971) and *The Other Mrs. Diefenbaker* (1983). I was an MP from 1974 to 1979, then a member of the National Parole Board from 1981 to 1985. My fifth career was that of researcher and writer inside the presidential campaign of George Bush in 1987 and 1988. At this stage, I am back doing what I love most, being a professional writer and author.

Now as my life moves towards its real and Final Deadline – a deadline that does not allow the return to the newsroom to correct the text – I know that my generation lived in the best of times and places. And after almost nine decades of life I am convinced that every decade was indeed better than the one before. Each one has the depth of perspective, more friends and always new stories. So growing old is not too bad and gives me the whole story – to date.

Here I am with my wonderful niece, Frances.

Acknowledgements

There are many people who helped me to produce this book, giving generously of their time, and I am grateful to all of them. I am so thankful to literally thousands whom I believe were the reason for my richness and unending joy in life.

In addition to the many who are mentioned in the book as mentors and helpful colleagues in my various careers, and to whom I am forever grateful, I especially want to thank Harry Sherman, who encouraged me in my writing after *Terror in the Name of God* was first published.

Special thanks to Peter Worthington who so eloquently wrote the Introduction to this book.

A special note of appreciation also to Barton Frank of Bellingham, Washington, who began 50 years ago to say, "Your stories are great … no one has writings like this."

I am indebted to the wonderful and helpful librarians and staff of the Library of Parliament in Ottawa, the Vancouver Public Library, and the Bellingham, Washington Public Library.

I am similarly indebted to the Archivists and Special Collections staff at the University of Manitoba.

Among the organizations which helped me are the Canadian Association of Parliamentarians in Ottawa (in particular Doug and Helen Rowland, Julie Martens, Susan Simms and Celine Brezeau Fraser) and all the people at the School of Orientation of the Public Service of Canada.

I could not have completed the book without my great "tech support" team: Paul Siczek, Pauline & Karl Siczek, Tony Kauwell, Bonnie Sainsbury, Gerri Sombke, and Fred Cohen.

Always my special thanks to my beloved sister, Hannah Milner Smith, my lifelong friend, who was always there for me. Even today, at age 94, her remarkable memory of facts and family has been invaluable to me.

I am grateful also to everyone who helped me by editing or checking sections of the book at various times and in its various stages of development, including Karen L. Brown of Exeter, Ontario, Beth Kauwell of Nanaimo, B.C., Michael Schumacher of Kenosha, Wisconsin, and the editorial staff of Seraphim Editions. I also thank Julie McNeill of McNeill Design Arts for her excellent design work in making the book such a handsome finished product.

This book would never have happened at all if it were not for Erika Roesner. Not only is she my dearest friend, but when this whole thing had come to a dead end after 25 or more years, she suddenly decided she would not allow it to die with me. Erika became my agent, personal manager and appointment secretary. I cannot say enough to express my gratitude to Erika and her husband, Wolfgang.

Erika went looking for a publisher for this book and found Maureen Whyte of Seraphim Editions. Maureen became so deeply involved in this work that she not only invited me to stay and work in her beautiful 100-year-old home in Hamilton, Ontario for more than a month, but did research on missing pieces of information that I could never have done without her help. I thank Maureen for accepting the book and bringing the project through to fruition.

I was sure from the start that this book would be published. All I needed was a deadline and all these special people. My heartfelt thanks go to all of them.

To all my friends, old and new, and to everyone who reads this book: Thank you for being part of my life.

Photograph Credits

Photos Courtesy of the University of Manitoba Archives & Special Collections
Simma Holt fonds PC 103

Front Cover Photos
1-5-21, 1-11-29, 1-5-20

Page 5   1-1-18
Page 29 1-1-20
Page 66 1-5-36
Page 70 1-5-25, 1-5-32
Page 71 1-4-37
Page 81 1-3-5
Page 125 1-5-3, 1-4-45, 1-5-30
Page 128 2-5-14, 2-5-3
Page 132 1-5-35
Page 139 1-5-21
Page 142 1-5-39
Page 144 3-10-1

Page 146 1-4-43
Page 164 1-5-20
Page 165 1-11-28, 1-11-29
Page 166 1-11-35, 1-11-24
Page 169 2-3-83
Page 175 2-3-61
Page 188 1-11-15
Page 200 2-25-7
Page 213 3-5-1

Page 198 Mss 103 31-6
Page 204 Mss 103 31-6

Page 35   Courtesy of Vegreville Regional Museum
Page 36   Courtesy of Vegreville Regional Musuem

Page 119   Canada Department of National Defence /
           Library and Archives Canada / PA-150931

Page 244   Courtesy of www.franceslitman.com
Page 247   Courtesy of www.franceslitman.com